Raspberry Pi OS Text Editors, Git, and LXC

The third volume in a new series exploring the basics of Raspberry Pi Operating System administration, this installment builds on the insights from Volumes 1 and 2 to provide a compendium of easy-to-use and essential guidance for Raspberry Pi system administration for novice users, with specific focus on Text Editors, Git/GitHub, and LXC/LXD.

The overriding idea behind system administration of a modern, 21st-century Linux system, such as the Raspberry Pi OS, is the use of systemd to ensure that the Linux kernel works efficiently and effectively to provide these three foundation stones of computer operation and management: computer system concurrency, virtualization, and secure persistence. This third volume includes a beginner's compendium of essential text-based Linux commands, a complete tutorial on the most important Raspberry Pi OS Text Editors, a description of uses of the git command, and a thorough explication of container virtualization with LXC/LXD and Docker.

This book is aimed at students and practitioners looking to maximize their use of the Raspberry Pi OS. With plenty of practical examples, projects, and exercises, this volume can also be adopted in a more formal learning environment to supplement and extend the basic knowledge of a Linux operating system.

Robert M. Koretsky is a retired lecturer in Mechanical Engineering at the University of Portland School of Engineering. He previously worked as an automotive engineering designer at the Freightliner Corp. in Portland, Oregon. He is married and has two kids and two grandkids.

Raspberry Pi OS System Administration with systemd
A Practical Approach
Series Editor: Robert M. Koretsky

Raspberry Pi OS System Administration with systemd: A Practical Approach
Robert M. Koretsky

Raspberry Pi OS System Administration with systemd and Python: A Practical Approach
Robert M. Koretsky

Raspberry Pi OS Text Editors, Git, and LXC: A Practical Approach
Robert M. Koretsky

For more information about this series, please visit: www.routledge.com/
Raspberry-Pi-OS-System-Administration-with-systemd/book-series/123

Raspberry Pi OS Text Editors, Git, and LXC

A Practical Approach

Robert M. Koretsky

CRC Press
Taylor & Francis Group
Boca Raton London New York

CRC Press is an imprint of the
Taylor & Francis Group, an **informa** business

A CHAPMAN & HALL BOOK

First edition published 2024
by CRC Press
2385 NW Executive Center Drive, Suite 320, Boca Raton FL 33431

and by CRC Press
4 Park Square, Milton Park, Abingdon, Oxon, OX14 4RN

CRC Press is an imprint of Taylor & Francis Group, LLC

ISBN: 978-1-032-59690-7 (hbk)
ISBN: 978-1-032-59691-4 (pbk)
ISBN: 978-1-003-45581-3 (ebk)

DOI: 10.1201/9781003455813

Typeset in Palatino
by Newgen Publishing UK

To my family.

Bob Koretsky

Contents

Series Preface

This series of books covers the basics of Raspberry Pi Operating System administration, and is geared towards a novice user. Each book is a complete, self-contained introduction to important system administration tasks, and to other useful programs. The foundation of all of them is the systemd super-kernel. They guide the user along a path that gives the 'why' and 'how to' of those important system administration topics, and they also present the following essential application facilities:

1) Raspberry Pi OS System administration with systemd, Volume 1
2) Raspberry Pi OS System administration with systemd and Python, Volume 2
3) Raspberry Pi OS Text Editing, Git, Virtualization with LXC/LXD, Volume 3

They can be used separately, or together, to fit the learning objectives/pace, and interests of the individual, independent learner, or can be adopted in a more formal learning environment to supplement and extend the basic knowledge of a Linux operating system in a classroom environment that uses the Raspberry Pi OS.

In addition, each book has In-Chapter Exercises throughout, and a Question, Problems, and Projects addendum to help reinforce the learning goals of the individual student, or reader.

An online GitHub site, with further materials and updates, program code, solutions to both In-Chapter Exercises and End-of-Chapter Problems, Questions, and Projects, plus other supplements, is provided for each volume. It can be found at:

www.github.com/bobk48/RaspberryPiOS

The fundamental prerequisites of each volume are (1) knowledge of how to type a syntactically-correct Linux command on the command line, (2) having access to a dedicated Raspberry Pi computer with the latest Raspberry Pi Operating System already installed and running on it, (3) being a privileged user on the system that is able to execute the **sudo** command to assume superuser status, and (4) having a basic knowledge of how to edit and save text files in the **nano** text editor.

All instructions in these volumes were tested on either a Raspberry Pi 4B, or a Raspberry Pi 400, both with 4GB of memory, and the latest version of the Raspberry Pi OS at the time.

Volume 3 Preface

Background

This book is a compendium of easy-to-use and essential Raspberry Pi OS supplements to system administration tasks for the beginner. The Raspberry Pi OS is derived from the Debian branch of Linux, and as of this writing, Debian Bullseye was the most current version of that operating system. To present the supplements to system administration topics and commands here, centered around Text Editing, Git/GitHub, and Virtualization with LXC/LXD and Docker, I have selected some very basic stuff, and a few more advanced concepts, topics, commands, and details that might not appear in a more complete system administration book, or a book on the auxiliary subject matter that might be found in another Raspberry Pi OS book.

The overriding idea behind system administration of a modern, 21st-century Linux system, such as the Raspberry Pi OS, is the use of systemd to ensure that the Linux kernel works efficiently and effectively to provide these three foundation stones of computer operation and management: computer system concurrency, virtualization, and secure persistence.

And this control of the kernel by a "super-kernel," which is what systemd essentially is, must also promote the highest level of system performance and speed, given the use cases the computer might be put to, and the perceived needs of the target user base that the computer serves. Unless that novice user, or even a more seasoned system professional, has not only a basic, but also a more complete knowledge of how systemd controls and oversees every process and operation of a modern Linux system, they will never be able to master administrating and implementing the kind of functionality that their use case(s) might ultimately require. Particularly for the user base on the system, and the demands that the user base makes.

Certainly out of the multitude of possible topics we could have presented, the ones you find detailed here have basically been selected in somewhat of a subjective way. That selective way was mainly guided by these concerns:

a. The secure maintenance, in terms of concurrency, virtualization, and persistence, of a single Raspberry Pi system that an ordinary novice user can install on her own dedicated hardware.

b. How important the topics are in a perceived ranking of essential system administration tasks.

c. How systemd plays into the maintenance regimen of the Raspberry Pi OS, and the hardware it's installed on, as chosen by that ordinary user.

d. The overall pedagogic integration of the selected topics presented on system administration with each other.

e. How well these topics serve to prepare a student for entry into any chosen Information Technology or Computer Science profession, or how someone already in those professions can use this book to better conform to the best practices of that profession. In other words, for educational and continuing education audiences.

f. To some degree, make it possible to extrapolate these topics (for audiences in e.) from a single Raspberry Pi system environment to a broader and larger-scaled computing environment, such as is found on small-to-medium-sized servers, or to cloud-based, virtual computing.

The topics presented in this volume are fundamental and supplementary to everything presented in the previous volumes, and can be summarized as follows:

1. Text-based and graphics-based editing of files, such as Python and C++ program code, using the Nano and Vi/Vim/Gvim text editors, and the Geany Integrated Development Environment (IDE).

2. File and code project control using the **git** command, and its deployment and integration with GitHub, via a text-based and web browser interfaces.

3. Virtualization techniques on the Raspberry Pi OS, using LXC/LXD containers, and Docker.

4. We also repeat for review Chapter Zero (0) from the previous volumes, which provides basic and essential file maintenance and system polling and inquiry commands for the beginner.

How to Read and Use This Book

Note

The premise and prerequisite of this book is that you understand what the correct form, or structure, of a Linux command is, and how to type one in on the console or terminal command line of a Raspberry Pi!

Just to review that here, the general syntax, or structure of a single Linux command (often referred to as a *simple command*) as it is typed on the command line, is as follows:

$ command [[-]option(s)] [option argument(s)] [command argument(s)]

where:

$ is the command line or shell prompt from the Raspberry Pi OS;
anything enclosed in [] is not always needed;
command is the name of the valid Linux command for that shell in lowercase letters;
[-option(s)] is one or more modifiers that change the behavior of command;
[option argument(s)] is one or more modifiers that change the behavior of **[-option(s)]**; and
[command argument(s)] is one or more objects that are affected by **command**.

Note the following seven essentials:

1. A space separates command, options, option arguments, and command arguments, but no space is necessary between multiple option(s) or multiple option arguments.

2. The order of multiple options or option arguments is irrelevant.

3. A space character is optional between the option and the option argument.

4. Always press the <Enter> key to submit the command for interpretation and execution.

5. Options may be preceded by a single hyphen - or two hyphens, --, depending on the form of the option. The short form of the option is preceded by a single hyphen, and the long form of the option is preceded by two hyphens. No space character should be placed between hyphen(s) and option(s).

6. A small percentage of commands (like **whoami**) take *no* options, option arguments, or command arguments.

7. Everything on the command line is case sensitive!

Also, it is possible, and *very* common to type *multiple* Linux commands (sometimes called *compound* commands, to differentiate them from simple commands) on the same command line, before pressing the **<Enter>** key. The components of a multiple Linux command are separated with input and output redirection characters, to channel the output of one into the input of another.

As stated in the Series Preface, the fundamental prerequisites of this volume are:

1. Knowledge of how to type a syntactically correct Linux command on the command line (as detailed above)

2. Having access to a dedicated Raspberry Pi computer with the latest Raspberry Pi Operating System already installed and running on it

3. Being a privileged user on the system, and as such are able to execute the **sudo** command to assume superuser status, and

4. Having a basic knowledge of how to edit and save text files in the Nano text editor. We give introductory instruction on how to use the Nano text editor in this volume.

An online GitHub site, with further materials and updates, program code, solutions to both In-Chapter Exercises and End-of-Chapter Problems, Questions, and Projects, plus other supplements, is provided for this book. It can be found at:

www.github.com/bobk48/RaspberryPiOS

All command line instructions in this volume were tested on either a Raspberry Pi 4B, or a Raspberry Pi 400, both with 4GB of memory, and the latest version of the Raspberry Pi OS at the time, which was Debian Bookworm.

Routes through the Book

Browse the Contents.

Select a topic that interests you.

Do the Examples, or all the command line materials presented for that topic.

Maybe pick another topic that interests you, and do the Examples and all the command line materials there.

Finally, go back to the beginning of the book. Do everything, from start to finish.

Rinse and repeat the above as necessary.

Have fun!

0

"Quick Start" into Sysadmin for the Raspberry Pi Operating System

In this introductory chapter, duplicated in the first two volumes of this series, we cover the essential Raspberry Pi OS commands that allow a system administrator to do file maintenance and perform other useful operations. This is a mandatory set of essentials that even an ordinary, non-administrative user would need to know to work efficiently in a character or text-based interface to the operating system. It should be evident to the reader, after completing this chapter, that correctly deployed, text-based commands are the predominant means that a system administrator has at her disposal to maintain the integrity of the system. We give a set of core examples, and show the basic format of essential commands and primitives here.

Objectives

To explain how to manage and maintain files and directories
To show where to get system-wide help for Raspberry Pi OS commands
To demonstrate the use of a beginner's set of utility commands
To cover the basic commands and operators

cat cd cp exit hostname -I ip login lp lpr ls man mesg mkdir more mv passwd, PATH pwd rm rmdir telnet unalias uname whatis whereis who whoami

0.1 Introduction

To start working productively with system administration on the Raspberry Pi OS, the beginner needs to have some familiarity with these sequential topics, as follows:

DOI: 10.1201/9781003455813-1

1. How to maintain and organize files in the file structure of the operating system. Creating a tree-like structure of folders (also called directories), and storing files in a logical fashion in these folders, is critical to working efficiently in the Raspberry Pi OS.

2. How to get help on text-based commands and their usage. With keyboard entry, in a command-based, Character User Interface (CUI) environment, being able to find out, in a quick and easy way, how to use a command, its options, and arguments by typing it on the keyboard correctly, is imperative to working efficiently.

3. How to execute a small set of essential utility commands to set up or customize your working environment. Once a beginner is familiar with the right way to construct file maintenance commands, adding a set of utility commands makes each session more productive.

To use this chapter successfully as a springboard into the remainder of the book, you should carefully read, follow, and execute the instructions and command line sessions we provide, in the order presented. Each section in this chapter, and the two subsequent chapters as well, builds on the information that precedes it. They will give you the concepts, command tools, and methods that will enable you to do system administration using the Raspberry Pi OS.

Throughout this book, we illustrate everything using the following version of the Raspberry Pi OS, on the hardware listed:

System:
Host: raspberrypi Kernel: 6.1.0-rpi6-rpi-v8 arch: aarch64 bits: 64
compiler: gcc v: 12.2.0 Desktop: LXDE v: 0.10.1 Distro: Debian GNU/Linux 12 (book-
    worm)
Machine:
Type: ARM System: Raspberry Pi 400 Rev 1.0 details: BCM2835 rev: c03130

In this chapter, the major commands we want to illustrate are first defined with an abbreviated syntax description, which will clarify general components of those commands. The syntax description format is as follows:

Syntax: The exact syntax of how a command, its options, and its arguments are correctly typed on the command line

Purpose: The specific purpose of the command

Output: A short description of the results of executing the command

Commonly used options/features: A listing of the most popular and useful options and option arguments

In addition, the following web link is to a site that allows you to type-in a single or multiple Raspberry Pi OS command, and get a verbose explanation of the components of that command:

https://explainshell.com/

In-Chapter Exercises

1. Type the following commands on your Raspberry Pi OS system's command line, and note the results. Which ones are syntactically incorrect? Why? (The Bash prompt is shown as the $ character in each, and we assume that **file1** and **file2** exist)

    ```
    $ la -ls
    $ cat
    $ more -q file1
    $ more file2
    $ time
    $ lsblk-a
    ```

2. How can you differentiate a Raspberry Pi OS command from its options, option arguments, and command arguments?

3. What is the difference between a single Raspberry Pi OS command and a multiple Raspberry Pi OS command, as typed on the command line before pressing <Enter>?

4. If you get no error message after you enter a Raspberry Pi OS command, how do you know that it actually accomplished what you wanted it to?

0.2 File Maintenance Commands and Help on Raspberry Pi OS Command Usage

After your first-time login to a new Raspberry Pi OS system, one of your first actions will be to construct and organize your workspace environment, and the files that will be contained in it. The operation of organizing your files according to some logical scheme is known as *file maintenance*. A logical scheme used to organize your files might consist of creating *bins* for storing files according to the subject matter of the contents of the files, or according to the dates of their creation. In the following sections, you will type file creation and maintenance commands that produce a structure similar to what

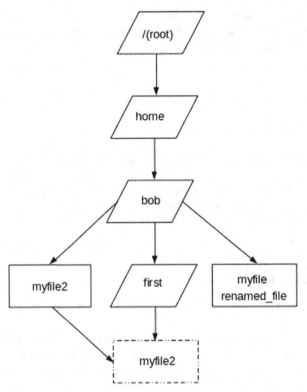

FIGURE 0.1
Example directory structure.

is shown in Figure 0.1. Complete the operations in the following sections in the order they are presented to get a better overview of what file maintenance really is. Also, it is critical that you review what was presented in the Preface regarding the structure of a Raspberry Pi OS command so that when you begin to type commands for file maintenance, you understand how the syntax of what you are typing conforms to the general syntax of any Raspberry Pi OS command.

0.2.1 File and Directory Structure

When you first open a terminal, or console, window, you are working in the *home directory*, or folder, of the autonomous user associated with the username and password you used to log into the system with. Whatever directory you are presently in is known as the *current working directory*, and there is only one current working directory active at any given time. It is helpful to visualize the structure of your files and directories using a diagram. Figure 0.1 is an example of a home directory and file structure for a user named **bob**. In this figure, directories are represented as parallelograms and plain files (e.g., files that contain text or binary instructions) are represented as rectangles. A *pathname*, or path, is simply a textual way of designating the location of a directory or file in the complete file structure of the Raspberry Pi OS system you are working on.

For example, the path to the file **myfile2** in Figure 0.1 is **/home/bob/myfile2**. The designation of the path begins at the root (/) of the entire file system, descends to the folder named **home**, and then descends again to the home directory of the user named **bob**.

As shown in Figure 0.1, the files named **myfile, myfile2**, and **renamed_file** are stored under or in the directory **bob**. Beneath **bob** is a *subdirectory* named **first**. In the following sections, you will create these files, and the subdirectory structure, in the home directory of the username that you have logged into your Raspberry Pi OS system with.

In-Chapter Exercise

5. Type the following two commands on your Raspberry Pi OS system:
    $ cd /
    $ ls

Similar to Figure 0.1, sketch a diagram of the directories and files whose names you see listed as the output of the second command. Save this diagram for use later.

0.2.2 Viewing the Contents of Files

To begin working with files, you can easily create a new text file by using the **cat** command. The syntax of the **cat** command is as follows:

cat [options] [file-list]
Purpose: Join one or more files sequentially or display them in the console window
Output: Contents of the files in **file-list** displayed on the screen, one file at a time
Commonly used options/features:
+E   Display $ at the end of each line
-n   Put line numbers on the displayed lines
--   **help** Display the purpose of the command and a brief explanation of each option

The **cat** command, short for concatenate, allows you to join files. In the example you will join what you type on the keyboard to a new file being created in the current working directory. This is achieved by the redirect character >, which takes what you type at the *standard input* (in this case the keyboard) and directs it into the file named **myfile**. You can consider the keyboard, and the stream of information it provides, as a file. As stated in the Preface, this usage is an example of a command, **cat** with no options, option arguments, or command arguments. It simply uses the command, a redirect character, and a target, or destination, named **myfile**, where the redirection will go.

This is the very simplest example of a *multiple command* typed on the command line, as opposed to a single command. In a multiple command, you can string together single Raspberry Pi OS commands in a chain with connecting operators, such as the redirect character shown here.

$ **cat > myfile**
This is an example of how to use the cat command to add plain text to a file
<Ctrl+D>
$

You can type as many lines of text, pressing **<Enter>** on the keyboard to distinguish between lines in the file, as you want. Then, on a new line, when you hold down **<Ctrl+D>**, the file is created in the current working directory, using the command you typed. You can view the contents of this file, since it is a plain text file that was created using the keyboard, by doing the following:

$ **more myfile**
This is an example of how to use the cat command to add plain text to a file
$

This is a simple example of the syntax of a single Raspberry Pi OS command.
The general syntax of the **more** command is as follows:

more [options] [file-list]
Purpose: Concatenate/display the files in **file-list** on the screen, one screen
              at a time
Output: Contents of the files in **file-list** displayed on the screen, one page
              at a time
Commonly used options/features:
+E/str   Start two lines before the first line containing **str**
-nN   Display N lines per screen/page
+N   Start displaying the contents of the file at line number N

The **more** command shows one screen full of a file at a time by default. If the file is several pages long, you can proceed to view subsequent pages by pressing the **<Space>** key on the keyboard, or by pressing the **Q** key on the keyboard to quit viewing the output.

In-Chapter Exercise

6. Use the **cat** command to produce another text file named **testfile**. Then join the contents of **myfile** and testfile into one text file, named **myfile3**, with the **cat** command.

0.2.3 Creating, Deleting, and Managing Files

To copy the contents of one file into another file, use the **cp** command. The general syntax of the **cp** command is as follows:

cp [options] file1 file2
Purpose: Copy **file1** to **file2**; if **file2** is a directory, make a copy of **file1** in this directory
Output: Copied files
Commonly used options/features:
-i If destination exists, prompt before overwriting
-p Preserve file access modes and modification times on copied files
-r Recursively copy files and subdirectories

For example, to make an exact duplicate of the file named **myfile**, with the new name **myfile2**, type the following:

```
$ cp myfile myfile2
$
```

This usage of the **cp** command has two required command arguments. The first argument is the source file that already exists and which you want to copy. The second argument is the destination file or the name of the file that will be the copy. Be aware that many Raspberry Pi OS commands can take plain, ordinary, or regular files as arguments, or can take directory files as arguments. This can change the basic task accomplished by the command. It is also worth noting that not only can file names be arguments, but *pathnames* as well. A pathname is the route to any particular place in the file system structure of the operating system. This changes the site or location, in the path structure of the file system, of operation of the command.

In order to change the name of a file or directory, you can use the **mv** command. The general syntax of the **mv** command is as follows:

mv [options] file1 file2
mv [options] file-list directory
Purpose: First syntax: Rename file1 to file2
Second syntax: Move all the files in file-list to directory
Output: Renamed or relocated files

Commonly used options/features:
-f   Force the move regardless of the file access modes of the destination file
-i   Prompt the user before overwriting the destination

In the following usage, the first argument to the **mv** command is the source file name, and the second argument is the destination name.

$ mv myfile2 renamed_file
$

It is important at this point to notice the use of spaces in Raspberry Pi OS commands. What if you obtain a file from a Windows system that has one or more spaces in one of the file names? How can you work with this file in Raspberry Pi OS? The answer is simple. Whenever you need to use that file name in a command as an argument, enclose the file name in double quotes ("). For example, you might obtain a file that you have "detached" from an e-mail message from someone on a Windows system, such as **latest revisions october.txt**.

In order to work with this file on a Raspberry Pi OS system – that is, to use the file name as an argument in a Raspberry Pi OS command – enclose the whole name in double quotes. The correct command to rename that file to something shorter would be:

$ mv "latest revisions october.txt" laterevs.txt
$

In order to delete a file, you can use the **rm** command. The general syntax of the **rm** command is as follows:

rm [options] file-list
Purpose: Removes files in **file-list** from the file structure (and disk)
Output: Deleted files
Commonly used options/features:
-f   Remove regardless of the file access modes of **file-list**
-i   Prompt the user before removing files in **file-list**
-r   Recursively remove the files in **file-list** if **file-list** is a directory; use with caution!

To delete the file **renamed_file** from the current working directory, type:

$ rm renamed_file
$

In-Chapter Exercise

7. Use the **rm** command to delete the files **testfile** and **myfile3**.

The most important command you will execute to do file maintenance is the **ls** command. The general syntax for the **ls** command is as follows:

ls [options] [pathname-list]
Purpose: Sends the names of the files and directories in the directory speci-
          fied by **pathname-list** to the display screen
Output: Names of the files and directories in the directory specified by
          pathname-list, or the names only if **pathname-list** contains file
          names only
Commonly used options/features:
-F   Display a slash character (/) after directory names, an asterisk (*) after
       binary executables, and an "at" character (@) after symbolic links
-a   Display names of all the files, including hidden files
-i   Display inode numbers
-l   Display long list that includes file access modes, link count, owner,
       group, file size (in bytes), and modification time

The **ls** command will list the names of files or folders in your current working directory or folder. In addition, as with the other commands we have used so far, if you include a complete pathname specification for the **pathname-list** argument to the command, then you can list the names of files and folders along that pathname list. To see the names of the files now in your current working directory, type the following:

```
$ ls
Desktop Documents Downloads Dropbox Music Pictures Public Templates Videos
$
```

Note that you will probably not get a listing of the same file names as we showed above here, because your system will have placed some files auto-matically in your home directory, as in the example we used, aside from the ones we created together named **myfile** and **myfile2**. Also note that this file name listing does not include the name **renamed_file** because we deleted that file.

The next command you will execute is actually just an alternate or modi-fied way of executing the **ls** command, one that includes the command name and options. As shown in the Preface, a Raspberry Pi OS command has options that can be typed on the command line along with the command to change the behavior of the basic command. In the case of the **ls** command, the options **l** and **a** produce a longer listing of all ordinary and system (dot) files, as well as providing other attendant information about the files.

Don't forget to put the space character between the **s** and the **-** (dash). Remember again that spaces delimit, or partition, the components of a Raspberry Pi OS command as it is typed on the command line!

Now, type the following command:

```
$ ls -la
total 30408
drwxr-xr-x   25   bob    bob    4096    May  5 07:53   .
drwxr-xr-x   5    root   root   4096    Oct 20 2022    ..
drwxr-xr-x   5    bob    bob    4096    Apr 23 16:32   .audacity-data
-rw-------   1    bob    bob    36197   May  5 07:51   .bash_history
-rw-r--r--   1    bob    bob    220     Apr  4 2022    .bash_logout
-rw-r--r--   1    bob    bob    3523    Apr  4 2022    .bashrc
-rw-r--r--   1    bob    bob    47329   Sep 19 2022    Blandemic.txt
drwxr-xr-x   2    bob    bob    4096    Apr  4 2022    Bookshelf
drwxr-xr-x   15   bob    bob    4096    Apr 17 14:05   .cache
drwx------   32   bob    bob    4096    Apr 28 07:08   .config
drwx------   3    root   root   4096    Jun 29 2022    .dbus
drwxr-xr-x   7    bob    bob    4096    Apr 27 05:21   Desktop
Output truncated...
```

As you see in this screen display (which shows the listing of files in our home directory and will not be the same as the listing of files in your home directory), the information about each file in the current working directory is displayed in eight columns. The first column shows the type of file, where d stands for directory, l stands for symbolic link, and – stands for ordinary or regular file. Also in the first column, the access modes to that file for user, group, and others is shown as r, w, or x. In the second column, the number of links to that file is displayed. In the third column, the username of the owner of that file is displayed. In the fourth column, the name of the group for that file is displayed. In the fifth column, the number of bytes that the file occupies on disk is displayed. In the sixth column, the date that the file was last modified is displayed. In the seventh column, the time that the file was last modified is displayed. In the eighth and final column, the name of the file is displayed. This way of executing the command is a good way to list more complete information about the file. Examples of using the more complete information are (1) so that you can know the byte size and be able to fit the file on some portable storage medium, or (2) to display the access modes, so that you can alter the access modes to a particular file or directory.

In-Chapter Exercise

8. Use the **ls -la** command to list all of the filenames in your home directory on your Raspberry Pi OS system. How does the listing you obtain compare with the listing shown above? Remember that our listing was done on a Raspberry Pi OS system.

You can also get a file listing for a single file in the current working directory by using another variation of the ls command, as follows:

$ **ls -la myfile**
-rw-r--r-- 1 bob bob 797 Jan 16 10:00 myfile
$

This variation shows you a long listing with attendant information for the specific file named **myfile**. A breakdown of what you typed on the command line is (1) **ls**, the command name, (2) **-la**, the options, and (3) **myfile**, the command argument.

What if you make a mistake in your typing, and misspell a command name or one of the other parts of a command? Type the following on the command line:

$ **lx -la myfile**
lx: not found
$

The lx: not found reply from Raspberry Pi OS is an error message. There is no **lx** command in the Raspberry Pi OS operating system, so an error message is displayed. If you had typed an option that did not exist, you would also get an error message. If you supplied a file name that was not in the current working directory, you would get an error message, too. This makes an important point about the execution of Raspberry Pi OS commands. If no error message is displayed, then the command executed correctly and the results might or might not appear on screen, depending on what the command actually does. If you get an error message displayed, you must correct the error before Raspberry Pi OS will execute the command as you type it.

Note
Typographic mistakes in commands account for a large percentage of the errors that beginners make!

0.2.4 Creating, Deleting, and Managing Directories

Another critical aspect of file maintenance is the set of procedures and the related Raspberry Pi OS commands you use to create, delete, and organize directories in your Raspberry Pi OS account on a computer. When moving through the file system, you are either ascending or descending to reach the directory you want to use. The directory directly above the current working directory is referred to as the *parent* of the current working directory. The directory or directories immediately under the current working directory are referred to as the *children* of the current working directory. The most common mistake for beginners is misplacing files. They cannot find the file names listed with the **ls** command because they have placed or created the files in a directory either above or below the current working directory in the file structure. When you create a file, if you have also created a logically organized set of directories beneath your own home directory, you will know where to store the file. In the following set of commands, we create a directory beneath the home directory and use that new directory to store a file.

To create a new directory beneath the current working directory, you use the **mkdir** command. The general syntax for the **mkdir** command is as follows:

mkdir [options] dirnames
Purpose: Creates directory or directories specified in **dirnames**
Output: New directory or directories
Commonly used options/features:
-m MODE   Create a directory with given access modes
-p   Create parent directories that don't exist in the pathnames specified in **dirnames**

To create a child, or subdirectory, named **first** under the current working directory, type the following:

$ mkdir first
$

This command has now created a new subdirectory named **first** under, or as a child of, the current working directory. Refer back to Figure 0.1 for a graphical description of the directory location of this new subdirectory.

In order to change the current working directory to this new subdirectory, you use the **cd** command. The general syntax for the **cd** command is as follows:

cd [directory]
Purpose: Change the current working directory to **directory** or return to the home directory when **directory** is omitted
Output: New current working directory

To change the current working directory to **first** by descending down the path structure to the specified directory named **first**, type the following:

$ cd first
$

You can always verify what the current working directory is by using the **pwd** command. The general syntax of the **pwd** command is as follows:

pwd
Purpose: Displays the current working directory on screen
Output: Pathname of current working directory

You can verify that **first** is now the current working directory by typing the following:

```
$ pwd
/home/bob/first
$
```

The output from the Raspberry Pi OS on the command line shows the pathname to the current working directory or folder. As previously stated, this path is a textual route through the complete file structure of the computer that Raspberry Pi OS is running on, ending in the current working directory. In this example of the output, the path starts at /, the root of the file system. Then it descends to the directory **home**, a major branch of the file system on the computer running Raspberry Pi OS. Then it descends to the directory **bob**, another branch, which is the home directory name for the user. Finally, it descends to the branch named **first**, the current working directory.

On some systems, depending on the default settings, another way of determining what the current working directory is can be done by simply looking at the command line prompt. This prompt may be prefaced with the complete path to the current working directory, ending in the current working directory.

You can ascend back up to the home directory, or the parent of the subdirectory **first**, by typing the following:

```
$ cd
$
```

An alternate way of doing this is to type the following, where the tilde character (~) resolves to, or is a substitute for, the specification of the complete path to the home directory:

```
$ cd ~
$
```

To verify that you have now ascended up to the home directory, type the following:

```
$ pwd
/home/bob
$
```

You can also ascend to a directory above your home directory, sometimes called the parent of your current working directory, by typing the following:

```
$ cd ..
$
```

In this command, the two periods (..) represent the parent, or branch above the current working directory. Don't forget to type a space character between the **d** and the first period. To verify that you have ascended to the parent of your home directory, type the following:

```
$ pwd
/home
$
```

To descend to your home directory, type the following:

```
$ cd
$
```

To verify that there are two files in the home directory that begins with the letters my, type the following command:

```
$ ls my*
myfile myfile2
$
```

The asterisk following the y on the command line is known as a *metacharacter*, or a character that represents a pattern; in this case, the pattern is any set of characters. When Raspberry Pi OS interprets the command after you press the **<Enter>** key on the keyboard, it searches for all files in the current working directory that begin with the letters my and end in anything else.

In-Chapter Exercise

9.   Use the **cd** command to ascend to the root (/) of your Raspberry Pi OS file system, and then use it to descend down each subdirectory from the root recursively to a depth of two subdirectories, sketching a diagram of the component files found on your system. Make the named entries in the diagram as complete as possible, listing as many files as you think necessary. Retain this diagram as a useful map of your particular Raspberry Pi OS distribution's file system.

Another aspect of organizing your directories is movement of files between directories, or changing the location of files in your directories. For example, you now have the file **myfile2** in your home directory, but you would like to move it into the subdirectory named **first**. See Figure 0.1 for a graphic description to change the organization of your files at this point. To accomplish this, you can use the second syntax method illustrated for the **mv file-list directory** command to move the file **myfile2** down into the subdirectory named **first**. To achieve this, type the following:

```
$ mv myfile2 first
$
```

To verify that **myfile2** is indeed in the subdirectory named **first,** type the following:

```
$ cd first
$ ls
myfile2
$
```

You will now ascend to the home directory, and attempt to remove or delete a file with the **rm** command.

Caution: you should be very careful when using this command because once a file has been deleted, the only way to recover it is from archival backups that you or the system administrator have made of the file system.

```
$ cd
$ rm myfile2
rm: myfile2: No such file or directory
$
```

You get the error message because in the home directory the file named **myfile2** does not exist. It was moved down into the subdirectory named **first**.

Directory organization also includes the ability to delete empty or nonempty directories. The command that accomplishes the removal of empty directories is **rmdir**. The general syntax of the **rmdir** command is as follows:

rmdir [options] dirnames
Purpose: Removes the empty directories specified in **dirnames**
Output: Removes directories
Commonly used options/features:
-p   Remove empty parent directories as well
-r   Recursively delete files and subdirectories beneath the current directory

To delete an entire directory below the current working directory, type the following:

$ rmdir first
rmdir: first: Directory not empty
$

Since the file **myfile2** is still in the subdirectory named **first, first** is not an empty directory, and you get the error message that the **rmdir** command will not delete the directory. If the directory was empty, **rmdir** would have accomplished the deletion. One way to delete a nonempty directory is by using the **rm** command with the **-r** option. The **-r** option recursively descends down into the subdirectory and deletes any files in it before actually deleting the directory itself. Be cautious with this command, since you may inadvertently delete directories and files with it. To see how this command deletes a nonempty directory, type the following:

$ rm -r first
$

The directory **first** and the file **myfile2** are now removed from the file structure.

0.2.5 Obtaining Help with the man Command

A very convenient utility available on Raspberry Pi OS systems is the online help feature, achieved via the use of the **man** command. The general syntax of the **man** command is as follows:

man [options][-s section] command-list
man -k keyword-list
Purpose: First syntax: Display Raspberry Pi OS Reference Manual
                    pages for commands in **command-list** one screen at a time
                    Second syntax: Display summaries of commands related to
                    keywords in **keyword-list**
Output: Manual pages one screen at a time
Commonly used options/features:
-k keyword-list   Search for summaries of keywords in **keyword-list** in a
                    database and display them
-s sec-num   Search section number **sec-num** for manual pages and
                    display them

To get help by using the **man** command, on usage and options of the **ls** command, for example, type the following:

$ man ls

LS(1)   User Commands   LS(1)

NAME
      ls - list directory contents

SYNOPSIS
      ls [OPTION]... [FILE]...

DESCRIPTION
      List information about the FILEs (the current directory
      by default).
      Sort entries alphabetically if none of -cftuvSUX nor –sort
      is specified.

      Mandatory arguments to long options are mandatory for
      short options too.

     -a, --all
          do not ignore entries starting with .

     -A, --almost-all
          do not list implied . and ..

     --author
Manual page ls(1) line 1 (press h for help or q to quit)

This output from Raspberry Pi OS is a Raspberry Pi OS *manual page*, or *manpage*, which gives a synopsis of the command usage showing the options, and a brief description that helps you understand how the command should be used. Typing **q** after one page has been displayed, as seen in the example, returns you to the command line prompt. Pressing the space key on the keyboard would have shown you more of the content of the manual pages, one screen at a time, related to the **ls** command.

To get help in using all the Raspberry Pi OS commands and their options, use the **man man** command to go to the Raspberry Pi OS reference manual pages.

The pages themselves are organized into eight sections, depending on the topic described, and the topics that are applicable to the particular system. Table 0.1 lists the sections of the manual and what they contain. Most users find the pages they need in Section 2.1. Software developers mostly use library and system calls and thus find the pages they need in Sections 2.2 and 2.3. Users who work on document preparation get the most help from Section 2.7. Administrators mostly need to refer to pages in Sections 2.1, 2.4, 2.5, and 2.8.

The manual pages comprise multi-page, specially formatted, descriptive documentation for every command, system call, and library call in Raspberry Pi OS. This format consists of eight general parts: name, synopsis, description, list of files, related information, errors, warnings, and known bugs. You

TABLE 0.1

Sections of the Manual

Section	What It Describes
1	User commands
2	System calls
3	Language library calls (C, FORTRAN, etc.)
4	Devices and network interfaces
5	File formats
6	Games and demonstrations
7	Environments, tables, and macros for troff
8	System maintenance-related commands

can use the **man** command to view the manual page for a command. Because of the name of this command, the manual pages are normally referred to as Raspberry Pi OS man pages. When you display a manual page on the screen, the top-left corner of the page has the command name with the section it belongs to in parentheses, as with LS(1), seen at the top of the output manual page.

The command used to display the manual page for the **passwd** command is:

$ **man passwd**

The manual page for the **passwd** command now appears on the screen, but we do not show its output. Because they are multi-page text documents, the manual pages for each topic take up more than one screen of text to display their entire contents. To see one screen of the manual page at a time, press the space bar on the keyboard. To quit viewing the manual page, press the **Q** key on the keyboard.

Now type this command:

$ **man pwd**

If more than one section of the man pages has information on the same word and you are interested in the man page for a particular section, you can use the **-S** option. The following command line therefore displays the man page for the read system call, and not the man page for the shell command read.

$ **man -S2 read**

The command **man -S3 fopen fread strcmp** sequentially displays man pages for three C library calls: **fopen**, **fread**, and **strcmp**.

To exit from the display of these system calls, type **<Ctrl-C>**.

Using the **man** command, and typing the command with the **-k** option, allows specifying a keyword that limits the search. It is equivalent to using the **apropos** command. The search then yields useful man page headers from all the man pages on the system that contain just the keyword reference. For example, the following command yields the on-screen output on our Raspberry Pi OS system:

```
$ man -k passwd
chgpasswd (8)               - update group passwords in batch mode
chpasswd (8)               - update passwords in batch mode
exim4_passwd (5)           - Files in use by the Debian exim4 packages
exim4_passwd_client (5)    - Files in use by the Debian exim4 packages
fgetpwent_r (3)            - get passwd file entry reentrantly
getpwent_r (3)             - get passwd file entry reentrantly
gpasswd (1)                - administer /etc/group and /etc/gshadow
openssl-passwd (1ssl)      - compute password hashes
pam_localuser (8)          - require users to be listed in /etc/passwd
passwd (1)                 - change user password
passwd (1ssl)              - compute password hashes
passwd (5)                 - the password file
passwd2des (3)             - RFS password encryption
update-passwd (8)          - safely update /etc/passwd, /etc/shadow and /etc/group
vncpasswd (1)              - VNC Server password utility
Output truncated...
```

0.2.6 Other Methods of Obtaining Help

To get a short description of what any particular Raspberry Pi OS command does, you can use the **whatis** command. This is similar to the command **man -f**. The general syntax of the **whatis** command is as follows:

whatis keywords
Purpose: Search the whatis database for abbreviated descriptions of each
                keyword
Output: Prints a one-line description of each keyword to the screen

The following is an illustration of how to use **whatis:**
The outputs of the two commands are truncated.

```
$ whatis man
man (7)   - macros to format man pages
man (1)   - an interface to the online
            reference manuals
$
```

You can also obtain short descriptions of more than one command by entering multiple arguments to the **whatis** command on the same command line, with spaces between each argument. The following is an illustration of this method:

```
$ whatis login set setenv
login (1)       - begin session on the system
login (3)       - write utmp and wtmp entries
setenv (3)      - change or add an environment variable
set: nothing appropriate.
$
```

The following in-chapter exercises ask you to use the **man** and **whatis** commands to find information about the **passwd** command. After completing the exercises, you can use what you have learned to change your login password on the Raspberry Pi OS system that you use.

In-Chapter Exercises

10. Use the **man** command with the **-k** option to display abbreviated help on the **passwd** command. Doing so will give you a screen display similar to that obtained with the **whatis** command, but it will show all apropos command names that contain the characters **passwd**.

11. Use the **whatis** command to get a brief description of the **passwd** command shown above, and then note the difference between the commands **whatis passwd** and **man -k passwd**.

0.3 Utility Commands

There are several important commands that allow the beginner to be more productive when using a Raspberry Pi OS system. A sampling of these kinds of utility commands is given in the following sections, and is organized as system setups, general utilities, and communications commands.

0.3.1 Examining System Setups

The **whereis** command allows you to search along certain prescribed paths to locate utility programs and commands, such as shell programs. The general syntax of the **whereis** command is as follows:

whereis [options] filename
Purpose: Locate the binary, source, and man page files for a command
Output: The supplied names are first stripped of leading pathname components and extensions, then pathnames are displayed on screen
Commonly used options/features:
-b   Search only for binaries
-s   Search only for source code

For example, if you type the command **whereis bash** on the command line, you will see a list of the paths to the Bash shell program files themselves, as follows:

```
$ whereis bash
bash: /bin/bash /etc/bash.bashrc /usr/share/man/man1/bash.1.gz
```

Note that the paths to a "built-in," or internal, command cannot be found with the **whereis** command.

When you first log on, it is useful to be able to view a display of information about your **userid**, the computer or system you have logged on to, and the operating system on that computer. These tasks can be accomplished with the **whoami** command, which displays your **userid** on the screen. The general syntax of the **whoami** command is as follows:

whoami
Purpose: Displays the effective user id
Output: Displays your effective user id as a name on standard

The following shows how our system responded to this command when we typed it on the command line.

```
$ whoami
bob
$
```

To find out the IP address of the Raspberry Pi you are working on, you can use the **ip** command. The general syntax of the **ip** command is as follows:

ip [OPTIONS] OBJECT {COMMAND | help}
Purpose: Show / manipulate routing, network devices, interfaces and tunnels.
Output: Information about your LAN.

To find out the IP address of the computer you are working on, type the following command in a terminal, or console window:

```
$ ip addr
1: lo: <LOOPBACK,UP,LOWER_UP> mtu 65536 qdisc noqueue state UNKNOWN group
default qlen 1000
    link/loopback 00:00:00:00:00:00 brd 00:00:00:00:00:00
    inet 127.0.0.1/8 scope host lo
     valid_lft forever preferred_lft forever
    inet6 ::1/128 scope host
     valid_lft forever preferred_lft forever
2: eth0: <BROADCAST,MULTICAST,UP,LOWER_UP> mtu 1500 qdisc mq state UP group
default qlen 1000
    link/ether dc:a6:32:ee:c6:6b brd ff:ff:ff:ff:ff:ff
    inet 192.168.1.2/24 brd 192.168.1.255 scope global dynamic noprefixroute eth0
     valid_lft 65558sec preferred_lft 54758sec
    inet6 fe80::78d9:c72e:75e2:82c/64 scope link
     valid_lft forever preferred_lft forever
3: wlan0: <BROADCAST,MULTICAST> mtu 1500 qdisc noop state DOWN group
default qlen 1000
    link/ether dc:a6:32:ee:c6:6c brd ff:ff:ff:ff:ff:ff
$
```

In the above output, the IP address 192.168.1.2 is the address on the LAN of this computer.

The following In-Chapter Exercises give you the chance to use **whereis**, **whoami**, and two other important utility commands, **who** and **hostname,** to obtain important information about your system.

In-Chapter Exercises

12. Use the **whereis** command to locate binary files for the Korn shell, the Bourne shell, the Bourne Again shell, the C shell, and the Z shell. Are any of these shell programs not available on your system?

13. Use the **whoami** command to find your username on the system that you're using. Then use the **who** command to see how your username is listed, along with other users of the same system. What is the on-screen format of each user's listing that you obtained with the **who** command? Try to identify the information in each field on the same line as your username.

14. Use the **hostname -I** command to find out the IP address of the host computer you are logged on to, on your LAN. Compares this to the output of the **ip addr** command on that same system.

0.4 Printing Commands

A very useful and common task performed by every user of a computer system is the printing of text files at a printer. This is accomplished using the configured printer(s) on the local, or a remote, system. Printers are controlled and managed with the Common UNIX Printing System (CUPS). We show this utility in detail in Chapter 1.

The common commands that perform printing on a Raspberry Pi OS system are **lpr** and **lp**. The general syntax of the **lpr** command is as follows:

lpr [options] filename
Purpose: Send files to the printer
Output: Files sent to the printer queue as print jobs
Commonly used options/features:
-P printer   Send output to the named printer
-# copies   Produce the number of copies indicated for each named file

The following **lpr** command accomplishes the printing of the file named **order.pdf** at the printer designated on our system as **spr**. Remember that no space is necessary between the option (in this case **-P**) and the option argument (in this case **spr**).

```
$ lpr -Pspr order.pdf
$
```

The following **lpr** command accomplishes the printing of the file named **memo1** at the default printer.

```
$ lpr memo1
$
```

The following multiple command combines the **man** command and the **lpr** command, and ties them together with the Raspberry Pi OS pipe (|) redirection character, to print the man pages describing the **ls** command at the printer named **hp1200**.

```
$ man ls | lpr -Php1200
$
```

The following shows how to perform printing tasks using the **lp** command.

The general syntax of the **lp** command is as follows:

lp [options][option arguments] file(s)
Purpose: Submit files for printing on a designated system printer, or alter
                pending print jobs
Output: Printed files or altered print queue
Commonly used options/features:
-d destination Print to the specified destination
-n copies   Sets the number of copies to print.

In the first command, the file to be printed is named **file1**. In the second
command, the files to be printed are named **sample** and **phones**. Note that
the **-d** option is used to specify which printer to use. The option to specify the
number of copies is **-n** for the **lp** command.

```
$ lp -d spr file1
request id is spr-983 (1 file(s))
$ lp -d spr -n 3 sample phones
request id is spr-984 (2 file(s))
$
```

0.5 Chapter Summary

In this introductory chapter, we covered essential Raspberry Pi OS commands
that allow a system administrator to do file maintenance, and perform other
useful operations. This is a mandatory set of essentials that even an ordinary,
non-adminstrative user would need to know to work efficiently in a character, or text-based interface to the operating system. Text-based commands
are the predominant means that a system administrator uses to maintain the
integrity of the system. We gave examples and showed the basic format of the
following commands and primitives:

cat cd cp exit hostname -I ip login lp lpr ls man mesg mkdir more mv passwd,
PATH pwd rm rmdir telnet unalias uname whatis whereis who whoami

Table 0.2 summarizes a basic set of useful commands necessary for the
beginner.

TABLE 0.2

Useful Commands for the Beginner

Command	What It Does
\<Ctrl+D\>	Terminates a process or command
alias	Allows you to create pseudonyms for commands
biff	Notifies you of new email
cal	Displays a calendar on screen
cat	Allows joining of files
cd	Allows you to change the current working directory
cp	Allows you to copy files
exit	Ends a shell that you have started
hostname	Displays the name of the host computer that you are logged on to
ip	Displays IP information of the current host
login	Allows you to log on to the computer with a valid username/password pair
lpr or lp	Allows printing of text files
ls	Allows you to display names of files and directories in the current working directory
man	Allows you to view a manual page for a command or topic
mesg	Allows or disallows writing messages to the screen
mkdir	Allows you to create a new directory
more	Allows viewing of the contents of a file one screen at a time
mv	Allows you to move the path location of, or rename, files
passwd	Allows you to change your password on the computer
pg	Solaris command that displays one screen of a file at a time
pwd	Allows you to see the name of the current working directory
rm	Allows you to delete a file from the file structure
rmdir	Allows deletion of directories
talk	Allows you to send real-time messages to other users
telnet	Allows you to log on to a computer on a network or the Internet
unalias	Allows you to undefine pseudonyms for commands
uname	Displays information about the operating system running the computer
whatis	Allows you to view a brief description of a command
whereis	Displays the path(s) to commands and utilities in certain key directories
who	Allows you to find out login names of users currently on the system
whoami	Displays your username
write	Allows real-time messaging between users on the system

1

Editing Text Files

1.0 Objectives

* To explain the general utility of editing text files on a Raspberry Pi system
* To show the basic capabilities of Nano
* To show the basic capabilities of Vi, Vim, and Gvim
* To present examples of C++ programs created, built, and run with Geany
* To provide a Geany an abbreviated reference source
* To illustrate some of the important ways of customizing these editors
* To cover the commands and primitives

   cp, geany, gvim, ls, nano, pwd, sh, vi, vim, who

1.1 Introduction and Quickstart

Questions: What is the salient difference, for a novice Raspberry Pi user, between a "text editor", an Integrated Development Environment (IDE), and a "word processor"? And why would that user want to deploy a text editor, when text files can be created using the Raspberry Pi IDE tools and facilities of Geany and Thonny?

Answers: Simply put, text editing is Character User Interface (CUI)-oriented, and IDEs and word processing are Graphical User Interface (GUI)-oriented. And there might be a circumstance where a purely-text based file is needed, that's not going to be executed as part of a C++ program or project, or a Python3 script file. For example, a simple Bash script, or an amendment to some system setup, or application resource file that's stored as text somewhere in the filesystem structure of your Raspberry Pi OS.

DOI: 10.1201/9781003455813-2

Even though Vi, Vim, and Gvim are highly customizable text editors, they don't have built-in project management features like Geany, or Visual Studio Code, for example. But you can use various plugins and techniques in those older editors to organize C++ source code files into projects. Here are some approaches you can consider when using those editors:

1. File System Organization: You can organize your C++ files in a directory structure that mimics your project's organization. Use subdirectories for different parts of your project (e.g., src, include, tests) and name files logically. Then, you can use Vim's file navigation commands to open files and navigate the project.

2. Use a Project Drawer Plugin: There are Vim plugins like NERDTree and Vim-vinegar that provide a file explorer or project drawer within Vim, making it easier to navigate and manage your project files.

3. Fuzzy File Finders: Plugins like fzf or CtrlP can help you quickly find and open files within your project by fuzzy searching filenames or paths.

4. Project-Specific Settings: You can create project-specific settings in your .vimrc or use a plugin like vim-projectionist to define project-specific configurations, file patterns, and settings.

5. Build Tools Integration: If you use a build system like CMake or Makefiles, you can integrate them into Vim to build and manage your project from within the editor.

6. Tag-Based Navigation: Vim has built-in support for ctags, which generates an index of symbols in your code. You can use plugins like CtrlP or fzf with ctags to navigate your codebase efficiently.

7. Session Management: Vim's built-in session management allows you to save and load workspace sessions. You can create a session for each project to save window layouts, opened files, and other settings.

8. Plugin Suites: Consider using plugin suites like SpaceVim or Janus, which come with various plugins and configurations tailored for specific programming languages, including C++.

9. Version Control Integration: If you use version control systems like Git, you can integrate Git with Vim to help you manage project files, branches, and commits.

10. Custom Scripts: You can create custom scripts or functions in Vimscript or other scripting languages (e.g., Python) to automate project-specific tasks.

While Vim itself doesn't provide a project management framework like Geany or Visual Studio Code, it offers a powerful and flexible environment where you can combine various plugins and custom configurations to suit your project organization needs. You can tailor your Vim setup to match your workflow and project structure effectively.

In this chapter we expose the ordinary novice Raspberry Pi user to basically three families of text editor: Nano, Vi/Vim/Gvim, and Geany. They are historically grounded in UNIX, when that operating system (OS) was purely text-based (similar to its extremely developed command line interface.) And with the advent of more sophisticated word processors in GUI environments, UNIX (and then Linux) text editors took on equivalent trappings in the mid-1980s. But Linux text editors never dispensed with a purely text-based mode of operation, as can be seen in the sections of this chapter. We use the following editors that are commonly available on our Raspberry Pi system: Nano, Vi, Vim, Gvim, and Geany.

1.2 Quick Start: The Simplest Path through These Editors

To stress how the keyboard keys are used in these editors, we provide the following reference to the keys used to execute commands or change modes:

1. Pressing the Escape key is signified as **<Esc>**

2. Pressing the Enter key is signified as **<Enter>**

3. Pressing the **<Ctrl>** key in combination with another single key is signified as **<Ctrl+X>**, where you hold down the **<Ctrl>** key and press the **X** key (or any valid key for that combination) at the same time.

4. Pressing the Alt key in combination with another single key is signified as **<Alt+X>**,

    where you hold down the **<Alt>** key and press the **X** key (or any valid key for that combination) at the same time.

5. A variant of points 3 and 4 is shown as **<Ctrl>+X a [b]**, where you first press and release **<Ctrl>** and **X** simultaneously, then press the **a** key, and optionally press the **b** key (or any valid combination of single keys or strings of characters).

What you type, or hold down on the keyboard, is shown in **bold** text. As a preliminary first example, the following sequence of key presses and typing makes use of the above references:

For Vi, Vim, and Gvim

*   At the shell prompt, run the program by typing **vi file1** then press **<Enter>**.
*   Type **A**

- Type some text.
- Press **<Esc>**
- Type **:** (colon)
- Type **wq** then press **<Enter>**.

You now have a file in your default directory named **file1** with the text you typed in it.

1.3 First Comments on Raspberry Pi Text Editors

The Raspberry Pi OS uses both a GUI, with powerful window management systems, and a CUI. Therefore, to do useful things such as execute multiple commands from within a script file, write email messages, or create C, or C++ language programs, you must be familiar with one or perhaps multiple ways of entering text into a file. In addition, you must also be familiar with how to edit existing files efficiently –that is, to change their contents or otherwise modify them in some way. Text editors allow you to view a file's contents, similar to the **more** command, so that you can identify the key features of the file, and then read and utilize the information contained in it. For example, a file without any extension, such as **foo** (rather than **foo.txt**) might be a text file that you can view with a text editor.

The editors that we consider here are all considered *full-screen display* editors. That is, on the display screen or monitor that you are using to view or edit a file, you are able to see a portion of the file, which fills most or all of the window allocated to the text editor screen display. You are also able to move the cursor, or point, to any of the text you see in this full-screen display, with either the arrow keys on the keyboard or with a mouse. That text material is usually held in a temporary storage area in computer memory called the editor *buffer*. If your file is larger than one screen, the buffer contents change as you move the cursor through the file. The difference between a file, which you edit, and a buffer is crucial. For text-editing purposes, a file is stored on disk as a sequence of data. When you edit that file, you edit a copy that the editor creates, which is in the editor buffer. You make changes to the contents of the buffer – and can even manipulate several buffers at once – but when you save the buffer, you write a new sequence of data to the disk, thereby saving the file.

Another important operational feature of all Raspberry Pi editors is that, traditionally, their actions are based on keystroke commands, whether they are a single keystroke or combinations of keys pressed simultan-eously or sequentially. Because one of the primary input devices in UNIX and Linux has been the keyboard, using the correct syntax of keystroke commands is absolutely mandatory. But the keyboard method of input, once you have become accustomed to it, is as efficient or, for some users, even more efficient than mouse/GUI input. Keystrokes also are more flexible, giving you more complete and customizable control over editing actions. Generally, you should choose the editor you are most comfortable with, in terms of the way you prefer to work with the computer. Of course, for most beginners, that will be Nano. However, your choice of editor also depends on the complexity and quantity of text creation and manipulation that you want to do. Practically speaking, editors such as Vi, Vim, and Gvim are capable of handling complex editing tasks in multiple windows on multiple files, and provide you with a visual software development environment, as well as document production and management capability. But to take advantage of that power, you have to learn the mechanics of the commands that are needed to perform those tasks and how they are implemented either graphically or by typing them – and retain that knowledge. The basic functions common to the text editors are listed in Table 1.1, along with a short description of each function.

For the text editors Vi, Vim, and Gvim, you can't immediately begin to enter text into the file you are editing. You have to be in *Insert mode* to do that. Vi, Vim, and Gvim have modes.

In Nano you can start typing text into the file immediately.

Nano is a *modeless* editor, and that's why it is easy to use. This basically means that you can immediately begin entering and editing text using the keyboard and some particular pointing device, such as a mouse or keyboard arrow keys.

We present the tutorial information on Nano in this chapter using typed commands.

It is very important to realize that Vi, Vim, and Gvim all generally use the same commands and have basically the same functionality. But Vim and Gvim are not only more graphical –allowing you to work more efficiently in

TABLE 1.1

General Text Editing Functions

Function	Description
Cursor movement	Moving the location of the insertion point or current position in the buffer
Cut or copy, paste	"Ripping out" text blocks or duplicating text blocks, reinserting ripped or duplicated blocks
Deleting text	Deleting text at a specified location or in a specified range
Inserting text	Placing text at a specified location
Opening, starting	Opening an existing file for modification, beginning a new file
Quitting	Leaving the text editor, with or without saving the work done
Saving	Retaining the buffer as a disk file
Search, replace	Finding instances of text strings, replacing them with new strings

GUI environments such as those on your Raspberry Pi system – but also have an improved and expanded command structure.

Note

Gvim was not pre-installed on our Raspberry Pi systems. But we used the APT package manager on the Raspberry Pi command line to install Gvim, as shown in the section on Gvim below.

The easiest and best way to install these editors on your system is by using the Add/Remove Software menu choice from the Raspberry Pi Preferences menu. The most expedient way of doing an installation of these editors, if they are not already installed on your Raspberry Pi system, is to use a graphical form of package management. This assumes that you are interacting with your Raspberry Pi using a desktop management system GUI. The most recent versions of the text editors we illustrate in this chapter at the time this book was written are as follows:

For Vim: Vim Version 8.2.2434

For Gvim: Vim-gtk 2:8.2.2434

In addition, be aware that if you are logging into a Raspberry Pi system via a terminal window, such as with ssh or PuTTY from another machine, many of the graphical modes and techniques of using these text editors will not be available to you. But that doesn't prevent you from using the traditional typed commands and keyboard edits that we show for Nano, for example!

1.4 Using Text Editors

Modern Linux uses both a GUI, with powerful window management systems, and CUI. Therefore, to do useful things such as execute multiple commands from within a script file, write email messages, or create C language programs, you must be familiar with one or perhaps multiple ways of entering text into a file. In addition, you must also be familiar with how to edit existing text files efficiently, that is, to change their contents or otherwise modify them in some way. Text editors allow you to view a file's contents, similar to the **more** command, so that you can identify the key features of the file, and then read and utilize the information contained in it. For example, a file without any extension, such as **foo** (rather than **foo.txt**), might be a text file that you can view with a text editor.

The editors that we consider here are all considered full-screen display editors. That is, on the display screen or monitor that you are using to view or edit a file, you are able to see a portion of the file, which fills most or all of the window allocated to the text editor screen display. You are also able to move the cursor, or point, to any of the text you see in this full-screen display, with either the arrow keys on the keyboard or with a mouse. That text material is usually held in a temporary storage area in computer memory called the editor *buffer*. If your file is larger than one screen, the buffer contents change as you move the cursor through the file. The difference between a file, which you edit, and a buffer is crucial. For text-editing purposes, a file is stored on disk as a sequence of data. When you edit that file, you edit a copy that the editor creates, which is in the editor buffer. You make changes to the contents of the buffer – and can even manipulate several buffers at once – but when you save the buffer, you write a new sequence of data to the disk, thereby saving the file.

Another important operational feature of all the editors discussed in this chapter is that, traditionally, their actions are based on keystroke commands, whether they are a single keystroke or combinations of keys pressed simultaneously or sequentially. Because one of the primary input devices in the Raspberry Pi OS is the keyboard, using the correct syntax of keystroke commands is mandatory. But the keyboard method of input, once you have become accustomed to it, is as efficient or, for some users, even more efficient than mouse/GUI input. Keystrokes also are more flexible, giving you more complete and customizable control over editing actions. Generally, you should choose the editor you are most comfortable with, in terms of the way you prefer to work with the computer. However, your choice of editor also depends on the complexity and quantity of text creation and manipulation that you want to do. Practically speaking, editors such as Vi, Vim, Gvim are capable of handling complex editing tasks in multiple windows on multiple files, and provide you with a visual software development environment, as well as document production and management capability. But to take advantage of that power, you have to learn the mechanics of the commands that are needed to perform those tasks and how they are implemented either graphically or by typing them – and retain that knowledge. The basic functions common to the text editors that we cover here are listed in Table 1.1, along with a short description of each function.

1.5 Nano

Our objectives in this section are to give a basic introduction to the Nano text editor, which is the simplest, and best for beginners What You See Is What You Get (WYSIWYG) editor in this chapter.

1.5.1 Introduction to Nano and Typographic Conventions

In this section, we introduce the simple text editor Nano, which comes pre-installed on our Raspberry Pi OS. To stress how the keyboard keys are used in the Nano editor, we repeat the following typographic convention reference for the keys used to execute commands in Nano:

1. Pressing the Escape key is signified as **<Esc>**
2. Pressing the Enter key is signified as **<Enter>**
3. Pressing the **<Ctrl>** key in combination with another single key is signified as **<Ctrl+X>**, where you hold down the **<Ctrl>** key and press the **X** key (or any valid key for that combination) at the same time.
4. Pressing the Alt key in combination with another single key is signified as **<Alt+X>**,

    where you hold down the **<Alt>** key and press the **X** key (or any valid key for that combination) at the same time.
5. A variant of points 3 and 4 is shown as <Ctrl>+X a [b], where you first press and release <Ctrl> and X simultaneously, then press the **a** key, and optionally press the **b** key (or any valid combination of single keys or strings of characters).

1.5.2 A Nano Quickstart

For many users, Nano would be the most efficient and adequate editor to deploy whenever a text editor is needed. Many of the tasks shown in the other standard text editors can be done quickly and easily by a novice user of a Raspberry Pi system using Nano.

To get started in Nano, either when you only have a CUI available, or when you are interacting with a Raspberry Pi via some desktop GUI, on the command line in a terminal window, type the following:

```
$ nano
```

You are immediately able to enter text into the editor, and move the cursor around with the arrow keys available on either a physical, or a "virtual" keyboard (e.g., such as is available on an iPad running the Termius terminal application). The first screen display presented by Nano is shown in Figure 1.1. You can also use the Delete key to delete text on the current line, at the first character before the current position of the cursor in the on-screen display of the text.

If you typed **nano file2**, where **file2** is the name of an already-existing text file, that text file is displayed on-screen, allowing you to make changes or additions to it.

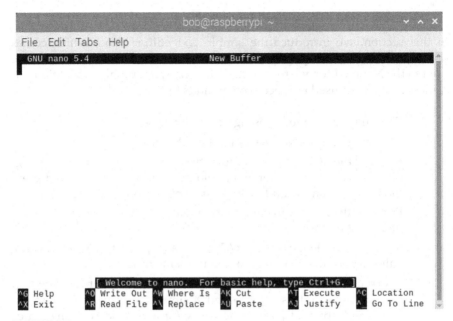

FIGURE 1.1
General appearance of the nano screen.

There are four main sections of the editor. The top line shows the program version, the current filename being edited, and whether or not the file has been modified. Next is the main editor window showing the file being edited. The status line is the third line from the bottom and shows important messages. The bottom two lines show the most commonly used commands executed via keyboard "shortcuts" in the editor.

Referring to Figure 1.1, at the bottom of the Nano screen display, there are several keyboard shortcut choices that you can make by holding down the Control (<**Ctrl**>, displayed as ^ on the Nano menu) key on your keyboard, in combination with a letter key.

Note
The two most important Nano shortcut choices presented are:

1.   The command <**Ctrl+O**>, which allows you to write (in other words, save) the contents of what is shown on-screen to a file in the current working directory, without leaving the Nano editor.

2.   The command <**Ctrl+X**> which allows you to exit from the editor, and return to the Raspberry Pi command prompt. If you've made changes to the current buffer, Nano will prompt you to save those changes (Yes/No), and then specify a file name to save the buffer to, with the default name presented for you to accept.

To get a more in-depth explanation of the other menu choices at the bottom of the Nano screen display, and of the capabilities of Nano itself, see the following sections. We also refer you to the various online help pages. A good place to start is "The Beginner's Guide to Nano, the Linux Command-Line Text Editor", currently found at the following website:

www.howtogeek.com/42980/the-beginners-guide-to-nano-the-linux-command-line-text-editor/

1.5.3 A Brief Nano Tutorial

The following subsections illustrate and explain some of the basic operations, as well as some of the features, of Nano.

1.5.3.1 Creating and Opening a New File

If you want to create a new file and open it using Nano, use the following command(s) from a terminal window:

```
$ nano
or
$ nano [filename]
```

The second command is also used to open an existing file, where filename is the name of the existing file. If you want to open a file which is not located in your current directory, then you have to use the absolute or relative path to that file. For example /home/bob/filename.

Figure 1.2 shows a file that has been opened with the second command shown above.

At the bottom of the editor window, keyboard shortcuts are displayed (they are not GUI menu choices!) that let you perform some basic operations. Examples of these are Cut, Paste, Write Out, Exit, etc.

1.5.3.2 How to Save a File

To save a file, use the keyboard shortcut <Ctrl+O>. When you use this key combination, the editor will prompt you for a filename (or confirm the name if it was already provided when the editor was started). Enter your filename, and press <Enter> to save the file with that name.

This is illustrated in Figure 1.3.

1.5.3.3 How to Cut and Paste Text

To cut and paste a particular line of existing text that has already been entered into the buffer, first bring the cursor to any character on that line by using the

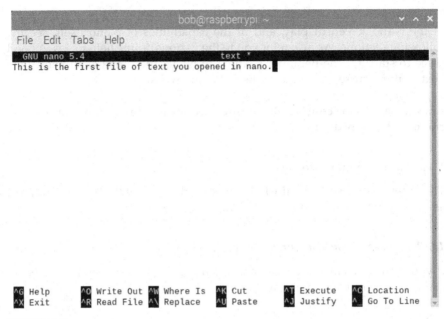

FIGURE 1.2

First opened file in nano.

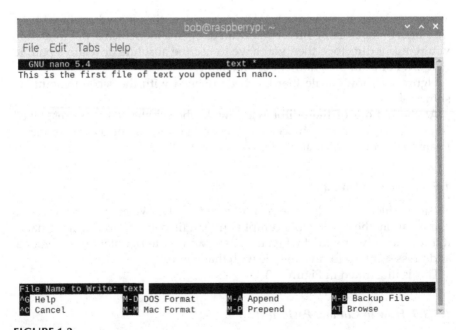

FIGURE 1.3

Writing out a file with a specific file name.

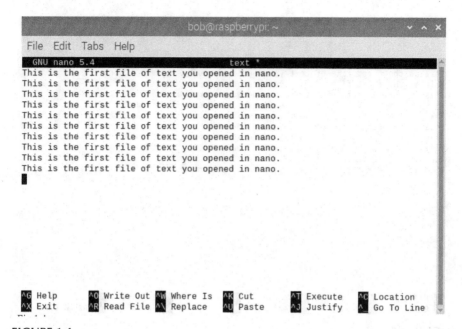

FIGURE 1.4

Cut and pasted text from one line to other lines.

arrow keys on the keyboard. Press **<Ctrl+K>** to cut that whole line out of the buffer, then position the cursor with the arrow keys to the place where you want to paste the "cut" line back into the buffer. Since in our example, there's only one line, now blank, in the buffer, the cursor is on line 1. Finally use **<Ctrl+U>** to paste the cut line back in.

For example, in Figure 1.4, if you want to cut the first line and paste it multiply to two lines below the first, go to the beginning of line 1 using the arrow keys on the keyboard, and then press **<Ctrl+U>**. Then, the position the cursor below the first line and press **<Ctrl+U>**. Repeat to do this multiply. In Figure 1.4, this paste was done nine times.

1.5.3.4 How to Search and Replace a Word

This feature allows you to search for a particular word in the buffer, as well as replace it with another word.

To search for a word in Nano, press **<Ctrl+W>**. Then, you will be asked to enter the word which you want to search for. After typing-in the word (we typed-in "opened"), press **<Enter>**, and Nano will take you to the first matched entry below or on the same line the cursor is positioned that matches that entry. In Figure 1.5, the cursor was on line 2, so Nano found the first instance of the word "opened," which was on the second line.

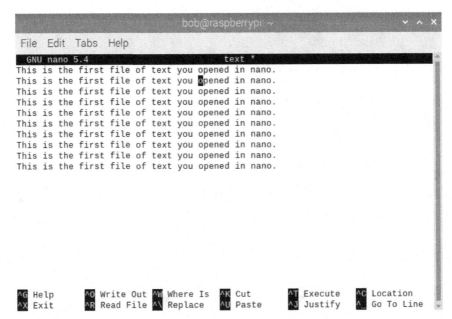

FIGURE 1.5
Searching for text.

You can also replace a word (or phrase) with another by pressing **<Ctrl+\>**. When you press this key combination, Nano prompts you for the word (or phrase) which you want to replace. After typing-in the word (or phrase), press **<Enter>**. You will be prompted for the replacement word (or phrase). After this, you will be prompted for various ways of doing the replacement, and then are asked to confirm the changes. Once confirmed, the replacement is done.

1.5.3.5 How to Insert Another File into Current One in the Buffer

To insert text from another, already-saved file into the buffer you are currently editing, do the following. Press **<Ctrl+R>**, and then give the complete pathname to the file which you want to insert into the current buffer, at the current position of the cursor in that buffer. Figure 1.6 illustrates this procedure.

As you can see in Figure 1.7, the text of a file "/home/bob/second_nano" was inserted at the cursor position (which in the file "text" from Figure 1.5 was placed on a blank line created after the last line of text already in that file).

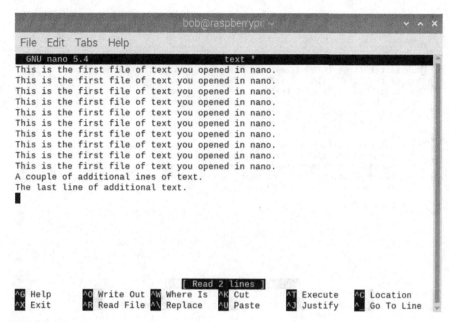

FIGURE 1.6

Inserting text from a file.

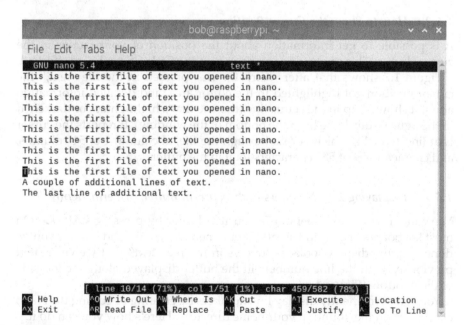

FIGURE 1.7

Cursor position report.

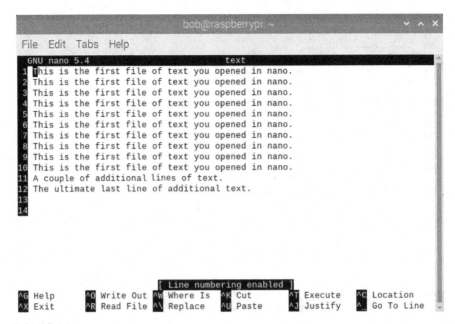

FIGURE 1.8
Display of line numbers in a buffer.

1.5.3.6 How to Show the Cursor Position

It is possible to get information about the position of your cursor in the current buffer. This can be done by pressing the **<Ctrl+C>** keyboard shortcut.

Figure 1.7 shows that after **<Ctrl+C>** was pressed in the file "text," the cursor position got highlighted in the editor area, and detailed information about it showed up in the status line (the one that's highlighted, or darkened in the figure – third line from the bottom of the window). It reports the cursor is at line 10 of 14, which is 78% through the file, at column 1 of 51 columns, and character 459 of 582 characters total in the buffer.

1.5.3.7 Displaying Line Numbers in the Current Buffer, or Permanently

You can show line numbers in the current buffer by pressing **<Alt+#>**. On most keyboards, the pound sign(#) is obtained using Shift and 3. After you've done this, the display looks as follows in the file "text" that we've created previously, with the line numbers in the buffer displayed along the left side of the window (Figure 1.8).

You can permanently display line numbers by creating or editing the Nano configuration file, found in your home directory. Here's how you can do it:

1.   Open a terminal window.

2. Type the following command to edit or create the Nano configuration file:

    `$ nano ~/.nanorc`

3. In the Nano configuration file, add the following line to enable line numbers:

    set linenumbers

4. Save the file by pressing **<Ctrl+O>**, then press Enter. To exit Nano, press **<Ctrl+X>**.

5. Use the **chmod** command to make sure the access privileges to the ~/.nanorc file are set to **u+x**.

6. The line numbers should now be permanently displayed whenever you open Nano to edit a file.

Note that if the ~/.nanorc file *doesn't* exist, you can create it by following the steps above. If it already exists, simply add the **set linenumbers** line to it.

In-Chapter Exercises

1.1 Launch Nano without specifying a file name on the command line, and then enter some text into the New Buffer. Save that text into a file in your current working directory.

1.2 Cut some text out of a displayed file in Nano, using Nano keyboard commands, and then paste it at another point in the display. What commands did you use to do this?

1.3 Replace a string of text in a displayed file in Nano with another string of text. What command(s) did you use to do this? Can this be done at multiple sites repetitively in the file, and simultaneously all at once?

1.4 Describe, in your own words, the concept of a buffer in Nano.

1.5 How did you select multiple characters in Nano for the commands executed in the exercises above? If you use a single-console, text-only method of logging into and interacting with the Raspberry Pi, how can you select multiple characters for the operations you are asked to do in the exercises above?

1.6 a. In only a single terminal display, how can you open multiple buffers in previously created text files in Nano, and switch between editing in them? b. What would be the major advantage of doing this?

1.6 Vi, Vim, and Gvim

The Vi, Vim, and Gvim text editors for the Raspberry Pi OS have almost all the features of a word processor, and have tremendous flexibility in creating text files. Initially, they are as easy to use as Nano, and can create simple text files for a novice user. Once you begin to exploit their more complex capabilities, their advantages allow you to create, manipulate, and use the kinds of text files that the full range of Raspberry Pi users, from absolute novice to seasoned veteran, commonly work with. We will proceed in the following sections and subsections to demonstrate Vi as a text-only interface editor, then move to a more graphical interface approach with Vim and Gvim.

As mentioned in Section 1.1, the notion of a *buffer* as a temporary storage facility for the text that you are editing is very useful and important in Vi, Vim, and Gvim.

Some examples of buffers in these three editors are as follows:

a.   The main buffer, sometimes referred to as the editing buffer, or the work buffer, is the main repository for the body of text that you are trying to create, or to modify from some previous permanently archived file on disk.

b.   The general purpose buffer is where your most recent "ripped-out" (cut/copied) text is retained.

c.   Indexed buffers allow you to store more than one temporary string of text.

1.6.1 Basic Shell Script File Creation, Editing, and Execution

Shell Script File: Practice Session 1.1 shows how to create a script file, or collection of Linux commands that are executed in sequence, and then execute the script. For this example, we assume that you are running the Bourne Again (bash) shell.

On your Raspberry Pi system, do Practice Session 1.1 for the bash shell, which is the default shell in that system, and don't change shells.

And don't worry too much if you make an error in Steps 2, 3, and 4; you can go through the rest of the script file discussion, and then come back to this example after you have learned some of the Vi text editing commands, and become more familiar with them.

Practice Session 1.1

Step 1: At the shell prompt, start vi by typing **vi firscrip** and then pressing **<Enter>**. The vi screen appears on your display.

Step 2: Type **A**. Then type **ls -la** and then press **<Enter>**.

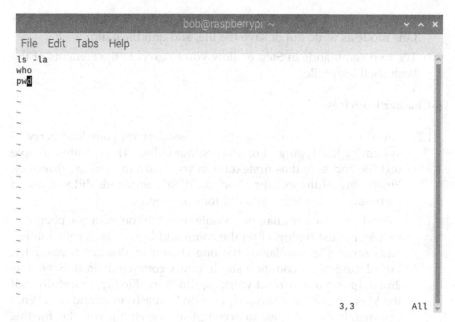

FIGURE 1.9
File firscrip after Step 4.

Step 3: Type **who** and then press **<Enter>**.

Step 4: Type **pwd** and then press the **<Esc>** key. At this point, your screen should look like that shown in Figure 1.9.

Step 5: Type **:wq** and then press **<Enter>**. You exit from Vi.

Step 6: At the shell prompt, type **chmod u+x firscrip** and then press **<Enter>**. Then type **./firscrip** and press **<Enter>**.

Step 7: Note the results. How many files do you have in your present working directory? What are their names and sizes? Who else is using your computer system? What is your present working directory?

In Practice Session 1.1, you accomplished these things:

* At Step 2, typing **A** took Vi out of *Command mode* (which is what Vi starts in by default) and placed it in one of the forms of Insert mode. In other words, anything that you typed at the keyboard was appended as text on the first line in the text area of the editor.

* When you pressed the **<Esc>** key in Step 4, Vi was taken out of Insert mode and put back into Command mode.

* When you typed: in Step 5, that was a valid Command mode prefix character for the two commands that followed, and put Vi in *Last Line mode*.

*   When you typed **wq** after the :, Vi interpreted those commands in Last Line mode as write out or save the file, and quit the editor.
*   The two commands in Step 6 allow you to execute the contents of the Bash shell script file.

In-Chapter Exercises

1.7   Launch Vi in a terminal, or console, window on your Raspberry Pi system by just typing **vi** on the command line. Then create a simple text file and save it as **firstext.txt** in your current working directory. Finally, gracefully exit the Vi editor. What commands did you use to accomplish everything you did for this exercise?

1.8   Launch Vi in a terminal, or console, window on your Raspberry Pi system by just typing **vi** on the command line. Then create another bash script file, similar to the one shown in Practice Session 1.1, but placing other common single Linux commands in it. Save it as **2ndscrip** in your current working directory. Finally, gracefully exit the Vi editor, and test this script file on the bash command line. What commands did you use to accomplish everything you did for this exercise?

1.6.2 How to Start, Save a File, and Exit

When you need to do Raspberry Pi text editing that gives you as much functionality as a typical word processor, you can use the Vi text editor. To start Vi from the command line, use the following general syntax (anything enclosed in square brackets [] is optional):

vi [options] [file(s)]
Purpose: Allows you to edit a new or existing text file(s)
Output: With no options or file(s) specified, you are placed in the Vi
              program and can begin to edit a new buffer
Commonly used options/features:
+n   Begin to edit file(s) starting at line number n
+/exp   Begin to edit at the first line in the file matching string exp

The operations that you perform in Vi fall into two general categories: *Command mode* operations, which consist of key sequences that are commands to the editor to take certain actions, and *Insert mode* operations, which allow you to input text.

The general organization of the Vi text editor, and how to start, exit, and switch modes, are illustrated in Figure 1.10. The general organization of Vim and Gvim, and how to start, exit, and switch modes in those editors, is the same as shown for Vi in Figure 1.10.

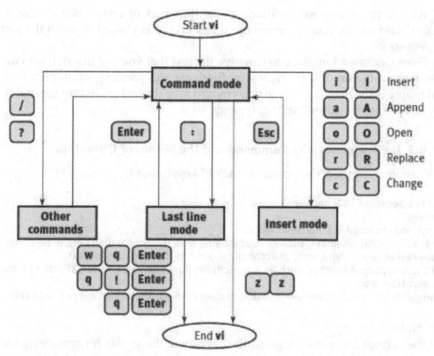

FIGURE 1.10
General organization of Vi, Vim, and Gvim.

For example, to change from Command mode, which you are in when you first enter the editor, to Insert mode, type a valid command, such as **A** to append text at the end of the current line. Certain commands that are prefixed with the:, /,?, or:! characters are echoed or shown to you on the last line on the screen and must be terminated by pressing **<Enter>**. *Last Line mode*, sometimes called *ex mode* because it is derived from an older, UNIX editor, the *ex editor*, allows you to execute certain commands and leave the editor. To change from Insert mode to Command mode, press the **<Esc>** key.

The keystroke commands that you execute in Vi are case sensitive; for example, uppercase **A** appends new text after the last character at the end of the current line, whereas lowercase **a** appends new text after the character the cursor is on.

To start Vi, at the shell prompt, type **vi** (and optionally designate some option[s] and file name[s]) and then press **<Enter>**. You are now in Command mode. To enter Insert mode, type **A** and you are now able to insert text on the first line of the file.

After entering text, you can press the **<Esc>** key to enter Command mode.

At any point in your creation or manipulation of text, when you're in Command mode, you can press the **u** key on the keyboard to undo the last operation.

From Command mode, you can save the text that you just inserted into the buffer to a file on disk by typing **:w filename** and pressing **<Enter>**, where **filename** is the name of the file you want to save the text to. To quit the editor, type **:q**. To quit without saving, type **:q!**

1.6.3 The Format of a Vi Command and the Modes of Operation

In Command mode, the generic syntax of keystrokes is:

[#1] operation [#2] target
where:
anything enclosed in **[ ]** is optional;
#1 is an optional number, such as 5, specifying how many operations are to be done;
operation is what you want to accomplish, such as deleting lines of text;
#2 is an optional number, such as 5, specifying how many targets are affected by the **operation**; and
target is the text that you want to do the operation on, such as an entire line of text.

Note
If the current line is the target of the operation, the syntax for specifying the target is the same as the syntax of the operation; for example, **dd** deletes the current line. Also, a variation on this generic syntax is the cursor movement command, whereby you can omit the numbers and operation and simply move the cursor by word, sentence, paragraph, or section.

Table 1.2 lists some specific examples of this generic syntax and variations used in Command mode.

As previously stated, when you start Vi, it is in Command mode. When you want to be in Insert mode instead of Command mode, press a valid key to accomplish the change. Some of these keys are shown in Table 1.3.

After inserting text, you can edit the text, move the cursor to a new position in the buffer, and save the buffer and exit the editor – all from within Command mode. When you want to change from Insert mode to Command mode, press the **<Esc>** key.

To save the buffer and exit the editor, press the: key (colon) to enter Last Line mode. The general commands that are useful in Last Line mode are shown in Table 1.4.

For now, we recommend that you use the arrow keys on the keyboard to move the cursor around in the buffer. It is possible to also use the **h, j, k,** and l keys on the keyboard to move the cursor. In Gvim, you can use the mouse and its buttons!

The following Practice Session introduces you to some of the commands presented in Tables 1.2 through 1.4. Feel free to use either Vi or Vim to do the steps of the following on your Raspberry Pi system:

TABLE 1.2

Examples of Vi Command Syntax

Command	Action
cw	Changees word.
cc	Changes line.
c$	Changes text from current position to the end of line.
C	Same as c$.
dd	Deletes the current line.
7 dd	Deletes 7 lines.
d$	Deletes text from current position to the end of line.
D	Same as d$.
5dw	Deletes 5 words.
d7,14	Deletes lines 7 through 14 in the buffer.
d}	Deletes up to next paragraph.
d^	Deletes back to beginning of line.
d/ pat	Deletes up to first occurrence of pattern.
dn	Delete up to next occurrence of pattern.
df x	Deletes up to and including x on current line.
dt x	Deletes up to (but not including) x on current line.
dL	Deletes up to last line on screen.
dG	Deletes to end of file.
Gqap	Reformats current paragraph to text width (Vim and Gvim).
g~w	Switch case of word (Vim and Gvim).
Guw	Change word to lowercase (Vim and Gvim).
gUw	Changes word to uppercase (Vim and Gvim).
p	Inserts the last deleted or yanked text after cursor.
Gp	Same as p, but leave cursor at the end of inserted text (Vim and Gvim).
gP	Same as P, but leave cursor at the end of inserted text (Vim and Gvim).
]p	Same as p, but match current indention (Vim and Gvim).
[p	Same as P, but match current indention (Vim and Gvim).
P	Inserts the last deleted or yanked text before cursor.
r x	Replaces character with x. Does not require the use of <Esc>!
R text	Replaces with new text (overwrite), beginning at cursor. <Esc> ends replace mode.
s	Substitutes character. <Esc> ends substitute mode.
4s	Substitute four characters. <Esc> ends substitute mode.
S	Substitutes the entire line. <Esc> ends substitute mode.
U	Undoesthe last change.
<Ctrl+R>	Redoes the last change (Vim and Gvim).
U	Restores the current line, if you have not moved off of it.
x	Deletes current cursor position.
X	Deletes back one character.
5X	Deletes previous 5 characters
.	Repeats last change.
~	Changes case and moves cursor right.
<Ctrl+A>	Increments number at the cursor (Vim and Gvim).
<Ctrl+X>	Decrements number at the cursor (Vim and Gvim).

TABLE 1.3

Important Keys Used to Switch from Command to Insert Mode

Key	Action
A	Appends text after the character the cursor is on.
A	Appends text after the last character of the current line.
C	Begins a change operation, allowing you to modify text.
C	Changes from the cursor position to the end of the current line.
i	Inserts text before the character the cursor is on.
I	Inserts text at the beginning of the current line.
o	Opens a blank line below the current line and puts the cursor on that line.
O	Opens a blank line above the current line and puts the cursor on that line.
R	Begins overwriting text.
s	Substitutes single characters.
S	Substitutes whole lines.

TABLE 1.4

Important Commands in Command Mode

Command	Action
: n, m w file	Write lines n to m to new file.
: n, m w >> file	Append lines n to m to existing file.
:r filename	Reads and inserts the contents of the file filename at the current cursor position.
:wq	Saves the buffer and quits.
:w	Saves the current buffer and remains in the editor.
:w filename	Saves the current buffer to filename.
:w! filename	Overwrites filename with the current text.
:w!	Writes file (overriding protection).
:w! file	Overwrites file with current text.
:w %.new	Writes current buffer named **file** as **file.new**.
:q	Quits Vi (fails if changes were made).
:q!	Quits Vi without saving the buffer.
:Q	Quits Vi and invokes ex.
:vi	Returns to Vi after Q command.
ZZ	Quits Vi, saving the file only if changes were made since the last save.
%	Replaced with current filename in editing commands.
#	Replaced with alternate filename in editing commands.

Practice Session 1.2

Step 1: At the shell prompt, type **vi firstvi** and then press <Enter>.

Step 2: Type **A**, then type **This is the first line of a vi file.** and then press <Enter>.

Step 3: Type **This is the line of a vi file.** and then press <Enter>.

Step 4: Type **is the 3r line of a vi**

Step 5: Press the **<Esc>** key.

Step 6: Type **:w** and then press **<Enter>**.

Step 7: Use the arrow keys on the keyboard to position the cursor on the character l in the word line on the second line of the file.

Step 8: Type **i** and then **2nd_**, where the _ is a space character

Step 9: Press the **<Esc>** key.

Step 10: Use the arrow keys to position the cursor anywhere on the third line of the file.

Step 11: Type **I** and then **This_**, where the _ is a space character.

Step 12: Press the **<Esc>** key.

Step 13: Use the arrow keys on the keyboard to position the cursor on the character r in 3r on this line.

Step 14: Type **a** and then **d**.

Step 15: Press the **<Esc>** key.

Step 16: Type **A** and then **_file.**, where the _ is a space character.

Step 17: Press the **<Esc>** key on the keyboard. Your screen display should look similar to Figure 1.11.

Step 18: Type **:wq**. You will be back at the shell prompt.

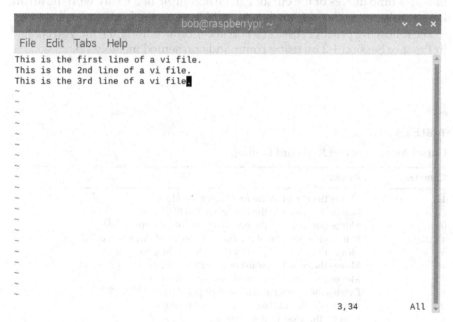

FIGURE 1.11
File firstvi.

The following In-Chapter Exercises ask you to apply some of the operations you learned about in the previous practice session.

In-Chapter Exercises

1.9   With Vi you begin editing a file that you created yesterday. You want to save a copy of it with a different filename while still in Vi, but you don't want to quit this editing session. How do you accomplish this result in Vi?

1.10   What happens if you accomplish five operations in Vi and then type **5u** when in Command mode?

1.11   In your own words, give a brief description of what the following Vi commands accomplish (use Tables 1.2 through 1.4 to guide you in your answers):

dd, d1,12, x, a, 5b, 3w,:q!, G, 1G

1.6.4 Cursor Movement and Editing Commands

In Command mode, several commands accomplish cursor movement and text editing tasks. Table 1.5 lists important cursor movement and keyboard editing commands. As we have already noted, character-at-a-time or line-at-a-time moves of the cursor can be accomplished easily with the arrow keys, or alternatively with the h, j, k, and l keys on the keyboard.

The following practice session lets you continue editing the file you created in Practice Session 1.2 by using commands presented in Table 1.5.

TABLE 1.5

Cursor Movement and Keyboard Editing

Command	Action
1G	Moves the cursor to the first line of the file.
G	Moves the cursor to the last line of the file.
0 (zero)	Moves the cursor to the first character of the current line.
<Ctrl+G>	Reports the position of the cursor in terms of line # and column #.
$	Moves the cursor to the last character of the current line.
w	Moves the cursor forward one word at a time.
b	Moves the cursor backward one word at a time.
x	Deletes the character at the cursor position.
dd	Deletes the line at the current cursor position.
u	Undoes the most recent change.
r	Replaces the character at the current cursor location with what is typed next.

Practice Session 1.3

Step 1: At the shell prompt, type **vi firstvi** and then press **<Enter>**.

Step 2: Type **G**. The cursor moves to the first character on last line of the file.

Step 3: Hold down the **<Ctrl>** and **g** keys at the same time. On the last line of the screen display, Vi reports the following:

"firstvi" 3 lines --100%-- 3,1 All

This is a report of the buffer that you are editing, the total number of lines in the buffer, the percentage of the buffer that this line represents, the current column position of the cursor, and other editor settings that are the default.

Step 4: Type **o**. A new line opens below the third line of the file, and you're in Insert mode.

Step 5: Type **This is the 5th line of a vi file.** Type **<Esc>**.

Step 6: Type **0** (zero). The cursor moves to the first character of the line you just typed in.

Step 7: Type **$**. The cursor moves to the last character of the current line.

Step 8: Type **O**. A new line opens above the current fourth line.

Step 9: Type **This is the 44th line of a va file.** Type **<Esc>**.

Step 10: Use the arrow keys to position the cursor over the first 4 in 44 on this line.

Step 11: Type **x**.

Step 12: Use the arrow keys to position the cursor over the a in va on this line.

Step 13: Type **r** and then type **i**.

Step 14: Type **dd**.

Step 15: Type **:wq** to go back to the shell prompt.

Step 16: At the shell prompt, type **more firstvi** and then press **<Enter>**. How many lines with text on them does **more** show in this file?

1.6.5 Yank and Put (Copy and Paste) and Substitute (Search and Replace)

Every word processor is capable of copying and pasting text, and also of searching for old text and replacing it with new text. Copying and pasting are accomplished with the Vi commands *yank* and *put*. In general, you use yank and put in sequence, and move the cursor (with any of the cursor movement commands or methods) only between yanking and putting. Some examples of the syntax for yank and put are given in Table 1.6.

TABLE 1.6

Example Yank and Put Command Syntax

Command Syntax	What It Accomplishes
y2W	Yanks two words, starting at the current cursor position, going to the right.
4yb	Yanks four words, starting at the current cursor position, going to the left.
yy or Y	Yanks the current line.
P	Puts the yanked text after the current cursor position.
P	Puts the yanked text before the current cursor position.
5p	Puts the yanked text in the buffer five times after the current cursor position.
Y	Copies the current line.
Yy	Copies current line.
"x yy	Copies the current line to register x.
Ye	Copies text to the end of word.
Yw	Like ye, but includes the whitespace after the word.
y$	Copies rest of line.
"x dd	Deletes current line into register x.
"x d	Deletes into register x.
"x p	Puts contents of register x.
y]]	Copies up to next section heading.
J	Join current line to the next line.
gJ	Same as J, but without inserting a space (Vim and Gvim).
:j	Same as J.
:j!	Same as gJ.

The simple Vi forms of search and replace are accomplished using the **substitute** command. This command is executed when Vi is in Last Line mode, where you preface the command with the: character, and terminate the command by pressing **<Enter>**. The format of the substitute command as it is typed on the status line is:

:[range]s/pattern/string[/option(s)][count]

where:

anything enclosed in [] is not mandatory;

: is the colon prefix for the Last Line mode command;

range is a valid specification of lines in the buffer (or the current line is the range);

s or **substitute** is the syntax of the substitute command;

/ is a delimiter for searching;

pattern is the text or objects you want to replace;

/ is a delimiter for replacement;

string is the new text or objects;

/option(s) is a modifier, usually **g** for global, to the command; and

count is the number of lines to execute the command on from the current position.

The grammatic constructions of pattern and string can be extremely explicit and complex, and may take the form of a *regular expression*. A regular expression in UNIX and Linux is a string that is used to describe sequences of characters. Some examples of the syntax for the substitute command, including Vim/Gvim-only constructions, are given in Table 1.7.

Practice Session 1.4 shows you how to use the Vi commands **yank** and **put** to copy and paste. It also allows you to do individual, and multiple searches, and replace text with the Vi **substitute** command.

Practice Session 1.4

Step 1: At the shell prompt, type **vi multiline** and then press **<Enter>**.

Step 2: Type **A** and then type **Windows is the operating system of choice for everyone.**

Step 3: Press the **<Esc>** key. You have left Insert mode and are now in Command mode.

Step 4: Press the **0** (zero) key. The cursor moves to the first character of the first line.

Step 5: Type **yy**. This action yanks, or copies, the first line to a special buffer.

Step 6: Type **7p**. This action puts, or pastes, the first line seven times, creating seven new lines of text containing the same text as the first line. The

TABLE 1.7

Example Syntax for the Substitute Command

Command Syntax	What It Accomplishes
:s/john/jane/	Substitutes the word jane for the word john on the current line, only once.
:s/john/jane/g	Substitutes the word jane for every word john on the current line.
:1,10s/big/small/g	Substitutes the word small for every word big on lines 1–10.
:1,$s/men/women/g	Substitutes the word women for every word men in the entire file.
:'<,'>s/this/that/g	Selects the range in Command mode first by typing <Ctrl+V> and using the arrow keys. Then type :. The word that will be substituted for the word this (Vim, Gvim only).
:s/ \<tim\>/tom/	Substitutes only the whole word tim with the word tom, not the partial match of tim in any string.
:%s/terrible/wonderful/gc	Interactive substitution using c option of the word terrible with the word wonderful (Vim, Gvim only).
:%s/^/ \=line(".") . ". "/g	Makes the line numbers of all lines in the buffer permanently part of each line (Vim, Gvim only).

cursor should now be on the first character of the eighth line. If it's not, use the arrow keys to put the cursor there.

Step 7: Type **1G**. This action puts the cursor on the first character of the first line in the buffer.

Step 8: Hold down the **<Shift>** and **;** keys at the same time. Doing so places a**:** in the status line at the bottom of the Vi screen display, allowing you to type a command.

Step 9: Type **s/everyone/students/** and then press **<Enter>**. The word everyone at the end of the first line is replaced with the word students.

Step 10: Use the arrow keys to position the cursor on the first character of the second line.

Step 11: Type **:s/everyone/computer scientists/** and then press **<Enter>**.

Step 12: Repeat Steps 8–10 on the third through eighth lines of the buffer, substituting the words engineers, system administrators, web servers, scientists, networking nerds, and mathematicians for the word everyone on each of those seven lines. Type **1G**.

Step 13: Type **:1,$s/Windows/Linux/g** and then press **<Enter>**. You have globally replaced the word Windows on all eight lines of the file with the word Linux. Correct?

Step 14: Your Vi screen display should now look like Figure 1.12. Type **:wq**. You have now saved the changes and exited from Vi.

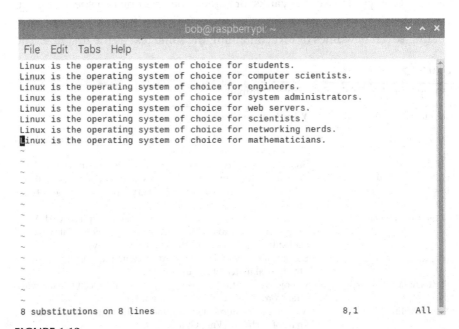

FIGURE 1.12
Multiline Vi file.

1.6.6 Vim and Gvim

Vim and Gvim are two examples among many of enhanced, "improved" versions of Vi. The following subsections illustrate some of the advantages of using Vim and Gvim over the traditional Vi editor.

1.6.6.1 Vim Enhancements

The following capabilities of Vim, which enhance Vi functionality, particularly the first one shown, are suggestions that you can use to expedite your editing tasks with Vim and Gvim over and above the capabilities of Vi:

* vimrc
If you want to enable any of the improved facilities of Vim and Gvim, you should create a ~/.vimrc file. Even if this file is empty, it will enable the facilities that we illustrate in this section!

* Help
In Vim Last Line mode, type help or press the **<F1>** function key.
Vim opens a help buffer that gives you extensive help on its facilities. In Last Line mode, when in the help buffer, type q to exit help.

* Multiple Windows
The Last Line mode command **split** splits the current window into two. You can then move the cursor up to a window with **<Ctrl+W> j** and down a window with **<Ctrl+W> k**. For example, the Last Line mode command **split new.c** splits the window and begins editing the file named **new.c**. To close a window, use the normal Vim exit commands **ZZ** or **:q!**.

* Multiple Levels of Undo
Unlike Vi, you can use the **undo** command to undo several steps back in the command history. For example, typing **u** in Command mode undoes the last action in Vim, and typing **3u** in Command mode undoes the last three actions you did in Vim. The undo level is set by default to 1000. You can redo multiply as well, using **<Ctrl+R>**. For example, 3 **<Ctrl+R>** redoes the last three actions that were undone with **u**.

* Visual Mode
Typing **v** causes Vim to enter *Visual mode*. You can then highlight a block of text and execute a Vim Command mode operation on it. The **v** command selects text by character. The **<Ctrl+V>** command selects text as a block. The V command selects the current line. See Section 1.5.6.2 for more details on this facility in Vim.

* The **incsearch** and **hlsearch** Environmental Options (Incremental Search and Highlight Search)
For the incremental search, by default, searching starts after you enter the string. With the option:

:set incsearch
incremental searches will be done. The Vim editor will start searching when you type the first character of the search string. As you type in more characters, the search is refined.

For the highlight search option, setting the option turns on search highlighting. This option is enabled by the command-

:set hlsearch
After the option is enabled, any search highlights the string matched by the search.

* The cindent Environmental Option and the = Command Option
Like Vi autoindent, the Vim editor does a more specific form of indentation. The cindent option is set with the command:

:set cindent
This turns on C programming language-style indentation. Each new line will be automatically indented the correct amount according to the C indentation standard.

* The **:make** Command
To compile a C program with an accompanying make file, and correct the errors, you can type this command in Last Line mode:

make
This runs the make command and captures the output. When the command finishes the editor starts editing the first file. The next step is to fix the error. After that you need to go to the line causing the next error. This is done using the command **cn** . This command will go to the location of the next error even if it is in another file. You can continue fixing problems and using **cn** until all your problems are resolved, or you want to do a recompile. If you want to see the current error message again, use the command **cc**

* Last Line Mode Command History
When you are in Last Line mode, you can use the **<Up>** arrow key to recall an older command line entry, and then can use the **<Down>** arrow key to go forward to newer commands. Then, when you press **<Enter>** after you have indexed to that previous command in the history, that previous command is executed again.

There are four histories you can utilize in Vim, but the two most important ones are for:

- Last Line mode command history
- / and? search command history

Your search history is most useful to you, particularly because if you type complex search criteria, you do not want to have to retype them every time you want to repeat that search!

The two other histories are for expressions and input lines for the **input()** function.

As an example, you have done a Last Line mode command, typed five more Last Line mode commands, and then want to repeat the first command again. To do this, in Last Line mode press the **<Up>** arrow key five times. Another way of doing this is to type the first few letters of the Last Line mode command you want to return to.

The **<Up>** arrow key will use the text typed so far and compare it with the lines in the history. Only matching lines will be used.

If you do not find the line you were looking for, use the **<Down>** arrow key to go back to what you typed and correct that. You can also type **<Ctrl+U>** to start all over again.

To see all the lines in your Last Line mode command history, while in Last Line mode, type: **history**

You will then see a complete history of the Last Line mode commands *for this session* at the bottom of the screen display.

Your entire search history for this session is displayed by typing history/ in Last Line mode.

<Ctrl+P> will work like the **<Up>** arrow key, except that it doesn't matter what you already typed. **<Ctrl+N>** works like the **<Down>** arrow key.

* The Last Line Mode Command Line Window

Typing any text in the Last Line mode command history to modify a previous command and then execute it is possible, but difficult for beginners.

A better way to use a modified form of a Last Line mode command from the history is to open the *command line window* while in Command mode by typing-

q:

Vim now opens a small utility window at the bottom of the screen. It contains the command line history and an empty line at the end.

In the buffer in this small utility window, you are in Insert mode, and can use Insert mode commands to modify text and also move commands. You can use the arrow keys to move around.

For example, move up the history tree with the **<Up>** arrow key to the :1,$s/Windows/Linux/g line, a command in the history of the creation of the file multiline.

Change the word Linux to Raspberry Pi OS in the Command Line Window. Now press **<Enter>** when on that line, and this command will be executed. The command line window will then close. The **<Enter>** command will execute the line under the cursor. This works if Vim is in Insert mode or in Command mode.

Unfortunately, changes you make in the command line window are lost! They do not result in any changes in the command history itself, but the command you execute when you are in the command line window will be added at the end of the history, similar to all other executed commands. Also, only one command line window can be open at a time.

The command line window is very useful when you want to see your old command history, index to a particular command, edit it, and execute it.

A search command in your history can be used to find something new if you index to it and modify it. For example, if in the command line window one of the lines contained **:s/everyone/computer scientists/**, you could index to it in the command line window and modify and execute it.

To exit from the command line window, type **:q!**

* Word Completion
When you are typing and you enter a partial word, you can cause Vim to search for a completion by using **<Ctrl+P>** (search for previous matching word) and **<Ctrl+N>** (search for next match).

* Record and Playback
The **.** (period) command repeats the previous change in Command mode. To accomplish multiple, complex changes in Vim Command mode, you can use the *record and playback* facility. There are three steps in record and playback:

1. The **q**(register) command starts recording keystrokes into the key named **register**. The register name must be a letter of the alphabet.
2. Type the commands you want to record in the register.
3. To end recording, press **q**.

You can now execute the macro by typing the command @register. For example, you have a list of filenames in a buffer that looks like this:

stdio.h
fcntl.h
unistd.h
stdlib.h

And what you want is the following:

#include "stdio.h"
#include "fcntl.h"
#include "unistd.h"
#include "stdlib.h"

You start by moving to the first character of the first line. Next, in Command mode, you execute the following commands:

qa
^
i#include "<Esc>
$
a"<Esc>
j
q

These commands do the following:

1. Start recording a macro in register a.
2. Move to the beginning of the line.
3. Insert the string #include " at the beginning of the line.
4. Move to the end of the line.
5. Append the double quotation mark (") character to the end of the line.
6. Go to the next line.
7. Stop recording the macro.

Now that you have done the work once, you can repeat the change by typing the command "@a" three times.

The "@a" command can be preceded by a count, which will cause the macro to be executed that number of times. In this case you would type: "3@a".

In-Chapter Exercises

1.12 How would you open a unique history window for the / and? commands?

1.13 Where does the cursor have to be positioned in the buffer if you want to execute a modified version of the substitute command :s/ **everyone/computer scientists/** correctly?

1.14 Can you include Last Line mode commands, such as substitute, or write to a file, in a record and playback session?

1.6.6.2 Vim Visual Mode

Because Vi does *not* have a graphical, or "visual," method of selecting and operating on blocks of text, we use Vim Visual mode. In Vim, Visual mode is the graphical and easy way to select a block of text in order to use a prescribed operator on it. The following will briefly describe Visual mode's features and give a simple example. Vim Visual mode allows you to apply commands to blocks of text that can be selected graphically, even though you may not be in a GUI environment. In general, all of the Vi commands and operating modes shown previously work in both Vim and Gvim.

Using Visual mode is done in three steps:

Step 1: Move the cursor to the start of the text block, mark the start of the block with "**v**" (character mode), "**V**" (line mode), or **<Ctrl+V>** (blockwise mode). The character under the cursor will be used as the start of the block.

Step 2: Depending on what kind of functionality is provided in the terminal or console window you are working in, move to the end of the text block, either with the arrow keys on the keyboard, with the h, j, k, or l keys on the keyboard, or with the mouse and mouse button(s). The text from the character where you start Visual mode, up to and including the character under the cursor, is highlighted. Generally **v** and **V** modes allow definition of non-rectangular blocks, whereas **<Ctrl+V>** allows definition of only rectangular blocks.

Step 3: Type a prescribed operator command. The highlighted characters from Step 2 will be operated upon depending on the nature of the prescribed operator listed.

You can use **<Esc>** to stop the definition of a block any time before you use a prescribed operator.

A simple example that illustrates how you can copy and paste using Visual mode follows in Practice Session 1.5.

Practice Session 1.5

Step 1: At the shell prompt type **vim visualtest1**, then press **<Enter>** on the keyboard.

Step 2: Type three or four arbitrary lines of text of uneven length (five to ten words each) into the buffer that opens on screen. Put some spaces at the beginning of some of the lines.

Step 3: Position the cursor on the first character of the first line of the buffer.

Step 4: Type **v**. On the last line display you will be notified that you have entered Visual mode! Now you can define the block that will be all or possibly only a portion of Step 2 text.

Step 5: Expand the highlighted area by using the input device of your choice until all the text you typed in Step 2 is highlighted. On our display, we used the arrow keys, and the highlighted area shows greyed-out (in fact, that's how we knew we were defining the area to be yanked.)

If you make a mistake in defining the block, use **<Esc>** to stop the block definition and begin highlighting again at the first character in the buffer until you get the block definition you desire.

Step 6: Type **y**.

Step 7: On the last line display you will see a report of how many lines you just yanked.

Step 8: Position the cursor anywhere on the last line of the buffer.

Step 9: Type **o**. A new line opens below the last line in the buffer. Press **<Esc>**.

Step 10: Type **p**. The yanked block from Step 6 is put back in the buffer, starting on the new line you opened in Step 9 and proceeding downward. Repeat if you so desire, to get a better feel for opening a blank line and pasting the yanked text. Save the file if you want to.

1.6.6.3 Using Gvim to Cut and Paste between Multiple Open Buffers

To illustrate the speed and efficiency of using Gvim as a modern graphical Raspberry Pi text editor, and to describe some of Gvim's functions, the following practice session allows you use Gvim to create text in two different files, open buffers into those files in two different windows, and copy and paste between those buffers.

To install Gvim on our Raspberry Pi systems, we used the following command:

```
bob@raspberrypi:~ $ sudo apt-get install vim-gtk
Output truncated...
```

Note
All of the typed-in Vim commands and operating modes shown previously work in both Vim and Gvim.

Practice Session 1.6

Step 1: At the shell prompt in a terminal window, type **gvim gvim1** and then press the **<Enter>** key.

Step 2: A new Gvim window opens on screen. In that window, type **A** and then type **This is the first line of text.** Then press the **<Enter>** key twice.

Step 3: Type **This is the third line of text.** Then press the **<Enter>** key.

Step 4: From the Gvim pull-down menu, make the choice **Window>Split**. You now are looking into two windows on the *same* buffer.

Step 5: From the Gvim pull-down menu, make the choice **File>Save**. Click the **OK** button in the Save window, if one appears. The buffer is saved to the file **gvim1**.

Step 6: Use the mouse and click anywhere in the lower window with the left mouse button. You are now working in the lower buffer.

Step 7: From the Gvim pull-down menu, make the choice **File>Save As**. In the Name: box at the top of the window that opens, change the name of the file to **gvim2**, and then make the **Save** button choice. The buffer is saved as **gvim2**, and you are looking into the buffer through two windows.

Step 8: The active buffer is still seen in the lower window. Use the mouse and **<Delete>** key on the keyboard to change the word first to the word second, and the word third to the word fourth in the lower window.

Step 9: Click anywhere in the top window.

Step 10: Make the Gvim pull-down menu choice **File>Open**. Scroll down and open **gvim1** in the current directory by selecting it and making the **OK** button choice. You should now be seeing **gvim1** in the upper window, and **gvim2** in the lower window.

Step 11: Click anywhere in the bottom window.

Step 12: Use the mouse and left mouse button to highlight the text This is the second line of text. Make sure the cursor is on the period as you finish selecting that line.

Step 13: Make the Gvim pull-down menu choice **Edit>Copy**. You have "yanked" a line of text in the lower buffer graphically.

Step 14: Click on the second blank line in the upper window buffer.

Step 15: Make the Gvim pull-down menu choice **Edit>Paste**. The line **This is the second line of text**. is now on the second line of the upper window buffer. You can use the Gvim pull-down menu choice **Edit>Undo** to correct mistakes in copying and pasting.

Step 16: Repeat Steps 11 through 15 to copy and paste the line This is the fourth line of text. from the lower window buffer to the upper window buffer, where it should be the fourth line of text. When you are done, your screen display should look similar to Figure 1.13.

Step 17: While the active window buffer is the upper window, make the Gvim pull-down menu choice **File>Save-Exit**.

Step 18: At the shell prompt in a terminal window, type **more gvim1**. What appears on screen? Do the same for the file **gvim2**. What appears on screen?

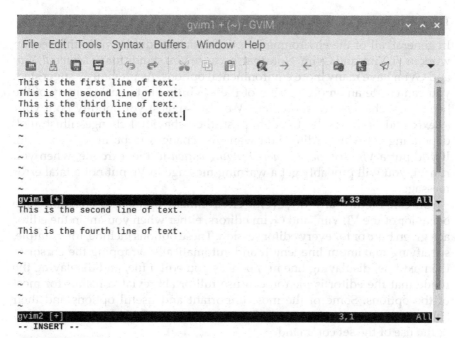

FIGURE 1.13
File gvim1 after Step 16.

A complete summary of Vi, Vim, and Gvim commands is given in later Table 1.10, which we conveniently append to the end of this chapter so that you may print it for use as a handy paper reference when doing text editing with these editors.

In-Chapter Exercises

1.15 Repeat Practice Session 1.6 for Gvim using another text file with content of your own choosing, and then cut and paste from it into three other files that you open simultaneously in the same Gvim terminal window. Save all four files when finished.

1.16 Similar to Practice Session 1.6, use non-graphical Vi in a terminal window on a non-GUI-based Raspberry Pi system, such as a server install, to achieve the same results. What commands did you use to do this? Which editor was easier to use to achieve the same results?

1.17 On a GUI-based Raspberry Pi, how could you achieve the same results as using Gvim in Practice Session 1.6 by using two, or more, sessions in separate terminal windows running Nano, or Vi in them?

1.6.7 Changing Vi, Vim, and Gvim Behavior

In general, all of the environment options commands shown in this section work in Vi, Vim, and Gvim. Note that, because Vim stands for *VI Mproved*, Vim and Gvim have many more environmental options. As previously suggested, you can create an empty version of the ~/.vimrc file to enable many of the behavioral changes we show here. We also suggest you modify both your ~/.exrc and ~/vimrc files to accomplish the behavioral changes illustrated, depending on which editor you want the changes to be implemented in. If you put a *Vim-specific behavior-changing option* in the .exrc file, when you run Vi, you will probably get a warning message in Vi, but not a fatal error message.

You can modify any of several environment options to customize the behavior of the Vi, Vim, and Gvim editors, either when you are in the editor at a given time or for every editor session. These options include, for example, specifying maximum line length and automatically wrapping the cursor to the next line, displaying line numbers as you edit a file, and displaying the mode that the editor is in. You can use full or abbreviated names for most of the options. Some of the most important and useful options and their abbreviations are summarized in Table 1.8. Also see Table 1.9 for a summary of the use of the **set** command.

The **set** command in Last Line mode changes environmental options. There are two types of environmental options that can be modified with the set command: toggle options, which are either "on" or "off," and options that require the use of an argument.

For example, after typing **:set showmode**, you have toggled the mode display "on," and the editor displays the current mode at the bottom of the screen. If you then type **:set noshowmode**, you have toggled the mode display "off." Similarly, after typing **:set nu**, Vi displays the line numbers for all the lines in the file. To turn "off" the line number display, type **:set nonu**. When the **:set ai** command has been executed, the next line is aligned with the beginning of the previous line. This useful feature allows you to easily indent source codes that you compose with Vi. Pressing **<Ctrl+D>** on a new line moves the cursor to the previous indentation level.

To see a listing of what all environment options in the editor are (the ones you have modified and the defaults) at any time, type **:set all**

There are a lot of them!

To see a listing of what environment options you have modified, either for this session only, or for all sessions, type **:set** When you use set to modify the environment options within an editor session, the options are set for that session only!

If you want to customize your environmental options for all Vi, Vim, and Gvim sessions, you need to put your options in the .exrc file in your home directory. You can use the **set** command to modify one or more options in the

TABLE 1.8

Important Environmental Options for Vi, Vim, and Gvim

Option	Abbreviation	Purpose
autoindent	ai	Aligns the new line with the beginning of the previous line.
ignorecase	ic	Ignores the case of a letter during the search process (with a / or the? command).
list	list	Displays invisible characters, such as ^I for <Tab> and a $ for end-of-line characters.
nolist	nolist	Turns off the display of invisible characters.
noignorecase	noic	Instructs cases to be case sensitive.
number	nu	Displays line numbers when a file is being edited; line numbers are not saved as part of the file.
nonumber	nonu	Hides line numbers.
scroll		Sets the number of lines to scroll when the <Ctrl+D> command is used to scroll the Vi screen up.
set		Displays all the Vi variables that are set.
all		Displays all set Vi variables and their current values.
showmode	smd	Displays the current Vi mode in the bottom right corner of the screen.
noshowmode	nosmd	Turns off the mode of operation display.
wrapmargin	wm	Sets the wrap margin in terms of the number of characters from the end of the line, assuming a line length of 80 characters.

.exrc file as follows (typing the two keyboard keys <Ctrl+C> terminates the creation of the **cat** command):

```
$ cat > .exrc
set wm=5 showmode nu ic
<Ctrl+C>
$
```

The **wm=5** option sets the wrap margin to 5, and is an example of a set command that requires an argument. That is, each line will be up to 75 characters long. The **ic** option allows you to search for strings without regard to the case of a character. Thus, after this option has been set, the **/Hello/** command searches for strings hello and Hello.

In-Chapter Exercises

1.18 After examining Tables 1.8 a and b, select a few of the environment options that most appeal to you and then place them in your **~/.exrc file**, whether it exists or not. Test them by running Vi.

1.19 If you haven't already done so, place the **set showmode** environment setting in your **~/.exrc** and in your **~/.vimrc** file, whether they exist or not. Run Vim and then Gvim. Do various operations in both those editors. Does the mode you are in appear in the mode line in both editors?

TABLE 1.9

Last Line Mode Syntax

Last Line Mode Syntax	What It Does
Abbr command	
:ab in out	Uses in as abbreviation for out in Insert mode.
:unab in	Removes abbreviation for in.
:ab	Lists abbreviations.
map!, map commands	
:map string sequence	Maps characters string as sequence of commands. Use #1, #2, etc., for the function keys.
:unmap string	Removes map for characters string.
:map	Lists character strings that are mapped.
:map! string sequence	Maps characters string to input mode sequence.
:unmap! string	Removes input mode map (you may need to quote the characters with <Ctrl+V>).
:map!	Lists character strings that are mapped for input mode.
Qx	Records typed characters into register specified by letter x (Vim and Gvim).
Q	Stops recording (Vim and Gvim).
@x	Executes the register specified by letter x. Use @@ to repeat the last @ command.
set command	
:set x	Enables boolean option x, show value of other options.
:set nox	Disables option x.
:set x=value	Gives value to option x.
:set	Shows changed options.
:set all	Shows all options.
:set x?	Shows value of option x.

1.6.7.1 Executing Shell Commands from within Vi, Vim, and Gvim

At times you will want to execute a shell command without quitting Vi, and then restarting it. You can do so in Command mode by preceding the command with:!. Thus, for example, typing **:! pwd** would display the pathname of your current directory, and typing :! **ls** would display the names of all the files in your current directory. After executing a shell command, the editor asks you to **Press ENTER or type command to continue,** and then you are returned to Command mode.

1.6.8 Vi, Vim, and Gvim Keyboard Macros

Vi, Vim, and Gvim offer a variety of *macro* facilities; a macro is a keystroke construction that uses one or more compact set keystrokes to represent another larger number of keystrokes that are substituted for the single or compact set. Macros are used in Vi, Vim, and Gvim for the following reasons:

1. During Insert mode, to construct an abbreviation. For example, in a text file where you use often-repeated blocks of the same text.

2. In Command mode, Vi, Vim, and Gvim commands can be associated with or *mapped* to other keys, such as the function keys at the top of the keyboard.

3. Complex commands and their arguments can be triggered by a single keystroke or a shorter sequence of keystrokes.

Here is a brief summary description of the various Vi, Vim, and Gvim macro operations, which are covered in the subsections below.

Text abbreviation (Section 1.5.8.1), which operates in Insert mode. An abbreviation works only in Vi, Vim, and Gvim Insert mode.

Keystroke mapping (Sections 1.5.8.2 and 1.5.8.3), which operates in Insert mode, and uses the **map!** and **map** Last Line mode commands. Once defined, a **map!** sequence is triggered only in Insert mode, and a **map** sequence is triggered only in Vi, Vim, and Gvim Command mode.

Macro Record (Section 1.5.8.4), which shows the definition and use of a recorded macro.

In those sections, we will describe and give examples of some of the Vi, Vim, and Gvim macro facilities, and also give an additional example of a specialized Vim macro feature that can be used in Gvim.

1.6.8.1 Text Abbreviation Macros Used in Insert Mode

To save keystrokes while entering text, in Last Line mode, use the **abbr**(eviate), or just **ab** command.

It has the following general syntactic form:

:ab[br] [abbreviation abbreviated]
where:
: gets you into Last Line mode;
[ ] designates optional components;
ab or **abbr** is the command for creating an abbreviation;
abbreviation is a valid string of contiguous (no spaces allowed) characters; and
abbreviated is the substitute text you want to be placed in the buffer.

Text abbreviations can be canceled with the Last Line mode **unabbr** command, followed by typing the abbreviation you want to cancel. Also, if you just type **abbr** in Last Line mode, you get a listing of all the abbreviations that are active.

To use the abbreviation, when you are in Insert mode, whenever you type the string that represents **abbreviation**, and follow it by a non-alphanumeric character, the substitution will take place. The editor will examine the next character after you type the abbreviation to see if it's non-alphanumeric or underscore, and if so, **abbreviation** will be erased, and the string that represents **abbreviated** will be substituted for it. Also, you are no longer in Insert mode.

For example, in Last Line mode, if you type **ab kts Know this stuff!** and then press **<Enter>**, **kts** is the abbreviation. Then anywhere in Insert mode, when you type **kts** and follow it by pressing the space key, the left or right arrow keys (all of which yield non-alphanumeric characters and are not the underscore keys on the keyboard for our Raspberry Pi system), the string **Know this stuff!** will be substituted on that line, and you will no longer be in Insert mode.

Note
As shown in the next section, this is different from keystroke mapping using the **map!** or **map** commands.

The following are some useful abbreviations for Python3 program file creation:

:ab 1 #!/usr/local/bin/python
:ab 2 from Tkinter import *
:ab 3 import os
:ab 4 import sys

1.6.8.2 Keystroke-Mapping Macros Used in Insert Mode

map! works on characters that are typed in Insert mode. As shown in the previous section, **abbr** won't substitute text until you type a non-alphanumeric after the abbreviation string. Notice the editor echoes each character of the abbreviation as you type it, just in case you really want the string of characters that represents abbreviation to be an actual string of characters that you want in your text. Keystroke mapping works in a more keystroke, time-dependent way. Keystroke mapping used in Insert mode is handled by the Last Line mode **map!** command, which takes the following general form:

:map! [substitution substituted]
where:
: gets you into Last Line mode;
[ ] designates optional components;
map is the command for creating a keyboard mapping;
substitution is a valid string of contiguous (no spaces allowed) characters; and
substituted is the substitute text you want to be placed in the buffer.

For example, in Last Line mode, if you type **map! ts This will save you time!** and then press **<Enter>**, **ts** is the substitution. Then, anywhere in Insert mode, when you type **ts** in a short amount of time (under approximately half a second), the string **This will save you time!** will be substituted on that line, and you will still be in Insert mode. If you type more slowly, the literal string **ts** will be inserted.

The keystroke sequence **<Ctrl+V>** will let you escape the mapping, as long as you precede the macro with it. So no matter how fast you type in **<Ctrl+V> ts**, you get the literal string **ts** inserted.

Remapping abbreviations can be canceled with the Last Line mode **unmap** command, followed by typing the substitution you want to cancel. Also, if you just type **map!** in Last Line mode, you get a listing of all the mappings that are active.

1.6.8.3 Keystroke-Remapping Macros Used in Command Mode

Command-mode remapping is accomplished with the map Last Line mode command.

The general form of the map command is as follows:

:map [substitution substituted]
where:
: gets you into Last Line mode;
[ ] designates optional components;
map is the command for creating a keyboard mapping;
substitution is a valid string of contiguous(no spaces allowed) characters; and
substituted is the substitute text you want to be placed in the buffer.

Some editor command keys cannot be remapped in Command mode. Two examples of these keys are **:** (colon) and **u**.

Remapping substitutions can be canceled with the Last Line mode **unmap** command, followed by typing the remapping you want to cancel. Also, if you just type **map** in Last Line mode, you get a listing of all the mappings that are active. You will see that the editor already has several mappings defined by default.

As an example, in Last Line mode, if you type **:map <F8>:wq<CR>** and then press **<Enter>**, the function key **<F8>** at the top of your keyboard is the **substitution**. The **substituted** is the command to write the buffer to a file and quit the editor. **<CR>** represents the **<Enter>** key. After this mapping is done, anytime you are in Command mode, when you press the function key **<F8>**, the buffer will be written to the default file and you will exit the editor.

Another interesting and useful example is the following Last line mode **map** command, which can be used so that when you press the function key

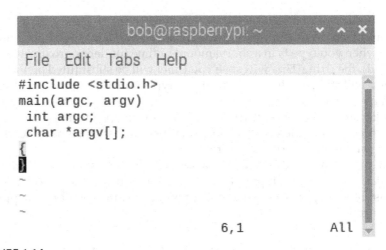

FIGURE 1.14
C Program skeleton done with the map Command.

<F3> during editor sessions, a skeleton C program construct is entered into a blank buffer, as shown in Figure 1.14:

:map <F3> <Esc>i#include <stdio.h><CR>main(argc, argv)<CR> int argc;<CR> char *argv[];<CR>{<CR>}<Esc>

where:

<Esc> is used to represent the Escape key.
<CR> is used to represent the <Enter> key.

When you press the function key <F3>, Vim will insert the desired skeleton C program construct into the buffer.

1.6.8.4 Vim/Gvim Macro Example

Here is a repeat of Practice Session 1.5, slightly enlarged, that uses a Vim-specific macro command sequence to accomplish kind of the same thing that Practice Session 1.5 did, but in another way.
Practice Session 1.7

Step 1: From the shell prompt, type **vim PiOS2** and then press <Enter> on the keyboard.

Step 2: In Vim, type **A** and then type the following ten lines of text, each on its own line:

computer scientists
students
hackers
systems analysts
newbies
Raspberry Pi gurus
computer programmers
systems administrators
network administrators
Raspberry Pi users

Step 3: Press **<Esc>**, then place the cursor anywhere on the first line of text.

Step 4: Type **q a**. This puts you in record mode, and associates the macro you are about to record with the **a** key.

Step 5: Type **I**. The cursor is now at the start of the first line in Insert mode.

Step 6: Type **Raspberry Pi OS is the operating system of choice for** with a single space after the **r** in the word **for**. Press **<Esc>**.

Step 7: Place the cursor anywhere on the second line of text.

Step 8: Type **q**. This ends record mode.

Step 9: Type **9@a**. This "plays back" the macro defined with the **a** key nine times, once on each of the lines below the first line, inserting the text string "**Raspberry Pi OS is the operating system of choice for.**" Your screen display should now look like Figure 1.15.

Step 10: Save the file, print it out, and memorize its contents.

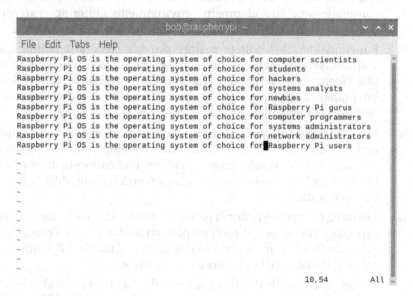

FIGURE 1.15
Practice Session 1.7 after Step 9.

1.7 Geany Introduction

To provide you with a useful comparison to the Raspberry Pi text editors, this section covers Geany, the freely available IDE that comes pre-loaded with the Raspberry Pi OS. We illustrate essential Geany operations in the context of the creation, and building, of C++ and Python programs and script files.

Note

This section is *not* a tutorial on C++, or Python! In fact, you don't even have to know about the syntax of those languages to be able to appreciate how Geany facilitates the development process of C++ and Python code. The fact that those languages are *structured*, with distinct syntactic forms whose production and creation are made easier and simpler to input by Geany, is the real lesson here.

To begin our discussion of Geany, it's worth noting the key differences between a Raspberry Pi OS text editor, like Nano or Vim, and a Raspberry Pi OS IDE like Geany.

It's also worth noting at this point that none of these apps are, strictly speaking, *word processors*, like LibreOffice Writer.

The five key differences between text editors and IDEs are as follows:

1. Scope and Complexity: Text editors like Vim, Emacs, or Nano are simpler and focused on text editing with minimal additional features. IDEs like Geany, Visual Studio Code, IntelliJ IDEA, or Eclipse are comprehensive development environments offering extensive features for coding, debugging, testing, and project management.

2. Functionality: Text editors mainly provide basic text editing capabilities, syntax highlighting, and search/replace functions. IDEs, like Geany, offer advanced features like compilation and linking, integrated debugging, version control, intelligent code completion, and project navigation.

3. Integration and Workflow: IDEs, like Geany, integrate various tools and services seamlessly within the development environment, streamlining the development workflow. Text editors usually rely on external tools for tasks like compilation and linking, debugging, or version control.

4. Learning Curve: Text editors generally have a steeper learning curve, especially for powerful but complex ones like Vim or Emacs. IDEs typically have a more intuitive and user-friendly GUI interface, making it easier for beginners to start coding.

5. Resource Usage: Text editors are usually lightweight and consume fewer system resources compared to full-fledged IDEs. IDEs tend to

be more resource-intensive, due to their comprehensive features and capabilities.

In general, IDEs on Linux provide a comprehensive set of tools and features to facilitate software development. Here are some key aspects:

1. Feature-Rich Environment: IDEs offer a wide array of features like code completion, syntax highlighting, integrated debugging, refactoring tools, version control integration, and project management capabilities.

2. Code Assistance and Productivity Tools: IDEs provide intelligent code completion, suggesting code snippets, variable names, and method signatures as you type. This enhances productivity and reduces errors.

3. Debugging and Testing: Debugging is seamlessly integrated within the IDE, allowing developers to set breakpoints, inspect variables, and step through code. Testing frameworks can be integrated for automated testing.

4. Project Management: IDEs often have built-in project management tools, making it easier to organize and navigate through complex codebases. This includes features like project-wide search, file hierarchy views, and class/module navigation. Some even offer integration of local projects with GitHub.

5. Integration with Build Systems: IDEs integrate with various build systems and tools, enabling developers to compile, link, build, and package their applications from within the IDE. This streamlines the development workflow.

6. Plugin Ecosystem: Most IDEs support an extensive ecosystem of plugins or extensions. Developers can customize their IDE by adding plugins for specific languages, frameworks, or tools, tailoring it to their needs.

7. Cross-Language Support: Many IDEs support multiple programming languages, allowing developers to work on projects with diverse technology stacks seamlessly.

Popular Linux IDEs include:

1. Geany: As stated in the Geany Manual, "Geany is a small and lightweight Integrated Development Environment. It was developed to provide a small and fast IDE, which has only a few dependencies on other packages. Another goal was to be as independent as possible from a particular Desktop Environment like KDE or GNOME. Geany only requires the GTK+ runtime libraries."

2.   Visual Studio Code (VSCode): A versatile and highly customizable IDE developed by Microsoft.

3.   IntelliJ IDEA: Known for its powerful features and support for Java and related technologies.

4.   Eclipse: An open-source IDE with a broad ecosystem and support for multiple languages.

5.   PyCharm: A specialized IDE for Python development.

To prepare you for working with Geany, we provide you with a listing of some typical IDE features as presented in the seven points above, such as

1.   User Interface: Geany has a clean and straightforward user interface, resembling a text editor but with additional IDE features. It's designed to be intuitive and easy to navigate.

2.   Code Editing Features:

     Syntax highlighting for a wide range of programming languages.

     Code folding to collapse and expand sections of code for better readability.

     Autocomplete functionality to suggest and complete code snippets.

3.   Build and Compile:

     Geany allows you to build and compile your projects directly within the IDE.

     It supports various build systems and compilers.

4.   Integrated Development Tools:

     Basic integrated tools include a terminal emulator and a file browser for easier

     navigation within the project.

5.   Plugin Support:

     Geany supports a range of plugins to enhance its functionality.

     These plugins can provide additional features like version control integration,

     project management, and more.

6.   Project Management:

     Geany offers project management features, enabling you to organize your files

     and resources effectively.

7.   Cross-Platform Support:

     Geany is available for Linux, Windows, and macOS, making it versatile and adaptable to different operating systems.

8. Extensible and Customizable:

Users can customize Geany to their preferences, adjusting settings, color schemes,

and installing plugins to tailor the IDE to their needs.

9. Documentation and Community:

Geany has good documentation and an active community, providing support and

assistance to users.

Geany is favored by developers looking for a lightweight and fast IDE without compromising essential features necessary for efficient coding. It's suitable for a variety of programming languages and project types.

1.7.1 Geany Usage

You can start Geany in the following ways:
* From the Desktop Environment menu:
  On your Desktop, using the Raspberry Menu, make the **Programming > Geany** choice.
* From the Raspberry Pi command line, type **geany** and press **<Enter>**.

1.7.2 The Geany Workspace

A picture is worth a million words. The Geany window, or workspace, is shown in Figure 1.16:

The workspace has the following parts, labeled as such in Figure 1.16:

1. The menu of pull-down text choices, File, Edit, Search, View, Document, Project, Build, Tools, Help.

2. A toolbar with several icons on it.

3. A sidebar that can show the following tabs:

   a. Documents – A document list, and

   b. Symbols – A list of symbols in your code. This is what is shown in Figure 1.16.

   c. Files – If you make the Geany menu choice **Tools > Plugin Manager**, you can put a check

   mark next to the File Browser plugin, and then Geany will include a file browser in this sidebar.

   See Section 1.6.4.10 for more information about obtaining and loading useful plugins.

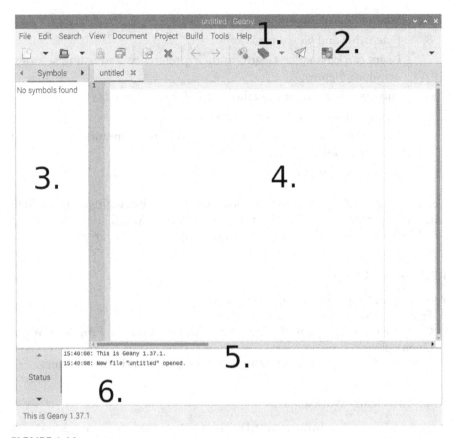

FIGURE 1.16
The Geany workspace.

4.   The main editor window.

5.   A message window, which can show the following tabs:

      a. Status – A list of status messages. This is what is shown in Figure 1.16.

      b. Compiler – The output of compiling or building programs.

      c. Messages –Results of 'Find Usage', ''Find in Files' and other actions.

      d. Scribble – A text scratchpad for any use.

      e. Terminal – A terminal window.

6.   A status bar

Note
By default, when you launch Geany, it loads all files from the last time Geany was launched. And, you can start several "instances" of Geany, but only the first instance will load files from the last session.

To run a second instance of Geany from the command-line, don't include any filenames as arguments, or disable opening files in a running instance using the appropriate command line option.

1.7.3 Five Easy Geanys and Some Geany Py

To begin this section, we present five Practice Sessions that allow you to get your feet wet with Geany as an IDE on the Raspberry Pi OS, in the context of C++ program development and execution. C++ as the illustrative language in this section was chosen because it's a modern Object-Oriented Programming (OOP) language. Of course, everything shown in this section can be applied, with the modification of different arguments and targets, to working with other compiled High Level Languages (HLLs,) such as C, C#, or intermediate languages like Python3 (which is both interpreted and compiled), Java, etc.

We then present a block of Python3 programs that you can use Geany to create, edit, and execute. These programs are taken directly from Volume 2, Chapter 2, where they were executed in various fashions, partly via the use of the Raspberry Pi IDE named **Thonny**.

1.7.3.1 Compiling and Executing C++ Programs

We provide some background material in this section on the development process of a C++ program, particularly the compilation and execution processes. Several C compilers are available on the Raspberry Pi OS, including gcc and g++. The most commonly used C++ compiler for the Raspberry Pi OS is the GNU C++ compiler, **g++**. All C++ compilers, such as the GNU compiler for C++ can also be used to compile C programs. The **g++** compiler invokes **gcc** with options necessary to make it recognize C++ source code. We solely utilize the **g++** compiler in Geany in this chapter. It's instructive at this point to see a synopsis of the man page for g++, as follows:

****

g++(1)

NAME
    gcc - GNU project C and C++ compiler
SYNOPSIS   top
    gcc [-c|-S|-E] [-std=standard]
        [-g] [-pg] [-Olevel]
        [-Wwarn...] [-Wpedantic]
        [-Idir...] [-Ldir...]
        [-Dmacro[=defn]...] [-Umacro]
        [-foption...] [-mmachine-option...]
        [-o outfile] [@file] infile...

Only the most useful options are listed here.

DESCRIPTION

When you invoke GCC, it normally does pre-processing, compilation, assembly and linking. The "overall options" allow you to stop this process at an intermediate stage. For example, the -c option says *not* to run the linker. Then the output consists of object files output by the assembler.

Other options are passed on to one or more stages of processing. Some options control the preprocessor and others the compiler itself. Yet other options control the assembler and linker; most of these are not documented here, since you rarely need to use any of them.

Most of the command-line options that you can use with GCC are useful for C programs; when an option is only useful with another language (usually C++), the explanation says so explicitly. If the description for a particular option does not mention a source language, you can use that option with all supported languages.

****

The Build command in Geany does all that, and can be combined with the **make** command, a Linux utility that allows *a combining of source files together to form a single executable image.* A synopsis of the man page for the **make** command is as follows:

****
make

SYNOPSIS
   make [-einpqrst] [-f makefile]... [-k|-S] [macro=value...]
      [target_name...]

DESCRIPTION

The make utility shall update files that are derived from other files. A typical case is one where object files are derived from the corresponding source files. The make utility examines time relationships and shall update those derived files (called targets) that have modified times earlier than the modified times of the files (called prerequisites) from which they are derived. A description file (makefile) contains a description of the relationships between files, and the commands that need to be executed to update the targets to reflect changes in their prerequisites. Each specification, or rule, shall consist of a target, optional prerequisites, and optional commands to be executed when a pre-requisite is newer than the target. There are two types of rule:

1. Inference rules, which have one target name with at least one
   <period> ('.') and no <slash> ('/')
2. Target rules, which can have more than one target name

OPTIONS

The following options, and option arguments, are supported:

-e   Cause environment variables, including those with null
       values, to override macro assignments within makefiles.

-f   makefile
       Specify a different makefile. The argument makefile is
       a pathname of a description file, which is also
       referred to as the makefile.

-i   Ignore error codes returned by invoked commands. This
       mode is the same as if the special target .IGNORE were
       specified without prerequisites.

-k   Continue to update other targets that do not depend on
       the current target if a non-ignored error occurs while
       executing the commands to bring a target up-to-date.

-n   Write commands that would be executed on standard
       output, but do not execute them. However, lines with a
       <plus-sign> '+' prefix shall be executed. In this
       mode, lines with an at-sign ('@') character prefix
       shall be written to standard output.

-p   Write to standard output the complete set of macro
       definitions and target descriptions. The output format
       is unspecified.

-q   Return a zero exit value if the target file is up-to-
       date; otherwise, return an exit value of 1. Targets
       shall not be updated if this option is specified.
       However, a makefile command line (associated with the
       targets) with a <plus-sign> ('+') prefix shall be
       executed.

-r   Clear the suffix list and do not use the built-in
       rules.

-S   Terminate make if an error occurs while executing the
       commands to bring a target up-to-date. This shall be
       the default and the opposite of -k.

-s   Do not write makefile command lines or touch messages
       (see -t) to standard output before executing. This mode
       shall be the same as if the special target .SILENT were
       specified without prerequisites.

-t   Update the modification time of each target as though a
       touch target had been executed.

COMMAND ARGUMENTS

The following arguments are supported:

target_name
    Target names, as defined in the EXTENDED DESCRIPTION
    section. If no target is specified, while make is
    processing the makefiles, the first target that make
    encounters that is not a special target or an inference
    rule shall be used.

macro=value
    Macro definitions, as defined in Macros.

If the target_name and macro=value operands are intermixed on the
make utility command line, the results are unspecified.

****

1.7.3.2 C++ and Geany Practice Sessions

Practice Session 1.8 Creating a C++ Program from Scratch

Objectives: To launch Geany on your Raspberry Pi system, and use it basically as a text editor to produce a simple C++ program. To then compile and
execute that program using the graphical menu facilities of the Geany IDE.

Prerequisites: Having Geany on your Raspberry Pi system, which it is by
default in the Raspberry Pi OS.

Background: As indicated in Section 1.6.1, the most useful aspects of Geany
as purely a replacement, or substitute for a text editor, are its capabilities
to expedite code creation, particularly for the HLLs like C++. Capabilities
like the coding assistance and productivity enhancement tools – intelligent
code completion, suggesting code snippets, variable names, and method
signatures as you type. This enhances productivity and reduces errors. And
of course, autoindentation, triggered by key block programming tokens such
as curly braces ({}) in C++. In this Practice Session, you'll get exposure to this
productivity enhancement, as well as Geany's capability to compile, link, and
execute structured programming code.

Procedure: The following steps allow you to easily create, build, and execute
a simple C++ program in Geany.

1. From the Raspberry Pi Menu, make the choice **Programming > Geany**
    to launch one instance of the Geany IDE. A file named "untitled" opens
    in the main editor window. Make the Geany menu choice **File > Save**

as..., and save the file in a convenient location on your Raspberry Pi, with the name **count1.cpp**. This convenient location now becomes Geany's current working directory. You can see that in the sidebar if the Documents heading is selected.

2. Make the Geany menu choice **Edit > Preferences > Editor > Completions**. Make sure a check mark is in the box next to **Curly brackets {}** under **Auto-close quotes and brackets**, and then click on the **OK** button in the lower right of the Preferences window.

This check mark signifies that auto-indentation is enabled, which will be triggered by the key C++ structured block programming token curly brace ({). Now, every time you type a left curly brace while entering text in the editor window, a matching right one will appear. And the subsequent new line of code will be indented by the specified default indentation.

3. In the main editor window of Geany, as shown in Figure 1.16, type in the following C++ program.

```cpp
#include <iostream>
#include <string>

int main() {
    std::string inputString;
    char targetLetter;

    // Prompt the user for input string
    std::cout << "Enter a string: ";
    std::cin >> inputString;

    // Prompt the user for the target letter
    std::cout << "Enter the letter you want to count: ";
    std::cin >> targetLetter;

    int count = 0;

    // Loop through the characters in the input string
    for (char ch : inputString) {
        // Check if the current character matches the target letter
        if (ch == targetLetter) {
            count++;
        }
    }

    // Display the count
    std::cout << "The letter '" << targetLetter << "' appears " << count <<\
 " times in the string." << std::endl;

    return 0;
}
```

Notice a few important things here.

a. Once you type the first {(curly brace), Geany automatically indents the second line of the C++ code. The same thing is true after you type in the second and third curly braces, automatically indenting those following lines of code after the curly braces.
b. By default, Geany applies a color coding scheme to the first line in the file as you type it in. Why is this true?
c. Fold regions appear at the left margin of the code. If you click on the – minus signs inside the fold boxes, the blocks of code incorporated automatically in those fold regions disappear temporarily. This is very useful for large, multi-line programs, where you can hide parts of the code, and only work on blocks of it.

4. After you're sure you've typed in everything shown above in step 3. correctly, make the Geany menu choice **File > Save.**

5. Make the Geany menu choice **Build > Build**, or press the Function key **<F9>.**

   If you typed in everything from step 3 correctly, the following message appears in the Geany message window:

   g++ -Wall -o "count1" "count1.cpp" (in directory: /home/bob/Desktop/cpp)

   Compilation completed successfully

6. Click on the paper airplane icon in the menu bar. This runs the program in a separate terminal window outside of the Geany window. For our example run here, we reproduce the output in that terminal window in the way we entered it as follows:

   Enter a string: **laksdjlkjfffffkajlskdjlka**
   Enter the letter you want to count: **f**
   The letter 'f' appears four times in the string.

   (program exited with code: 0)
   Press return to continue

7. Press **<Enter>** in the terminal window to continue. Run the program with several input string values to further test it.

   Note
   If you enter a space character anywhere in the input string, you won't get the proper output! Why is that?

8. Make the Geany menu choice **File > Close All**.

9. Quit Geany by making the Geany menu choice **File > Quit**.

Conclusion:
You launched Geany on your Raspberry Pi system, and used Geany as a text editor to produce a simple C++ program. Then you used the Build Menu choice to compile the code, and the Run icon to execute that program, using the graphical menu facilities of Geany.

Practice Session 1.9 Opening, Building, and Running a Previously Saved C++ Programming

Objectives: To open an existing file with C++ code in it, build an image from that source, and execute the built image using Geany graphical menu choices.

Prerequisites:

1. Having Geany available on your Raspberry Pi system,
2. Having completed Practice Session 1.8,
3. Downloading the appropriate source code files for this chapter from www.github.com/bobk48/RaspberryPiOS

Background:
It's often necessary to load a file into Geany that you've previously worked on, or that someone in your DevOps team has given you. In this exercise, you will download and open a C++ file that calculates the Greatest Common Factor (GCF) of four interactively entered integers, using the Euclidean algorithm. Once you build and run the file, you're prompted for the four integers, and it displays the GCF in a terminal window external to the Geany window.

Note
Once you exit Geany, without closing anything, upon the next launch of a single instance of Geany, that file is automatically loaded again, facilitating further work you might want to do on or with it. That's a convenient feature of the IDE. Since at the end of Practice Session 1.8, you closed everything before exiting Geany, on a subsequent launch of a single instance of the app, the file named "untitled" is opened again.

Procedures:

1. In your web browser, navigate to the www.github.com/bobk48/ RaspberryPiOS, and download the file GCF4.cpp to a convenient directory on your Raspberry Pi system..
2. Launch Geany, either from the **Raspberry Pi Programming > Geany** menu, or from the command line.
3. From the Toolbar at the top of the Geany window, make the **File > Open an existing file** menu choice, and use the Raspberry Pi navigator screen to choose the file **GCF4.cpp** from Step 1. It loads into the main editor window.

4.   From the Toolbar at the top of the Geany window, make the **Build the
      current file** menu choice (It looks like a brown brick.) In the message
      window at the bottom of the screen two messages appears, similar to
      the following:

      g++ -Wall -o "2nd" "GCF4.cpp" (in directory: /home/bob/Desktop/cpp)
      Compilation finished successfully.

      The directory shown will be the directory you downloaded the
      source code files to, not the pathname of that we illustrate here!

5.   From the Toolbar at the top of the Geany window, click on the **Run
      or view the current file** icon. (It looks like a paper airplane.)

6.   A terminal window appears on screen, showing the output results of
      our test running the GCF4 code, as follows.

      Enter the first number: 3
      Enter the second number: 27
      Enter the third number: 9
      Enter the fourth number: 81
      The Greatest Common Factor of 3, 27, 9, and 81 is 3

      (program exited with code: 0)
      Press return to continue

      Press **<Enter>** to close the terminal window.

7.   Run the program again to test other sets of integers.

8.   Make the Geany menu choice **File > Close** and then the choice **File >
      Quit** .

Conclusion:
You downloaded and opened a file with C++ code in it, built an image from
that C++ source, and executed the built image using Geany graphical menu
choices, to find the Greatest Common Factor of four integers.

Practice Session 1.10 Geany Project Basics in C++

Objectives: To create a C++ program that finds the Least Common
Denominator (LCD) of three entered fractions, and to place that program in a
new project, and its attendant folder(s) in Geany.

Prerequisites
Completion of Practice sessions 1.8 and 1.9.

Background:
As mentioned in the section on vi, vim, and gvim, even though those editors
are highly customizable text editors, they don't have built-in project management features like Geany.

Files are managed individually in Geany, even though you can view files and folders in the Documents sidebar display, there is no usable folder context, so you can't add folders through Geany unless you do it via the command line. Geany has a built-in terminal that can be accessed from the Messages area at the bottom of the Geany window (Item 5 in Figure 1.16). Because Geany does not allow you to add folders from the File browser if you've enabled that plugin, you can use this terminal for folder management. Scroll the menu on the left of the messages window, using the arrows, to the Terminal item to open a view into that terminal. Then use Linux file maintenance commands to do folder management, or other operations you might want to accomplish.

Note
See Section 1.6.4.10 to enable the File browser sidebar, which allows you to navigate to files and directories where you can view the contents of Geany's current working directory, or the directory of the current project.
    A project is a Geany convenience feature that allows you to save your file state, and IDE settings that may be specific to your project.

Procedures:

1.   Launch Geany. As described in the Background to this Practice Session, Geany has a built-in terminal that can be accessed from the Messages area at the bottom. Because Geany does not allow you to add folders from the file browser if you've loaded that plugin, you can use this terminal for folder management. Scroll the menu on the left of the messages window, using the arrows, to the Terminal item to open a view into that terminal.

2.   From the terminal in the Messages area of Geany, create a project directory.

      bob@raspberrypi:~ $ **mkdir project2**

      Change to the folder second.

      bob@raspberrypi:~ $ **cd project2**

3.   So we can see the files we're working with if we switch to the Files sidebar display, and navigate to the new **projects2** folder.

      Create a new file called **third.cpp**. There are two steps to accomplish this:

      a.   Make the Geany menu choice **File > New** This creates a new tab with the name 'untitled'

      b.   Make the Geany menu choice **File > Save As...** In the Raspberry Pi file window that opens on screen, in the Name area, type third.cpp. Navigate to the **project2** directory. It's empty! Then click on the Save button in the Save File window. This will allow you to save your file **third.cpp** into the new **project2** folder.

4.   Add the following C++ code into the editor area, save your new file as **third.cpp** into your **project2** folder:

```
#include <iostream>

// Function to find the greatest common divisor (GCD) of two numbers
int findGCD(int a, int b) {
    if (b == 0) {
        return a;
    }
    return findGCD(b, a % b);
}

// Function to find the least common multiple (LCM) of two numbers
int findLCM(int a, int b) {
    return (a * b) / findGCD(a, b);
}

int main() {
    int num1, den1, num2, den2, num3, den3;

    // Input three fractions
    std::cout << "Enter the first fraction (numerator denominator): ";
    std::cin >> num1 >> den1;
    std::cout << "Enter the second fraction (numerator denominator): ";
    std::cin >> num2 >> den2;
    std::cout << "Enter the third fraction (numerator denominator): ";
    std::cin >> num3 >> den3;

    // Find the LCD of the denominators
    int lcm12 = findLCM(den1, den2);
    int lcd = findLCM(lcm12, den3);

    // Output the LCD
    std::cout << "The LCD of the three fractions is: " << lcd << std::endl;

    return 0;
}
```

5.   Projects

a.   For this example, with the **third.cpp** file still open, from the Geany menu, choose **Project >New...**
In the New Project window that opens, type **third** into the Name: bar. Change the Filename: entry to /home/bob/project2/third.geany, and the Base path: entry to /home/bob/project2/third/

b. Then click on the Create button in the New Project window.
c. A Question box will open, asking you if you want to "Move the current documents into the new project's session?". Select 'Yes' to add **third.cpp** to the new project.
d. Another Question box opens, saying that The path "home/bob/project2/third/" does not exist. Create the project's base path directory? Click the OK button.

Note
Of course, your pathnames will be slightly different, depending on the names of your home directory.

An explanation of the contents of the New Project window is as follows:

Name - this is the project name
FileName - The name and location of the project file.
BasePath - This is the folder where your project files belong. The **third.cpp** file is in the home/bob/project2 folder.
Now you have a project file that will load your source files and set your project directory when you load it.

So at this point, in the */home/*bob/project2 directory, as viewed int the Geany terminal window, you have the following files:
    third third.cpp third.geany
    You must delete the directory named **third** with the following command in a terminal window:

$ rmdir third

Note
This ordinarily would be the project directory that would hold all of your code, but for the sake of this Practice Session, and the next, where we clone project directories, we take the liberty of deleting that created directory because we created a project directory by hand, and didn't use the *default projects folder* to contain our new project, and its attendant files and subfolders.

6. Build

The Geany menu choice **Build > Build** will create an executable image. You can make the Geany menu choice **Build > Build**, or press the function key on the keyboard **<F9>,** to accomplish this. First click on the arrow buttons again to scroll up in the sidebar until "Messages" is displayed. Then, make the Geany menu choice **Build > Build**.

The following message appears in the Messages area at the bottom of the Geany window, **IF** you have faithfully and correctly typed in the code from Step 4:

```
g++ -Wall -o "third" "third.cpp" (in directory: /home/bob/project2)
Compilation finished successfully.
```

7. Executing

So now that you have an executable image of this C++ program, you can execute it simply by clicking on the paper airplane icon (**Run or view the current file**) in the Geany Toolbar area. When we did that on our Raspberry Pi system, we got the following output in a separate terminal that opened off the Geany window:

```
Enter the first fraction (numerator denominator): 2 3
Enter the second fraction (numerator denominator): 3 4
Enter the third fraction (numerator denominator): 15 16
The LCD of the three fractions is: 48


------------------
(program exited with code: 0)
Press return to continue
```

8. Press the **<Enter>** key to close the terminal window.
9. Make the Geany menu choice **File > Close All**, then quit Geany.

It's interesting to notice at this point that even though you ostensibly closed everything before quitting, on the next launch of Geany, you are placed back in the Project named **third**.

Conclusion: You created a C++ program that finds the LCD of three entered fractions, and placed that program in a newly created project, with its attendant directory in Geany. This technique is admittedly a hybrid version of the way it is ordinarily done.

Practice Session 1.11 Cloning Geany Projects

Objectives: To clone, or copy, an already-created Geany project that contains C++ program files, into another folder so that you can modify the copied C++ programs in this new project folder for an alternative use case.

Prerequisites:

1. Completion of Practice Sessions 1.8 through 1.10.

Background: To clone an entire project directory in this Practice Session, we use the **cp -r** Linux command, so that all the files created in the previous Practice Exercise in the project directory from there are duplicated into a new cloned project directory. The purpose of doing this is so that you can reuse the same code in a new project, and modify it, while retaining the original code in the original project directory. In this Practice Session, we also switch to the terminal display in the Message area at the bottom of the Geany window to execute Raspberry Pi OS commands. If you want to, you can open a separate terminal outside of Geany to accomplish this. We also utilize the Files sidebar of the Geany window to navigate to directories, and display their contents.

Note
See Section 1.6.4.10 to enable the File browser sidebar, which allows you to navigate to files and directories where you can view the contents of Geany's current working directory, or the directory of the current project.

Procedures:

1. At the Raspberry Pi command line in a terminal display in the Message area, change the current working directory to the projects folder you created in Practice Session 1.10. This Practice Session assumes that your projects folder, when you change to the one created in Practice Session 1.10, is at /*home*/bob/project2/, but on your Raspberry Pi system, it will be slightly different, depending on where you created it in Practice Session 1.10.

2. Create a new subdirectory of your home directory, named **project3**, with the following command:

    $ cp -r project2 project3

    project3 will be where your cloned project files will exist, after you execute this command.

3. Change the current working directory to **project3** in the sidebar Files sidebar display. The following files should now be shown in that new directory:

    third third.cpp third.geany

The file **third** is the executable image of the compiled program **third.cpp**, and the file **third.geany** is a Geany project file that holds information about the project.

4.   Launch Geany, and in the Files sidebar display, navigate to /*home*/bob/ project3, and double click on the project3 icon. You should now see the listing of files there as **third, third.cpp**, and **third.geany** in the Files sidebar display.

5.   Select the file **third.cpp**, and double click on it to open it. The C++ code should appear in the Geany main editor pane.

6.   Make the Geany menu choice **Build > Build**, or press the Function key **<F9>**.

You should get the following messages in the terminal area

```
g++ -Wall -o "third" "third.cpp" (in directory: /home/bob/project3)
Compilation finished successfully.
```

6.   Execute the program named **third** by clicking on the paper airplane icon.

7.   The output we got, displayed in a separate terminal window, is exactly the same as we got in Practice Session 1.3 when we input the three fractions values, and should be as follows:

```
Enter the first fraction (numerator denominator): 2 3
Enter the second fraction (numerator denominator): 3 4
Enter the third fraction (numerator denominator): 15 16
The LCD of the three fractions is: 48


------------------
(program exited with code: 0)
Press return to continue
```

8.   Press the **<Enter>** key to close the terminal window.

9.   You are now free to modify the code of this file, save it with a different name, recompile and relink the newly modified file, and execute it with the Geany's Build facility. You have two versions of the C++ program in this cloned project directory, the original copied over from the project2 directory, and perhaps a modified one.

10.   Make the Geany menu choice **File > Close All**, then **Project > Close**. Finally, quit Geany.

Conclusion: In a hybridized way, you cloned, or copied, an already-created Geany project directory that contained a C++ program file, into another directory so that you can then modify the original C++ program in that new directory.

Practice Session 1.12 Building Multiple C++ Modules into One Executable Image in a Project

Objectives: To use Geany and a makefile to write and execute a C++ program with two separate modules, which can be compiled with **make** into one executable program, where integers are input into the first module, and printed out by the second module.

Prerequisites: Completion of Practice Sessions 1.8 through 1.11.

Background:
There is an automated Geany menu choice that accomplishes the process of building multiple modules into a single executable image. That is done in Geany via the use of a *makefile*. A makefile is traditionally a UNIX or Linux script used in software development to automate the build process of a program or project. It contains a set of rules and dependencies that define how to compile and link the source code files to produce the final executable image, or library.

In the context of C++ compilation and linking, a makefile typically includes the following components:

Targets: These are the desired end products of the build process, such as executable images or libraries.

Dependencies: These are the files that the target depends on, including source code files, header files, and other dependencies.

Rules: These define how to build the target based on its dependencies. Each rule typically specifies the compiler flags, source files, and other build instructions necessary to generate the target.

The makefile's primary purpose is to streamline and automate the compilation and linking process. When a developer invokes the Linux **make** command in a terminal, for example, **make** reads the makefile, determines which targets need to be rebuilt based on their dependencies and modification times, and executes the necessary build commands accordingly.

This ensures that only the modified or affected files are compiled and linked, saving time and resources during the development process.

For example, a simple makefile for a C++ program might look like as follows:

```
CC = g++  # C++ compiler
CFLAGS = -Wall -O2  # Compiler flags

TARGET = my_program  # Name of the target executable
SOURCES = main.cpp helper.cpp  # Source files

all: $(TARGET)

$(TARGET): $(SOURCES)
    $(CC) $(CFLAGS) -o $(TARGET) $(SOURCES)

clean:
    rm -f $(TARGET)
```

In this example:

CC is the compiler being used (here, g++).
CFLAGS are the compiler flags for optimization and warnings.
all is a target that depends on **$(TARGET)** (the executable).
$(TARGET) depends on **$(SOURCES)** (the source files). The rule specifies how to compile and link the sources into the target executable.
clean is a target that can be used to remove the target executable.

By using this makefile, invoking **make** in the terminal would compile and link the C++ source files (main.cpp and helper.cpp) into the my_program executable using the specified compiler and flags. Invoking **make clean** would remove the executable.

See Section 1.6.3.1 for more information on the **make** command.

Procedures:

1. Launch Geany, type in the following three C++ source code files, and using the Geany menu **File > Save**, save them separately as **input_module.cpp**, **output_module.cpp**, and **main.cpp**, respectively:

    input_module.cpp:

    ```
    // input_module.cpp
    #include <iostream>

    int getInput() {

        int num;
        std::cout << "Enter an integer: ";
        std::cin >> num;
        return num;
    }
    ```

---

output_module.cpp:

```cpp
// output_module.cpp
#include <iostream>

void printOutput(int num) {
    std::cout << "The entered integer is: " << num << std::endl;
}
```

---

main.cpp:

```cpp
// main.cpp
#include <iostream>

// Declare the functions from the modules
extern int getInput();
extern void printOutput(int num);

int main() {
    int num = getInput(); // Get input from the first module
    printOutput(num);     // Print the input using the second module

    return 0;
}
```

4. Create a file in Geany, named **makefile**, that contains the following:

   ```
   my_program: main.cpp input_module.cpp output_module.cpp
   g++ -o my_program main.cpp input_module.cpp output_module.cpp
   ```

   This makefile will compile main.cpp, input_module.cpp, and output_module.cpp into one executable called my_program. There should now be four tabs above the main Geany editor window.

5. Make the Geany menu choice **Build > Set Build Commands**. The Project Properties window opens on screen. Edit the Execute commands line 1. to read **"./my_program"**

   Then, make the OK button choice in the Project Properties window.

6. Make the Geany menu choice **Build > Make**

7. Click on the **Run or view the current file** icon in the toolbar to run the program. A separate terminal opens on screen, and a prompt appears as shown below, asking you to enter an integer. We entered the integer 42. The program will print the entered integer as follows:

Enter an integer: **42**

The entered integer is: 42

8.   Press **<Enter>** on the keyboard to close the open terminal the program has generated.

9.   Make the Geany menu choice **File > Close All**, then quit Geany.

Conclusion: This Practice Session demonstrates how to use Geany and a makefile to create a C++ program with two separate modules, one for input and one for output, and how to pass an integer from one module to another for processing and display.

1.7.3.3 A Geany Py

In this section, we use the Geany IDE to create and execute a number of Python programs and script files. Python is an interpreted language that's basically an OOP language, which can also very easily incorporate the procedural (imperative) model. The latter is much easier to understand for beginners.

Disclaimer:
Again, the objective here in this section, as it was for C++, is *not* to teach the basics of the Python language. Our goal is to illustrate how Geany can be used as a graphical code editor to expedite the creation and execution of Python programs, and script file code.

1.7.3.3.1 Geany Py Preliminary Considerations

In order to prepare Geany for use with Python, you need to set up some preliminary things first. These preliminaries allow you to use Geany for the creation and execution of Python code in a manner very similar to the use of Thonny, the other IDE already available by default in the Raspberry Pi OS. You must install Python2 using APT, because Python2 is not installed by default on the Debian-Bookworm based Raspberry Pi OS.

There are basically five ways to execute Python code from within an IDE such as Geany. They are as follows, as delineated in detail in Chapter 2, Section 2.2.6 of Volume 2 of this series:

Way 1 (Interactive Mode)
In the Geany terminal, you launch either Python2 or Python3, and type a single line of Python code on the Python command line (>>>) in the Geany terminal. Or maybe multiple lines of Python code, to see the results immediately. A good reason to use this mode is that you can test small fragments of Python code, one line, or a couple of lines, at a time, directly in the current Python interpreter which is either the default Python interpreter, or another one that you've installed and selected. This is equivalent to executing Python in a Raspberry Pi terminal.

Remember, to submit a line of Python code to its interpreter, at the end of the line, press **<Enter>** on the keyboard.

Way 2 (Script Mode)
This mode uses the **Run or view file...** icon on the Geany toolbar to execute the multiple line Python code found in this section.

Note
Before you begin to type any code into the Geany editor window, you should make the Geany menu choice **File > Save As ...** *first*, and make sure you save the at-this-point blank **untitled** file with the **.py** extension, and a meaningful name in a predetermined, and easily accessible directory. That way, Geany knows to deploy the appropriate build and execute parameters for the lines of Python code you're going to type into the Geany editor window.

Then, you can perform a check. Make the Geany menu choice **Build > Set Build Commands**, and in the **Set Build Commands** window, the following should appear:

On lines 1. **Compile** and 3. **Lint** of the Python commands area for Python3, for example:

python3 -m py_compile "%f"
pep8 --max-line-length=80 "%f"

In the Error regular expression area-

(.+):([0-9]+):([0-9]+)

On the line number 1. of the Execute commands area for Python3, for example-

python3 "%f"

You can also modify those commands to have either Python3 (and perhaps its latest version) or Python2 build and execute your code.

So, in the above entries, change the python3 entries to python if you want Python2 to build and execute your code. You must install Python2 using APT, because Python2 is not installed by default on the Debian-Bookworm based Raspberry Pi OS. After making changes in the **Set Build Command** window, click on the **OK** button at the bottom of the window to close it.

You type multiple, properly formatted and syntactically correct Python commands into the Geany editor window. This is traditionally called a *script file* (and is saved with a file name ending in **.py**). Then you click on the Geany **Run** Toolbar icon, and the results of the execution of the Python commands are seen in a separate window that opens on screen.

A good reason to use this mode is if you have programs or scripts with more than a few lines of code in them, and you do *not* want to type that code in every time you want to run it.

Of course, when you use the Geany Toolbar **Save** icon, you can resave the multiple line Python code into a meaningfully named file in Geany's current working directory, and then at some later time, use **Geany's Open an existing file** Toolbar icon to bring that file back into the editor window, if you want to modify it.

Way 3 (Import Script Mode)
Similarly to Way2 (Script Mode), you use Geany as a code, or text editor, to create and save multiple Python commands in a script file, in the Geany current working directory.

Then in the Geany terminal, you execute Python2 or Python3, and at the Python3 command prompt there, you bring the script file into Python with the Python3 **import** command. A good reason to use this mode is if your script files contain function definitions. A simple example of this is as follows:

```
# A function with two arguments
def mult_numbers(num1, num2):
    product  = num1 * num2
    print('Product: ',product)
```

A good reason to use this mode is to bring those structures and functions into the current interactive Geany Python session environment, or namespace.

How do you know what the Geany current working directory is?

It's set to a default, and can be changed to any directory you want in the filesystem of your Raspberry Pi OS, to retrieve, or save, Python3 script files from or to. To find out, and be able to reset the current working directory in Geany, in the Geany terminal at the prompt, type the following commands:

```
>>> import os
>>> os.getcwd()
'/home/bob/Public'
>>>
```

We see from the above output that the current working directory, where Geany retrieves and saves script files to from the Script Area, is */home/*bob/ Public.

To change that current working directory to */home/*bob/Documents, for example, type the following command on the command line in the Geany terminal, after you've typed in the previous two commands:

```
>>>os.chdir("/home/bob/Documents")
```

Way 4 (Bash Mode)
We use this Mode a few times in this section. This is an alternative way of executing Python scripts, which depends upon the working environment within which you are executing Python. That alternative, very similar to the way of

executing a Bash, or other script file, is to include this line as the first line in the Python script file (if you want to use Python3 to execute your code):

#! /usr/bin/env python3

You must also be sure that you have execute privilege on the file with the **.py extension**, such as **first.py**, using the **chmod u+x first.py** command. Then, to execute that script file, on the Bash command line in the Geany terminal, type the following:

$./first.py

> This method uses Bash to execute the script file.
>
> The main advantage of this method is that, depending on which version of Python you want to run, you can place the command name for that version in the first line of the script file. For example, if you want to use Python Version 3.11.3 (if you've installed that version!) to run the script file, you could modify the first line in the script file to read-

#! /usr/bin/env python3.11

> There are portability issues with this method, for example when the working environment is in conflict with what version of Python you want to execute the script file code with. But for beginners, you can ignore those issues for now.

This method of executing the Python code is sometimes called running it as a *user-written library module*.

Way 5 (Compiling a Script File into Bytecode for Bash Execution)
It is possible to run a Python script file in Geany that you have used the interpreter to compile into a portable form of executable code, to execute from the Bash command line. It's called the *bytecode form*. We don't use it here in this section. But we offer help on how to use this mode in Chapter 2, Section 2.2.6 of Volume 2 of this series.

1.7.3.3.2 *Other Preliminary Considerations*
To *autoindent* lines of Python code in the Geany editor window, do the following:

1. Launch Geany and open a new file you want to enter Python code into.
2. To ensure that Geany will recognize the code in the files you create and execute in this section as Python language code, make the Geany menu **Document > Set Filetype > Scripting Languages > Python**

source file choice. Also, make sure there's a check mark on the Document menu next to Auto-indentation.

3.   To check the auto-indentation, when you type Python code and press **<Enter>**, Geany should automatically indent the next line based on the structured programming context.

1.7.3.3.3 *Python Code Examples*

In this section, we offer a range of Python script files, and program code, most of which uses the procedural (imperative) model, and some of which uses the OOP paradigm, that can be created and executed in Geany with the modes we specified in Section 1.6.3.3.1.

The following code for the first example is a more involved use of OOP: creating a class, and then using some methods to manipulate the objects in that class. After setting up the preliminaries as shown in Section 1.6.3.3.1, type in the following code, using the Geany editor window, into a file that you use Geany to name **firstclass.py**.

Practice Session 1.13

```
#!/usr/bin/python3
class Structure:
  'Common base class for all Python Structures'
  StrucCount = 0

  def __init__(s, name, number):
    s.name = name
    s.number= number
    Structure.StrucCount += 1

  def displayCount(s):
    print ("Total Structures %d" % Structure.StrucCount)

  def displayStructure(s):
    print ("Name : ", s.name,  ", Number : ", s.number)
```

Then, in the Geany terminal, execute Python3, and run the code with the following instructions:

(You can leave out the comments):

```
>>> import firstclass
>>> Stru1 = firstclass.Structure("Arithmetic Operators", 17)   #creates the
                                                               first object
>>> Stru2 = firstclass.Structure("Logical Operators", 10)      #creates the
                                                               second object
>>> Stru1.displayStructure()
Name : Arithmetic Operators , Number : 17                 #displays the first object
>>> Stru2.displayStructure()                              #displays the second object
```

```
Name : Logical Operators, Number : 10
>>> print ("Total Structures %d" % firstclass.Structure.StrucCount) #prints
total structures
Total Structures 2
>>> Stru1.inst = 7                              #creates a new attribute of Stru1
>>> hasattr(Stru1, 'inst')                        #checks object for attribute
True
>>> getattr(Stru1, 'inst')                        #gets the value of the attribute
7
>>> getattr(Stru1, 'name')                        #gets the value of the attribute
'Arithmetic Operators'
>>>
```

The following is an example of function definitions in Python2, which must be installed with APT if you are using a Debian-Bookworm based Raspberry Pi OS.

Practice Session 1.14
In the Geany editor window, type in the following code:

```python
def add(a, b):
    c = a + b
    return(c)
def subtract(a, b):
    c = b - a
    return(c)
def multiply(a, b):
    c = a * b
    return(c)
def divide(a, b):
    c = a / b
    return(c)
```

Name this file **math1.py**. Then, run Python2 in the Geany terminal with the command **python**, and type the following three lines of Python code:

```python
>>> import math1
>>> z = math1.add(3, 4)
>>> z
7
>>>
```

The following is an example of conditional execution in Python.

Practice Session 1.15
Type in the following code in the Geany editor window.

```
x = 1
if x == 0:   # the == is a logical, or Boolean operator
    print ("x equal 0")
elif x == 1: #one or more of these optional blocks are allowed
    print ("x equal 1")
else:      #the optional block
    print ("x is something else")
```

When you're finished correctly typing the above in, click on the **Run or view the current file** icon in the Geany Toolbar.

x equal 1

It is also possible to nest Python conditional execution blocks inside of one another.

For example, for the code execution below, enter the following correctly into a file named **two7.py** in Geany. Geany indents according to the Rule of Four!

Then, in Geany click on the Run Toolbar icon:

Practice Session 1.16

```
w = 36
y = 13
z = 20
if w < 37:
    print ("w is less than 37")
    if y > 13:
      print ("y is greater than 13")
    elif y == 13:
      print ("y is equal to 13")
    else:
      print ("y is less than 13")
    if z > 21:
      print ("z is greater than 21")
    elif z == 21:
      print ("z is equal to 21")
    else:
      print ("z is less than 21")
else:
    print ("w is greater than or equal to 37")
```

The following is what should appear on your display in the Geany terminal:

w is less than 37
y is equal to 13
z is less than 21
>>>

Here's a Python3 program that uses the sys module to allow you to enter some text, and have it echoed on the command line:

Practice Session 1.17

```
#!/usr/bin/python3
import sys
s = input("Enter input:")
print ("You entered:", s)
r = input("Enter another line:")
words = r.split(' ')
print ("The first word is:", words[0])
print ("The second word is:", words[1])
rest = (' '.join(words[2: ]))
print ("The rest of the line is:", rest)
sys.exit() #normal exit status
```

On our Raspberry Pi system, using Python 3.9.2, we ran the Python3 code in Geany. We named the file **ex27.py**. We obtained the following output, with the supplied text shown in **bold**:

```
$ ./ex27.py
Enter input: Linux rules!
You entered: Linux rules!
Enter another line: Raspberry Pi rules!
The first word is: Raspberry
The second word is: Pi
The rest of the line is: rules!
Process ended with exit code 0.
$
```

Here's another Python3 program that uses the sys module, and some of its methods to allow you to enter some text, and have it echoed on the command line:

Practice Session 1.18

```
#!/usr/bin/python3
import sys
x = (sys.argv)
print ("The command name is: ", sys.argv[0])
print ("The value of the command line arguments are: ", x[1:10])
print ("Another way to display values of all the arguments: ", sys.argv[1:])
print ("Yet another way is: ", sys.argv[slice(1,15)])
sys.exit ()
```

On our Raspberry Pi system and Geany, using Python 3.9.2, we ran the Python3 code in the Geany terminal, after we named it **ex28.py**. Remember to give yourself access privileges on the file ex28.py with the command **chmod**

u+x ex28.py if necessary! We obtained the following output, with the argument list to the **./ex28.py** command as shown:

```
$ ./ex28.py a b c d e f g h i j k l m n
The command name is: ./ex28.py
The value of the command line arguments are: ['a', 'b', 'c', 'd', 'e', 'f', 'g', 'h', 'i']
Another way to display values of all the arguments: ['a', 'b', 'c', 'd', 'e', 'f', 'g', 'h', 'i', 'j',
'k', 'l', 'm', 'n']
Yet another way is: ['a', 'b', 'c', 'd', 'e', 'f', 'g', 'h', 'i', 'j', 'k', 'l', 'm', 'n']
$
```

The following is a neat-looking graphics plot done by Python. You first need to install the following necessary libraries, using pip, on the Raspberry Pi command line:

```
$ pip install matplotlib numpy
Output truncated ...
$
```

Practice Session 1.19

```
import numpy as np
import matplotlib.pyplot as plt
from mpl_toolkits.mplot3d import Axes3D

# Generate x values
x = np.linspace(-2*np.pi, 2*np.pi, 100)
# Compute sine and tangent for each x
sin_x = np.sin(x)
tan_x = np.tan(x)

# Create a 3D plot
fig = plt.figure()
ax = fig.add_subplot(111, projection='3d')

# Plot the sine and tangent functions
ax.plot(x, sin_x, tan_x)

# Set labels for axes
ax.set_xlabel('X')
ax.set_ylabel('Sine(X)')
ax.set_zlabel('Tangent(X)')

# Show the plot
plt.show()
```

After you enter the above code into the Geany editor window, click on the **Run** Toolbar icon. The output we got is shown in Figure 1.17.

Here is an example (the code of which we named **ex35.py**) of carrying out simple system administration, in this case using Python 2.7.12. In order for you to execute this program on a Debian-Bookworm based Raspberry Pi OS,

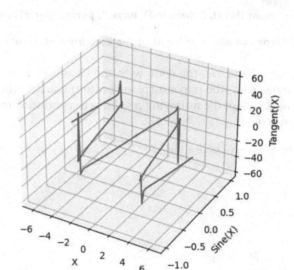

FIGURE 1.17
3D matplotlib.pyplot of Sine and Tangent functions.

you need to use APT to install Python 2. It customizes a shell command to show permissions set on files in the current working directory that match a certain pattern:

Practice Session 1.20

```
#!/usr/bin/python
import stat, sys, os, glob
try:
   #Getting search pattern from user and assigning it to a list
   pattern = input("Enter the file pattern to search for:\n")
   matching_Files = glob.glob(pattern)
   print ("Files:")
   print (matching_Files)
   print ("************************************")
   for file in matching_Files:
      mode=stat.S_IMODE(os.lstat(file)[stat.ST_MODE])
      print ("\nPermissions for file ", file, ":")
      for level in "USR", "GRP", "OTH":
```

```
        for perm in "R", "W", "X":
            if mode & getattr(stat,"S_I"+perm+level):
                print (level, " has ", perm, " permission")
            else:
                print (level, " does NOT have ", perm, "permission")
except:
    print ("Error - check your input of file matching pattern")
```

Once we saved and ran the code with the Geany **Run or view the current file ...** toolbar icon (the paper airplane button) using Python 2.7.12, and the input shown, we got the following results in a separate terminal window that opened on screen:

```
Enter the file pattern to search for:
*.py
Files:
2_1.py
2_16.py
2_17.py


*******************************
Permissions for file  2_1.py :
USR   has  R  permission
USR   has  W  permission
USR   does NOT have  X permission
GRP   has  R  permission
GRP   does NOT have  W permission
GRP   does NOT have  X permission
OTH   has  R  permission
OTH   does NOT have  W permission
OTH   does NOT have  X permission

Output truncated...
```

For the Python3 code in Practice Sessions 1.21 through 1.23, you don't have to install the Python3 Tkinter libraries, as shown on the following Raspberry Pi command line:

```
bob@raspberrypi:~ $ sudo apt-get install python3-tk
Reading package lists... Done
Building dependency tree... Done
Reading state information... Done
python3-tk is already the newest version (3.11.2-3).
The following packages were automatically installed and are no longer required:
    linux-headers-6.1.0-13-arm64 linux-headers-6.1.0-13-common
    linux-headers-6.1.0-14-arm64 linux-headers-6.1.0-14-common
    linux-headers-6.1.0-15-arm64 linux-headers-6.1.0-15-common
Use 'sudo apt autoremove' to remove them.
0 upgraded, 0 newly installed, 0 to remove and 1 not upgraded.
bob@raspberrypi:~ $
```

The following APT command must be done-
bob@raspberrypi:~ $ **sudo apt-get install tk-dev**
Output truncated...
bob@raspberrypi:~ $

The following simple example shows a complete tkinter Python script, and the widget it creates. You should create, and then execute these six lines of code in the Geany editor window (after saving the untitled file with a **.py** extension), and run it with the Toolbar **Run or view the current file ...** icon.

Practice Session 1.21

```
import tkinter
from tkinter import ttk
w = tkinter.Tk()
w.title("Python GUI")
ttk.Label(w,text="My first tkinter gui window").grid(column=0, row=0)
w.mainloop()
```

When this widget was generated on our Raspberry Pi 400, it appeared in the upper-left corner of the display screen, just below the raspberry in the Raspberry Pi menu, but we could manually move it wherever we wanted on the screen display.

To close the widget, just click on the "destroy window" button in your style of GUI window in which the widget was created. You may have to expand the window to see all of the window manipulation buttons, but we didn't need to do that on our Raspberry Pi 400.

The next simple example allows a user to add two real numbers as text, that has been entered interactively, on lines inside the tkinter widget. And, as in Example 1.21, you can enter the code in Geany's editor window, and use the **Run or view the current file ...** icon to launch it.

Practice Session 1.22

```
import tkinter as tk
from tkinter import ttk
from functools import partial

# This is the data generating module, which computes the sum.
def add_it(label_result, n1, n2):
    num1 = (n1.get())
    num2 = (n2.get())
    result = float(num1)+float(num2)
    label_result.config(text="Sum = %f" % result)
    return
```

```
# This grids the widget object where indicated, then returns it.
def mkgrid(r, c, w):
        w.grid(row=r, column=c, sticky='news')
        return w

root = tk.Tk()
root.title('Real Number Adder')
# The rest hooks the adder into the grid manager widgets.
add1_lab = mkgrid(0, 0, ttk.Label(root, text="addend 1",
                            anchor='e'))
add2_lab = mkgrid(1, 0, ttk.Label(root, text="addend 2",
                            anchor='e'))
add1= mkgrid(0, 1, ttk.Entry(root))
add2= mkgrid(1, 1, ttk.Entry(root))
spacer = mkgrid(0, 2, ttk.Label(root, text="))
labelResult = ttk.Label(root)
labelResult.grid(row=7, column=2)
add_it = partial(add_it, labelResult, add1, add2)
add_but = mkgrid(1, 2, ttk.Button(root, text="Add them",
                            command=add_it))
# Starts the root main event loop
root.mainloop()
```

The results of running this tkinter script file are shown in Figure 1.18.

Even though Practice Session 1.22 ostensibly uses the procedural (imperative) programming model, syntax, and data abstraction, you should begin to see that tkinter GUI scripts are basically composed of OOP class instance objects. All of the methods that are applied to those instances come from the methods applied to the core widgets in tkinter.

The following example will construct a Fahrenheit-to-Celsius temperature conversion GUI with tkinter. And, as in Practice Sessions 1.21 and 1.22, you can enter the code in Geany's editor window, and use the **Run or view the current file ...** Toolbar icon to launch it.

FIGURE 1.18
tkinter adder script output results.

Practice Session 1.23

```
import tkinter as tk
from tkinter import ttk
# This computes the Celsius temperature from the Fahrenheit.
def findcel():
        famt = ftmp.get()
        if famt == ":               #not double quote, 2 single quotes
                cent.configure(text=")
        else:
                famt = float(famt)
        camt = (famt - 32) / 1.8
# A method(configure) applied to an object (cent) that is converted to a string
# tr(camt).
        cent.configure(text=str(camt))
# This grids the widget object where indicated, then returns it.
def mkgrid(r, c, w):
        w.grid(row=r, column=c, sticky='news')
        return w
root = tk.Tk()
root.title('Temp Conversion')
# The rest hooks the temps into the grid graphics manager widgets.
flab = mkgrid(0, 0, ttk.Label(root, text="Fahrenheit Temperature",anchor='e'))
clab = mkgrid(1, 0, ttk.Label(root, text="Celsius Temperature",anchor='e'))
ftmp = mkgrid(0, 1, ttk.Entry(root))
cent = mkgrid(1, 1, ttk.Label(root, text= "", relief='sunken',anchor='w'))
elab = mkgrid(0, 2, ttk.Label(root, text="))
fbut = mkgrid(1, 2, ttk.Button(root, text="Compute Celsius",command=\
findcel))
# Starts the root main event loop
root.mainloop()
```

The results of running this tkinter script file are shown in Figure 1.19.

Again, even though the previous example is ostensibly a procedural (imperative) model program design, you should be able to recognize from this line-by-line description and explanation that the underlying core widgets from tkinter are OOP classes that we have instanced as objects.

The example used methods applied to those classes, but the structure of our script file was still functional and declarative in nature.

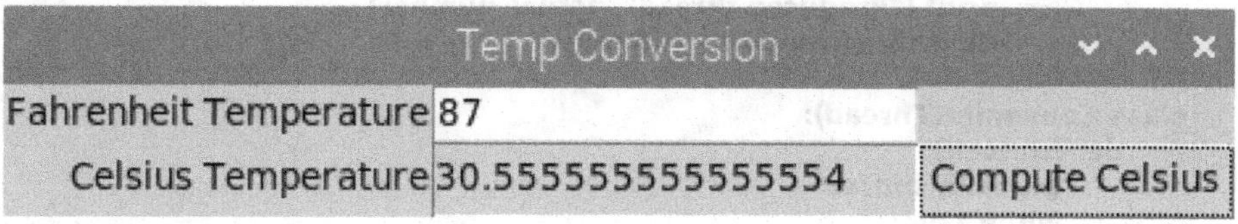

FIGURE 1.19
tkinter temperature conversion output results.

The following Python3 code brings together much of the syntax and structure from this section. It illustrates a Python3 solution to the *producer-consumer problem*, using an FIFO queue with the **queue.Queue** class, in a multi-threaded program. It uses OOP, and the threading module and its methods, to start two threads: Producer and Consumer.

An overview of how Python3 uses the Queue class to obtain a solution to the producer-consumer problem, taken from the reference material, is as follows:

> The Producer places a piece of data on the queue using the .**put** method. The utility and advantage the queue module is most visible here- .**put** locks the queue, checks to see if the queue is full, and calls an internal .**wait()** to pause the producer if the queue is full. The Consumer then uses the .**get** method to acquire the lock before removing data from the queue, and .**get** checks for an empty queue. If the queue is empty, the consumer is put in a wait state.
>
> .**get()** and .**put()** also implement the notification logic to allow "talking" between Producer and Consumer threads.

In this final Geany-run Python3 example, create the code in a file named **ex45. py** in the Geany editor, and run it (and also terminate it, and the Python3 process it spawns using **<Ctrl>+C**) using the **Run or view the current file ...** icon:

Practice Session 1.24

```python
from threading import Thread
import time
import random
import queue

q_buffer = queue.Queue()

class Producer(Thread):
    def run(self):
        numbers = range(5)
        global q_buffer
        while True:
            actual_number = random.choice(numbers)
            q_buffer.put(actual_number)
            print ("Produced thread", actual_number)
            time.sleep(random.random())

class Consumer(Thread):
    def run(self):
        global q_buffer
        while True:
            actual_number_gotten = q_buffer.get()
            q_buffer.task_done()
```

```
            print ("Consumed thread", actual_number_gotten)
            time.sleep(random.random())

Producer().start()
Consumer().start()
```

Output from the above example is as follows:

```
Produced thread 1
Consumed thread 1
Produced thread 0
Produced thread 4
Consumed thread 0
Consumed thread 4
Produced thread 3
Consumed thread 3
Produced thread 0
Consumed thread 0
Produced thread 4
Consumed thread 4
Produced thread 4
Consumed thread 4
Produced thread 2
Produced thread 1
Consumed thread 2
Produced thread 1
<Ctrl>+C
```

1.7.4 Geany Abbreviated Reference Encyclopedia

The following sections are abstracts and condensed versions of portions of the Geany documentation, found at the following website:

www.geany.org/manual/current/index.html

We've selected those portions rather subjectively, and not necessarily alphabetically, based upon what we've presented previously in Geany.

1.7.4.1 Indentation

Geany allows each document to indent either with a tab character, multiple spaces or a combination of both. This is critical when you're coding in a structured language, such as C++ or Python.

1. The Tabs setting indents with one tab character per indent level, and displays tabs as the indent width.
2. The Spaces setting indents with the number of spaces set in the indent width for each level.

3. The Tabs and Spaces setting indents with spaces as above, then converts as many spaces as it can to tab characters at the rate of one tab for each multiple of the `Various preference` setting.

indent_hard_tab_width (default 8) and displays tabs as the *indent_ hard_tab_width* value.

The default settings can be overridden per-document using the Geany **Document** menu. They can also be overridden by on a per project basis.

The indent mode for the current document is shown on the status bar, when a file is being edited in the editor window, as follows:

TAB
   Indent with Tab characters.
SP
   Indent with spaces.
T/S
   Indent with tabs and spaces, depending on how much indentation is on a line.

Applying new indentation settings
After changing the default settings you may wish to apply the new settings to every document in the current session. To do this, use the Geany **Project > Apply Default Indentation** menu item.

Detecting indent type
The **Detect from file** indentation preference can be used to scan each file as it's opened and set the indent type based on how many lines start with a tab vs. 2 or more spaces.

Auto-indentation
When enabled, auto-indentation happens when pressing **<Enter>** on the keyboard when in the editor window. It adds a predetermined amount of indentation to the next line, so the user doesn't always have to indent each line manually. Of course, if you initially save the file with a .cpp or .py extension, then Geany recognizes the file to be C++ or Python code, and indents according to the structured programing rules of those languages.

Geany has four types of auto-indentation:

1. **None**

Disables auto-indentation completely.

2. **Basic**

Adds the same amount of whitespace on a new line as on the previous line. For the Tabs and the Spaces indent types the indentation will use the same combination of characters as the previous line. The Tabs and Spaces indentation type converts as explained above.

3. **Current chars**

Does the same as *Basic* but also indents a new line after an opening brace '{', and de-indents when typing a closing brace '}'. For Python, a new line will be indented after typing ':' at the end of the previous line.

4. **Match braces**

Similar to *Current chars* but the closing brace will be aligned to match the indentation of the line with the opening brace. This requires the filetype to be one where Geany knows that the Scintillalexer understands matching braces (C, C++, D, HTML, Pascal, Bash, Perl, TCL).

1.7.4.2 Search, Replace, and Go to

This section describes search-related commands from the Search menu and the main editor window's pop-up menus:
Find, Find selection, Find usage, Find in files, Replace, Go to symbol definition, Go to symbol declaration, and Go to line

There are also two toolbar entries:
Search bar and Go to line entry
Using the Search bar is the quickest way to find some text. You can perform a *case-insensitive* search in the current document during text entry. Pressing **<Enter>** will search again, and pressing
<Shift>-<Enter> will perform searching backward.
The Find dialog window is used for finding text in one or more open documents, and is shown in Figure 1.20.

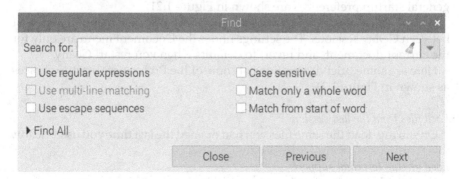

FIGURE 1.20
Find dialog window.

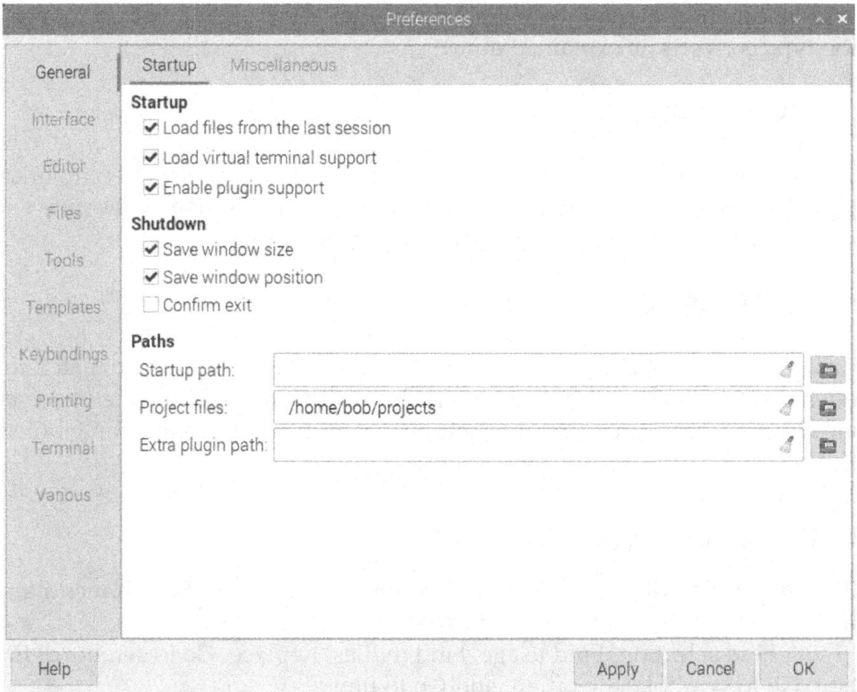

FIGURE 1.21
General startup preferences.

1.7.4.3 Preferences

You adjust Geany's settings using the Geany pull-down menu choice **Edit > Preferences**. Any changes you make there can be applied by clicking on either the **Apply** or the **OK** button. These settings will be persistent between Geany editing sessions. Most settings here have a **help** "pop-up" message. Just hover with your mouse over the item in the window to get help on it. The general startup preferences are shown in Figure 1.21.

You may also adjust some View settings (under the View menu) that persist between Geany sessions. The settings under the Document menu are only for the current document, and revert to defaults when you restart Geany.

Here are some brief descriptions of some of the Preferences Startup choices as shown in Figure 1.21.

Load files from the last session
On startup, load the same files you had opened the last time you used Geany.

Load virtual terminal support
Load the library for running a terminal in the message window area.

Enable plugin support
  Allow plugins to be used in Geany.

Shutdown
Save window position and geometry
  Save the current position and size of the main window so next time you open
  Geany it's in the same location.

Confirm Exit
  Have a dialog pop-up to confirm that you really want to quit Geany.

Paths
Startup path
  Path to start in when opening or saving files. It must be an absolute path.

Project files
  Path to start in when opening project files.

1.7.4.4 Interface preferences

The following Edit > Preferences menu is for the Interface tab, as shown in
Figure 1.22.

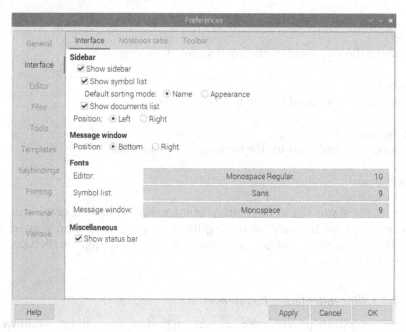

FIGURE 1.22
Interface preferences.

Abbreviated descriptions of the settings are as follows:

Sidebar
Show sidebar
    Whether to show the sidebar at all.

Show symbol list
    Show the list of functions, variables, and other information in the current
    document you are editing.

Show documents list
    Show all the documents you open currently. This can be used to change
    between documents, and to perform some common operations such as
    saving, closing, and reloading.

Position
    Whether to place the sidebar on the left or right of the editor window.

Message window
Position
    Whether to place the message window on the bottom or right of the editor
    window.

Fonts
Editor
    Change the font used to display documents.

Symbol list
    Change the font used for the Symbols sidebar tab.

Message window
    Change the font used for the message window area.

Miscellaneous
Show status bar
    Show the status bar at the bottom of the main window. It gives informa-
    tion about the file you are editing like the line and column you are on,
    whether any modifications were done, the file encoding, the filetype, and
    other information.

1.7.4.5 Editor Indentation Preferences

Abbreviated descriptions of the indentation preferences settings, as shown in
Figure 1.23, are as follows:

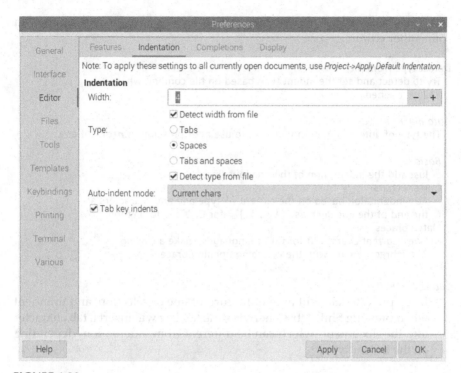

FIGURE 1.23
Indentation preferences.

Indentation group

Width
    The width of a single indent size in spaces. By default the indent size is equivalent to spaces.

Detect width from file
    Try to detect and set the indent width based on file content, when a file is opened.

Type
    When Geany inserts indentation, whether to use:

* Just Tabs
* Just Spaces
* Tabs and Spaces, depending on how much indentation is on a line

The *Tabs and Spaces* indent type is also known as *Soft tab support* in some other editors.

Detect type from file
  Try to detect and set the indent type based on file content, when
  a file is opened.

Auto-indent mode
  The type of auto-indentation you wish to use after pressing **<Enter>**, if any.

  Basic
    Just add the indentation of the previous line.
  Current chars
    Add indentation based on the current filetype and any characters at
    the end of the line such as ` `{` `, ` `}` ` for C, ` `:` ` for Python.
  Match braces
    Like *Current chars* but for C-like languages, make a closing
    ` `}` ` brace line up with the matching opening brace.

Tab key indents
  If set, pressing tab will indent the current line or selection, and unindent
  when pressing Shift-tab. Otherwise, the tab key will insert a tab character
  into the document (which can be different from indentation, depending
  on the indent type).

1.7.4.6 Editor Completions Preferences

Abbreviated description of the Editor Completions settings, as shown in Figure 1.24, are as follows:

Auto-close quotes and brackets
Geany can automatically insert a closing bracket and quote characters when you open them. For instance, you type a curly brace "{," Geany will automatically insert a closing curly brace "}." This allows you to conform to the syntax of a C++ program. With the following options, you can define for which characters this should work, depending on the coding requirements of the document or program you're working on.

Parenthesis ( )
  Auto-close parenthesis when typing an opening one
Curly brackets { }
  Auto-close curly brackets (braces) when typing an opening one
Square brackets [ ]
  Auto-close square brackets when typing an opening one
Single quotes ' '
  Auto-close single quotes when typing an opening one
Double quotes " "
  Auto-close double quotes when typing an opening one

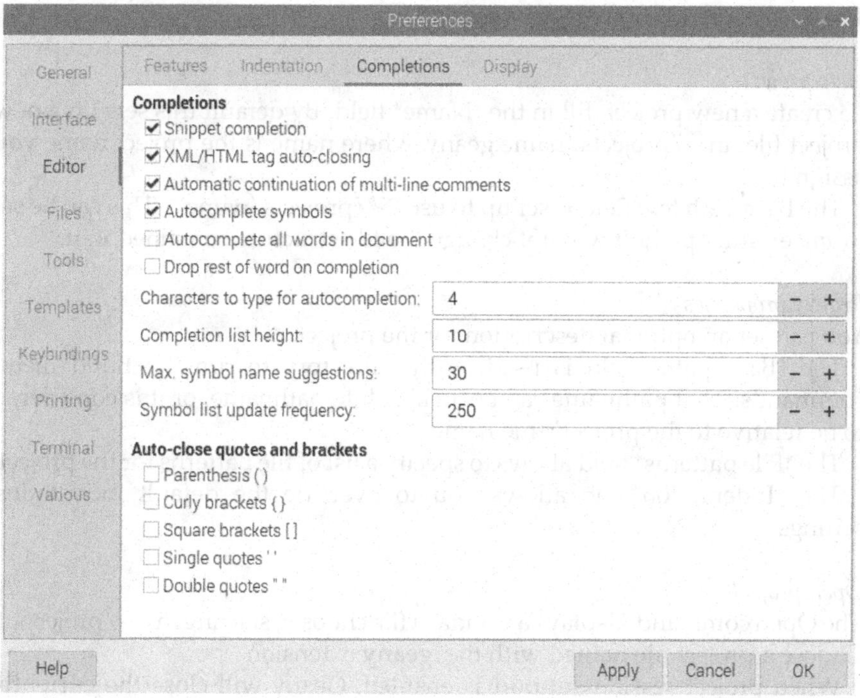

FIGURE 1.24
Editor completions.

1.7.4.7 Project Management

Project management in Geany involves the following:

1. Storing and opening session files on a project basis.
2. Overriding default settings with individual project settings.
3. Configuring the Geany **Build menu**, so that software suites can be configured and individually applied on a per-project basis.

As long as a project is "open," the **Build menu** will use the items defined in that project's settings, instead of the defaults. See Section 1.6.4.9, **Set Build menu**, for information on configuring the **Set Build menu**.

Note
The current project's settings are saved when it is closed, or when Geany is shutdown. When restarting Geany, the previously opened project file that was in use at the end of the last session will be reopened.

The Project menu choices are as follows.

New project
To create a new project, fill in the *Name* field. By default this sets up a new project file, in ~/projects/name.geany, where name is the project name you assign to it.

The Base path text field is set up to use ``~/projects/name``. This can be set to *any* existing path. It will not change the file structure contained in it.

Project properties
You can set an optional description for the project.

The *Base path* field is used as the directory to run the Build menu commands. That pathname can be an absolute pathname, or it is considered to be relative to the project's file name.

The *File patterns* field allows to specify a list of file patterns for the project.

The *Indentation* tab allows you to override the default indentation settings.

Open project
The Open command displays a standard file chooser, starting in ``~/projects``. Choose a project file named with the **.geany** extension.

When project session support is enabled, Geany will close the currently opened files and open the session files associated with the project.

Close project
Project file settings are saved when the project is closed. When project session support is enabled, Geany will close the project session files and open any previously closed default session files.

1.7.4.8 Build Menu

After creating and editing code with Geany, the next step is to compile, link, build, interpret, and run it.

This is the most important aspect of using an IDE like Geany, above and beyond the traditional UNIX and Linux text editors. Even more critical and useful than the same capabilities in an extremely developed text editor like Gnu emacs.

As Geany supports many languages, each with a different approach to such operations, and as there are also many language-independent software building systems, Geany does not have a built-in build system, nor does it limit which system you can use. Instead the build menu provides a configurable and flexible means of running any external commands to execute your preferred build system.

This section provides a description of the default configuration of the **Build Menu** and then covers how to configure it, and where the defaults fit in.

Running the commands from within Geany has two benefits:

* The current file is automatically saved before the command is run.
* The output is captured in the Compiler notebook tab and parsed for warnings or errors.

Indicators

Indicators are red squiggly underlines which are used to highlight errors which occurred while compiling the current file. So you can easily see where your code failed to compile. You can remove them by selecting *Remove Error Indicators* in the Document menu.

*1.7.4.8.1 Default **Build Menu** Items*

Depending on the current file's filetype, the default Build menu will contain the following items:

* Compile
* Build
* Lint
* Make All
* Make Custom Target
* Make Object
* Next Error
* Previous Error
* Execute
* Set Build Menu Commands

Compile

The Compile command has different uses for different kinds of files. For compilable languages such as C and C++, the Compile command is set up to compile the current source file into a binary object file.

Java source files will be compiled to class file bytecode.

Interpreted, or intermediate languages such as Perl, Python, and Ruby will compile to bytecode if the language supports it, or will run a syntax check, or if that is not available will run the file in its language interpreter.

Build

For compilable languages such as C and C++, the Build command will link the current source file's equivalent object file into an executable image. If the object file doesn't exist, the source will be compiled and linked in one step, producing just the executable binary.

Note

Purely interpreted languages do *not* use the Build command. If you need complex settings for your build system, or several different Build settings applicable to multiple source code files, then create a **makefile** and use the **make** command; this technique will also be useful for users to build your software.

Lint

Source code lint programs are basically used to find code that doesn't correspond to certain style guidelines: non-portable code, common or hard to find errors, variables used before being set, unused functions, division by zero, constant conditions, etc. Lint programs inspect the code and issue warnings much like the compilers do. This is formally referred to as static code analysis.

Some common lint programs are preconfigured in the Build menu (``pep8`` for Python, ``cppcheck`` for C/C++, JSHint for JavaScript, ``xmllint`` for XML, ``hlint`` for Haskell, ``shellcheck`` for shell code, ...), but all these are standalone tools you need to obtain before using.

Make

This runs the **make** command in the same directory as the current file.

Make Custom Target ...

This is similar to running 'Make' but you will be prompted for the make target name to be passed to the Make tool. For example, typing 'clean' in the dialog prompt will run "make clean".

Make Object

Make Object will run "make current_file.o" in the same directory as the current file, using the filename for 'current_file'. It is useful for building just the current file without building the whole project.

Next Error

The next error item will move to the next detected error in the file.

Previous Error

The previous error item will move to the previous detected error in the file.

Execute

Execute will run the corresponding executable file, shell script or interpreted script in a terminal window.

After your program or script has finished executing, the run script will prompt you to press the return key. This allows you to review any text output from the program before the terminal window is closed.

Note
The execute command output is not parsed for errors.

1.7.4.9 Set Build Commands

Most of the configuration of the Build menu is done through the **Set Build Commands** menu choice. When no project is open, you can edit the configuration via that menu. You can edit the configuration of an open project in the Build tab of the Project Properties dialog box. That menu item also shows the project dialog when a project is open. Both use the same dialog box shown in Figure 1.25.

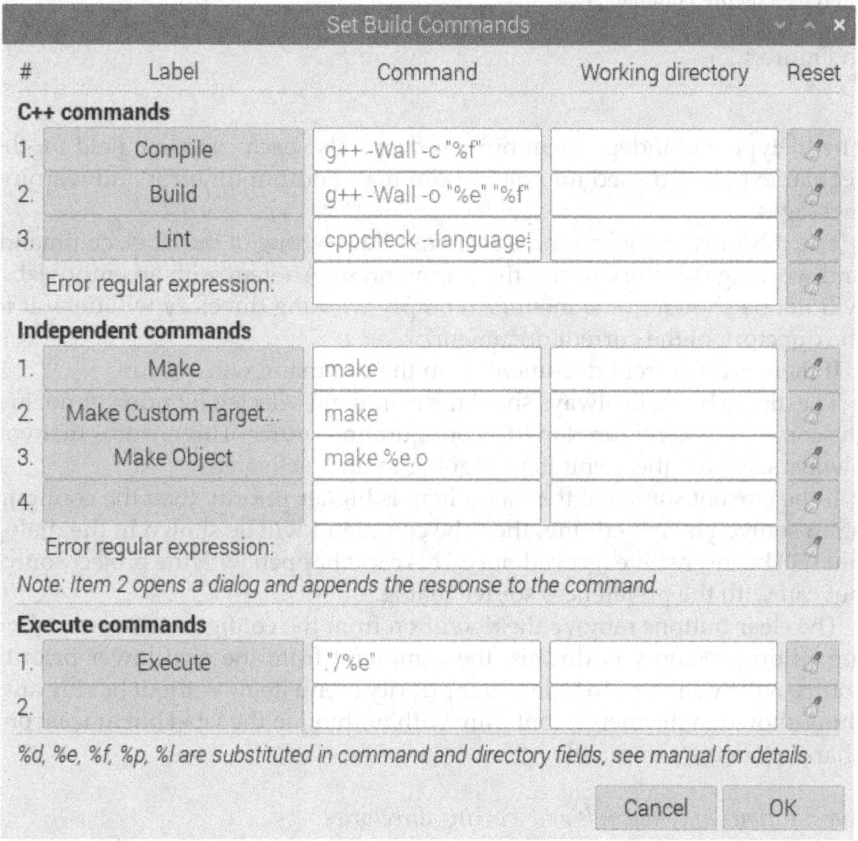

#	Label	Command	Working directory	Reset
		Set Build Commands		
C++ commands				
1.	Compile	g++ -Wall -c "%f"		
2.	Build	g++ -Wall -o "%e" "%f"		
3.	Lint	cppcheck --language:		
	Error regular expression:			
Independent commands				
1.	Make	make		
2.	Make Custom Target...	make		
3.	Make Object	make %e.o		
4.				
	Error regular expression:			

Note: Item 2 opens a dialog and appends the response to the command.

#	Label	Command	Working directory	Reset
Execute commands				
1.	Execute	"./%e"		
2.				

%d, %e, %f, %p, %l are substituted in command and directory fields, see manual for details.

Cancel　　OK

FIGURE 1.25
Set build commands dialog box.

The dialog box is divided into three sections:

Filetype build commands (selected based on the current document's filetype).
In Figure 1.25:

g++ -Wall -c "%f"
g++ -Wall -o "%e" "%f"
cppcheck --language=c++

Independent build commands (available regardless of filetype).

In Figure 1.25-

make

Filetype execute commands.

In Figure 1.25-
."/%e"

The filetype and independent build sections also each contain a field for the regular expression used for parsing command output for error and warning messages.

The columns in the first three sections allow setting of the label, command, and working directory to run the command in. An item with an empty label will not be shown in the menu. An empty working directory will default to the directory of the current document.

If there is no current document, then the command will not run.

The dialog box will always show the command selected by priority, not just the commands configured in this configuration source. This ensures that you always see what the menu item is going to do if activated.

If the current source of the menu item is higher priority than the configuration source you are editing, then the command will be shown in the dialog but will be insensitive (greyed out). This can't happen with the project source but can with the preferences source dialog.

The clear buttons remove the definition from the configuration source you are editing. When you do this, the command from the next lower priority source will be shown. To hide lower priority menu items without having anything shown in the menu, configure with nothing in the label but at least one character in the command.

Substitutions in commands and working directories
Before the command is run, the first occurrence of each of the following two character sequences in each of the command and working directory fields is substituted by the items specified below:

* %d – the absolute path to the directory of the current file.

* %e – the name of the current file without the extension or path.

* %f – the name of the current file without the path.

* %p – if a project is open, the base path from the project.

* %l – the line number at the current cursor position.

Note
If the base path that is set is not an absolute path, then it is taken as relative to the directory of the project file. This allows a project file stored in the source tree to specify all commands and working directories relative to the tree itself, so that the whole tree including the project file, can be moved and even checked into and out of version control without having to re-configure the build menu.

1.7.4.10 Plugins

To install all plugins, or a specific one, on your Raspberry Pi system, first you have to know which one you want. You can type in the following command in a terminal window to get a listing:

```
$ apt-cache search geany
```

or you can go to the following web page to get a listing:

https://plugins.geany.org/install.html

To install a wide variety of all the plugins available, use the following command:

```
$ sudo apt-get install geany-plugins
```

To install a specific plugin, after you've chosen one of them, such as the **autoclose** plugin, use the following command:

```
$ sudo apt install geany-plugin-autoclose
```

Plugins are loaded at startup. Some plugins add menu items to the Geany Tools menu when they are loaded.

The Plugin Manager, shown in Figure 1.26, is launched by making the Geany **Tools > Plugin Manager** choice, lets you choose which plugins should be loaded at startup. You can also load and unload plugins on a per use basis using this manager window. Once you click the checkbox for a specific plugin in the manager window, it's loaded or unloaded according to its previous state. An interesting and useful feature of the Plugin Manager window is that if you hover your mouse near one of the plugins listed, a brief description of it, along with pertinent information about the plugin, appears on screen.

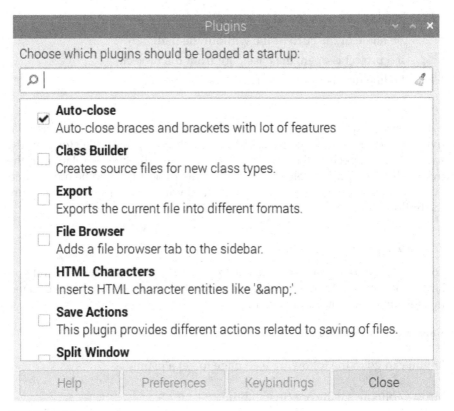

FIGURE 1.26
Plugin manager window.

1.7.4.11 Customizing the Toolbar

You can add, remove, and reorder the elements in the toolbar using the following graphical way:

Make the Geany menu choice **Edit > Preferences**, and click on the Interface sidebar menu in the Preferences window that opens. When you choose the Toolbar heading, a window opens, and Customize Toolbar button on it to the right. Click on that button, and the Customize Toolbar sub-window opens, as shown in Figure 1.27.

In Figure 1.27, in the column to the left, all *Available Items* for inclusion on the Toolbar are shown, and in the right column, all *Displayed Items* are shown. Between the two columns, left- and right-facing arrows allow you to interchange items between Available and Displayed Items. Once you use the arrows to interchange Toolbar items, the new Toolbar item appears on the extreme left of the Toolbar items that are already displayed at the top of the Geany window. Make the Close button choice to confirm your addition(s) or subtraction(s).

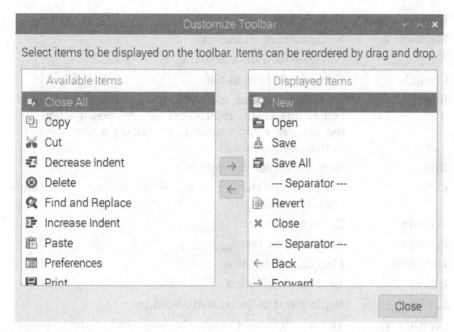

FIGURE 1.27
Customize toolbar sub-window.

Here's a listing of Available Toolbar Elements, as of version 1.37.1 of Geany:

Element name	Description
New	Create a new file
Open	Open an existing file
Save	Save the current file
SaveAll	Save all open files
Reload	Reload the current file from disk
Close	Close the current file
CloseAll	Close all open files
Print	Print the current file
Cut	Cut the current selection
Copy	Copy the current selection
Paste	Paste the contents of the clipboard
Delete	Delete the current selection
Undo	Undo the last modification
Redo	Redo the last modification

Element name	Description
NavBack	Navigate back a location
NavFor	Navigate forward a location
Compile	Compile the current file
Build	Build the current file, includes a submenu for Make commands. Geany remembers the last chosen action from the submenu and uses this as default action when the button itself is clicked.
Run	Run or view the current file
Color	Open a color chooser dialog, to interactively pick colors from a palette
ZoomIn	Zoom in the text
ZoomOut	Zoom out the text
UnIndent	Decrease indentation
Indent	Increase indentation
Replace	Replace text in the current document
SearchEntry	The search field belonging to the 'Search' element (can be used alone)
Search	Find the entered text in the current file (only useful if you also use 'SearchEntry')
GotoEntry	The goto field belonging to the 'Goto' element (can be used alone)
Goto	Jump to the entered line number (only useful if you also use 'GotoEntry')
Preferences	Show the preferences dialog
Quit	Quit Geany

1.8 Summary

In this chapter, we covered Nano, Vi/Vim/Gvim, and Geany, the most useful group of text editors, and an IDE that the Raspberry Pi OS offers. We achieved this in both a command line, text-based way and a graphical way, for these editors and the IDE. They are useful because Raspberry Pi systems use both a text-driven and GUI-based OS. Common operations done by an ordinary user, such as editing script files, writing email messages, or creating and compiling C++ or Python language programs, are done with text editors and an IDE.

In text editors, a full-screen display editor shows a portion of a file that fills most or all of the screen display. The cursor, or point, can be moved to any of the text shown in the screen display. Editing a file involves editing a copy that the editor creates, called a buffer. Keystroke commands are one of the primary ways of interacting with these editors. Using a GUI to interact with these editors is time efficient and easy to learn. The editor(s) used should fit the user's personal criteria, particularly if the user is new to the Raspberry Pi OS.

The most important functions that are common to the Raspberry Pi text editors are:

Cursor movement, cut/copy and paste, deleting text, inserting text, opening an existing file, starting a new file, quitting, saving, and search and replace.

The most important functions common to Raspberry Pi IDEs are:

1. Feature-Rich Environment: IDEs offer a wide array of features like code completion, syntax highlighting, integrated debugging, refactoring tools, version control integration, and project management capabilities.

2. Code Assistance and Productivity Tools: IDEs provide intelligent code completion, suggesting code snippets, variable names, and method signatures as you type. This enhances productivity and reduces errors.

3. Debugging and Testing: Debugging is seamlessly integrated within the IDE, allowing developers to set breakpoints, inspect variables, and step through code. Testing frameworks can be integrated for automated testing.

4. Project Management: IDEs often have built-in project management tools, making it easier to organize and navigate through complex codebases. This includes features like project-wide search, file hierarchy views, and class/module navigation.

5. Integration with Build Systems: IDEs integrate with various build systems and tools, enabling developers to compile, build, and package their applications from within the IDE. This streamlines the development workflow.

6. Plugin Ecosystem: Most IDEs support an extensive ecosystem of plugins or extensions. Developers can customize their IDE by adding plugins for specific languages, frameworks, or tools, tailoring it to their needs.

7.   Cross-Language Support: Many IDEs support multiple program-ming languages, allowing developers to work on projects with diverse technology stacks seamlessly.

We provide summary tables of commands and operations for Vi/Vim/Gvim as Table 1.10.

TABLE 1.10

Vi, Vim, and Gvim Command Summary

Vi Syntax	
Command	**Action**
cw	Changes word.
cc	Changes line.
c$	Changes text from current position to end of line.
C	Same as c$.
dd	Deletes current line.
7 dd	Deletes seven lines.
d$	Deletes text from current position to the end of line.
D	Same as d$.
5dw	Deletes five words.
d7,14	Deletes lines 7 through 14 in the buffer.
s	Substitutes character. \<Esc> ends substitute mode.
4s	Substitutes four characters. \<Esc> ends substitute mode.
S	Substitutes entire line. \<Esc> ends substitute mode.
u	Undoes the last change.
\<Ctrl+R>	Redoes the last change (Vim and Gvim).
U	Restores the current line, if you have not moved off of it.
x	Deletes current cursor position.
X	Deletes back one character.
5X	Deletes previous five characters
.	Repeats last change.
~	Changes case and move cursor right.
\<Ctrl+A>	Increments number at the cursor (Vim and Gvim).
\<Ctrl+X>	Decrements number at the cursor (Vim and Gvim).

Vi Mode Keys	
Key	**Action**
a	Appends text after the character the cursor is on.
A	Appends text after the last character of the current line.
c	Begins a change operation, allowing you to modify text.
C	Changes from the cursor position to the end of the current line.
i	Inserts text before the character the cursor is on.
I	Inserts text at the beginning of the current line.
o	Opens a blank line below the current line and puts the cursor on that line.
O	Opens a blank line above the current line and puts the cursor on that line.

TABLE 1.10 (Continued)

Vi, Vim, and Gvim Command Summary

Vi Command Mode

Command	Action
:wq	Saves the buffer and quits.
:w	Saves the current buffer and remains in the editor.
:w filename	Saves the current buffer to filename
:q	Quits Vi (fails if changes were made).
:q!	Quits Vi without saving the buffer.
:Q	Quits Vi and invoke ex.
:vi	Returns to Vi after Q command.
ZZ	Quits Vi, saves the file only if changes were made since the last save.

Vi Cursor Movement

Command	Action
1G	Moves the cursor to the first line of the file.
G	Moves the cursor to the last line of the file.
0 (zero)	Moves the cursor to the first character of the current line.
<Ctrl+G>	Reports the position of the cursor in terms of line # and column #.
$	Moves the cursor to the last character of the current line.
w	Moves the cursor forward one word at a time.
b	Moves the cursor backward one word at a time.
x	Deletes the character at the cursor position.
dd	Deletes the line at the current cursor position.
u	Undoes the most recent change.
r	Replaces the character at the current cursor location with what is typed next.

Vi Yank and Put

Command Syntax	What It Accomplishes
y2W	Yanks two words, starting at the current cursor position, going to the right.
4yb	Yanks four words, starting at the current cursor position, going to the left.
yy or Y	Yanks the current line.
p	Puts the yanked text after the current cursor position.
P	Puts the yanked text before the current cursor position.

Vi Substitute

Command Syntax	What It Accomplishes
:s/john/jane/	Substitutes the word jane for the word john on the current line, only once.
:s/john/jane/g	Substitutes the word jane for every word john on the current line.

TABLE 1.10 (Continued)

Vi, Vim, and Gvim Command Summary

Vi Environment Options	
Last Line Mode Syntax	**What It does**
Abbr command	
:ab in out	Uses in as abbreviation for out in Insert mode.
:unab in	Removes abbreviation for in.
:ab	Lists abbreviations.
map!, map commands	
:map	Lists character strings that are mapped.
:map! string sequence	Maps characters string to input mode sequence.
:unmap! string	Removes input mode map (you may need to quote the characters with <Ctrl+V>).
:map!	Lists character strings that are mapped for input mode.
Set Command	
:set x	Enables boolean option x, shows value of other options.
:set	Shows changed options.
:set all	Shows all options.
:set x?	Shows value of option x.

2

Version Control for Software Code Using Git and GitHub

2.0 Objectives

* To introduce forms of source code version control for the Raspberry Pi OS, particularly the **git** command, and GitHub
* To detail the basic concepts and structure of a Git repository
* To illustrate the Git staging model
* To define a Directed Acyclic Graph (DAG)
* To provide numerous practical examples of using the **git** command
* To show strategies of managing a Git repository with branches via example
* To give a tutorial on GitHub use
* To allow you to use GitHub to obtain the supplementary materials for this book

Commands and primitives covered:
git

Anything that you are required to type on the command line is shown in bold type.

2.1 Introduction to Version Control

Studies have shown that about two-thirds of the cost of a software product is spent on maintenance. The maintenance of a software product comprises corrective maintenance and enhancement. In corrective maintenance, the errors and bugs found after the deployment of a software product are fixed. In enhancement, the product is enhanced to include more features, such as an improved user interface. Regardless of its type, maintenance means changing and/or revising the source code for the product and generating new executables. This means using a version control system (VCS). As you revise source code, you may need to undo changes made to it and go back to an earlier version of the software. If an individual or team of programmers is working on a piece of software, they should be able to locally and autonomously maintain editable (modifiable) versions that can be joined together at a convenient time.

Git and GitHub are atomic-level, distributed, content-oriented VCSs. *Atomic-level* means that when you take a snapshot of the software package, everything in it is captured in the snapshot at a single instance in time. *Distributed* means that the entire software package you are working with is available to all collaborators locally at all times. *Content-oriented* means that when you join different branches of work on the software, only the content of lines in the files along the branches you are merging are considered. Here, content means "with form," and context means "with meaning." Git only considers content when it operates on your software files and directories; the individual(s), collaborator(s), or *integrator(s)* of the software project are responsible for the merged context of the files in the software package. The combining of different lines of development of a project that causes content conflicts are indicated by Git with several useful strategies and mechanisms, and their resolution is aided by many tools that are available as add-ons to Git. But only the people writing and testing how the software works, the content creators, and those people managing that process are responsible for resolving merged-context conflicts.

In-Chapter Exercise

    2.1. Give a detailed example of what you think is content tracking in a revision control system. Then contrast that example with what you think is context tracking.

Git, as a source code maintenance tool, is a software database for tracking changes made to a set of source code files over time. Although programmers most often use it to coordinate changes to software source code, you can use Git to track any kind of content.

Git can

1.   Examine the state of your source code project at earlier points in time.
2.   Show the differences among various states of the project, and the files present at those states.
3.   Split the project development into multiple independent lines, called branches, which can evolve separately.
4.   Regularly recombine branches by merging, or reconciling, the changes made in two or more branches.

5. Allow many people to work on a project simultaneously, sharing and combining their work as needed.

Git is a member of the newer generation of distributed VCSs. Older systems such as SCCS, RCS, CVS, and Subversion are centralized, meaning that there is a single, central copy of the project content and history to which all users must refer. If the central copy is unavailable, all users must wait until the central copy is online again. Distributed systems such as Git *have no central copy*. Each user has a complete, independent copy of the entire project history, called a *repository*, and full access to all version control facilities. Network access is only needed to share changes among members of the same development team or group.

Git's distributed nature accommodates many different styles of interaction, or *workflows*. Individuals can share work directly between their personal repositories. Git is the technology behind the social coding website GitHub, which includes many well-known open-source projects, most notably for the Linux kernel.

We discuss Git and GitHub in an example-based tutorial presentation.

For Git and GitHub, the following subsections will include:

1. How Git is used, and how it works on a Raspberry Pi system.
2. A high-level overview of the Git terminology, data structures, objects, and actions.
3. Illustrations, both graphical and textual, of the Git staging model, what a directed acyclic graph (DAG) is, and a finer-grained view of the object store contents.
4. A short and a long example of how to create, edit, branch, and merge branches of a Git repository.
5. An exploration of GitHub as a remote repository.
6. Three basic examples of how to use the **git clone**, **git push**, and **git pull** commands and options to transfer repository contents between a local repository and GitHub online.

To get the most useful information out of this chapter, you are encouraged to first read through the high-level background materials in first three subsections. Then do the examples in the subsequent three sections, as many times as necessary to become comfortable using Git and GitHub. Finally, be sure to do all In-Chapter Exercises and the problem set on Git and GitHub at the end of this chapter.

2.2 What Is Git Used for and How Does It Work?

Git is used to manage one or more source code project repositories, each packaged into its own directory that you create for the source code files in that project.

The concept of a project contained in its entirety in a Raspberry Pi OS single directory on the file system is very critical and important.

A repository is a database containing all the information needed to archive and manage the revisions and history of a project. In Git, as with most VCSs, a repository archives a complete copy of the entire project, with all of the revisions to it.

Git maintains a set of configuration settings and files within each repository. Unlike file data and other repository metadata, configuration settings are not transferred from one repository to another during a cloning, or duplicating, operation. Instead, Git manages and inspects the configuration and setup information on a per-site, per-user, and per-repository basis. Within a repository, Git maintains two primary data structures, the *object store* and the *index*. The object store is designed to be efficiently copied during a clone operation as part of the mechanism that supports a fully distributed VCS. The index is transitory information, is private to a repository, and can be created or modified on demand as needed. All of this repository data is stored at the root of the working directory of the repository, in a hidden subdirectory named **.git**.

Simply put, with Git and GitHub, you can manage your source code repositories and work in an independent, collaborative, or integrated and efficiently managed way. A majority of the introductory material we present here is aimed at the independent developer. From a learning point of view, you need to first know how to use Git in an independent way. Then we also show some collaborative workflows, particularly with GitHub.

Note

We do not touch on the integrative management techniques and commands of Git or GitHub, nor do we explain the details of what an integrator of a software system does. Those kinds of tasks and activities, pertinent to the particular coding language and systems that comprise them, are well beyond a basic knowledge of commands and techniques that a beginner would need to know about to work effectively with Git and GitHub.

In-Chapter Exercise

2.2 What do you think the role of an integrator of a project would be, in terms of what a revision control system accomplishes for a software code development and maintenance program, and the project that envelops it? Generically, and not bound by a language like C, C++, Python, or to any kind of project, such as a web-based application, or for the operating system itself.

2.3 Basic Git Terminology

Following are the definitions of essential, and very basic Git terms used throughout our examples. These terms are further partitioned into categories that reflect the basic structure of the Git repository itself.

2.3.1 Top-Level Terminology

Repository: The repository is encapsulated, and wholly contained in a single working directory, and has inside of itself the source code files you want to maintain and control, the object store, and the index, as shown in Figure 2.1. The advantage of having the repository self-sufficient inside of its own container is that the container can be shared locally and globally.

A repository can also be thought of as a collection of commits, each of which is an archive of what the project's working tree looked like at a past date, whether on your Raspberry Pi, or another one. It also defines HEAD, which identifies the branch or commit the current working tree stemmed from. It contains a set of branches and tags to identify certain commits by name.

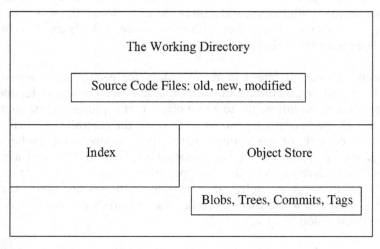

FIGURE 2.1
The structure of the repository.

Working Directory: The working directory is any directory on your file system that has a repository associated with it, typically indicated by the presence of a subdirectory within it named **.git**. It includes all the files and subdirectories in that directory.

Object Store: Holds the changes in your source code over time, as you perform more commit operations. It is found in the .git subdirectory of your working directory. Its primary components or data structures are blobs, trees, commits, and tags.

The Index (Staging Area): This is a cache, or intermediate area, between your working tree and your repository. You can add changes to the index and build your next commit step by step. When your index content is complete, you then commit from the index. It is also used to keep information during failed merges (your side, their side, and current state). Unlike other, similar tools you may have used, Git does not commit changes directly from the working tree into the repository. Instead, changes are first made in the index. Think of it as a way of double-checking your additions or modifications, one by one, before doing a commit. You can also call it the staging area.

Blobs: Each version of a file is represented as a blob. Blob, a contraction of "binary large object," is a term that's commonly used in computing to refer to some variable or file that can contain any data and whose internal structure is ignored by the program. A blob is treated as being opaque. A blob holds a file's data but does not contain any metadata about the file or even its name.

Trees: A tree object represents one level of directory information. It records blob identifiers, path names, and a bit of metadata for all the files in one directory. It can also reference other subtree objects recursively and thus build a complete hierarchy of files and subdirectories.

Commits: A commit object holds metadata for each change introduced into the repository, including the author, committer, commit date, and log message. Each commit points to a tree object that captures, in one complete snapshot, the state of the repository at the time the commit was performed. The initial commit, or root commit, has no parent. Most commits have one commit parent. However, as we explain later, a commit, called a merge commit, can reference more than one parent. A commit is the state of your project, or of your working tree at some point in time. The state of HEAD at the time your commit is made becomes that commit's parent. This is what creates the revision history.

Tags: A tag is also a name for a commit, similar to a branch, except that it always names the same commit, and can have its own shorthand descriptive text name. A tag object assigns an arbitrary, human-readable name to a specific object, usually a commit. Although the 40-digit-long hexadecimal number is an exact reference to a commit, a more tractable, understandable, and familiar tag name like Ver-1.0-Beta is more useful for humans.

Working Tree: A working tree is a data structure component that represents the state of your source code files and directories at any given point in the history of the repository. Sometimes referenced as the contents of the index, it can be best thought of for beginners in Git as the data structure tree that loads or fills the working directory with its files and directories when you either create or checkout a commit.

Adding: Putting files from the working directory into the index for staging.

Branch: A branch is just a name for a line of commits, also called a reference. It is the parentage of a commit that defines its history – hence, the typical notion of a "branch of project development." It can be simply thought of as a different line of development in the project. A branch in Git is just a "label" that points to a commit. You can get the full history through the parent pointers. A branch by default is only local to your repository.

Checking Out: Bringing a branch of the repository into the working directory is called checking out.

Directed Acyclic Graph: A DAG is a graph of the state of a repository, showing all commits and the parent–child relationships of the commits. It is also a good graphic representation of the branches, tags, and location of HEAD, if those are included in the graph. See Section 2.3.3 for more complete and descriptive information.

Master: The main line of development in most repositories is done on a branch called the master. It is the default name for the main branch of development.

HEAD: Your repository uses HEAD to define what is currently checked out. If you check out a branch, HEAD symbolically refers to that branch, indicating that the branch name should be updated after the next commit operation. If you checkout a specific commit, HEAD refers to that commit only. This is referred to as a detached HEAD, and occurs, for example, if you check out a tag name.

Clone: A clone is a replicated copy of the entire repository, with all of its data structures, files, configurations, and so on.

Merge: The opposite of branch – that is, the fusion of branches and their commits.

In-Chapter Exercise

2.3 What do you think would be the quickest and easiest way to delete an entire a local repository on your Raspberry Pi system? What command would you use to accomplish this?

2.3.2 The Git Staging Model

Git has three main states that your files can be in: *modified, staged,* and *committed.* Modified means that you have changed the file but have not committed it to your database yet. Staged means that you have designated a modified file in its current version to go into your next commit snapshot. Committed means that the data is safely stored in your Git repository database. It is held as a data structure consisting of the four types of objects in your object store.

The three main sections of a Git project are seen in Figure 2.2. They are the *working directory* (where you initially add, create, or modify files), the *index* or *staging area* (where you prepare files to be put into the repository), and the *repository* (i.e, in a database held in the .git subdirectory of your working directory).

The *object store,* in your .git subdirectory of your working directory, is where Git stores the metadata and object database for your project. This is the most important part of Git, and it is what is copied when you clone a repository to collaborate with other members of a software development team or group. The working directory contains a single checked-out copy of one version

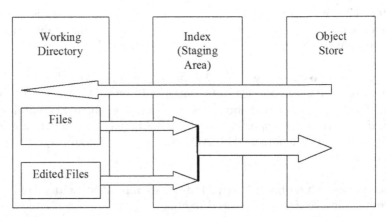

FIGURE 2.2
Working directory, index (staging area), and repository.

of the project. These files are pulled out of the compressed database in the repository directory and placed on disk for you to use or modify, using the **git checkout** command. The index is a file contained in the .git subdirectory of your working directory that stores information about what will go into your next commit.

The basic Git workflow is as follows:

1. You place new files into, delete files from, or modify files in your working directory.
2. You stage the files, adding snapshots of them to your index.
3. You do a commit, which takes the files as they are in the staging area and stores that snapshot permanently to your object store.

If a particular version of a file is in the object store, it is considered committed. If it is modified, but has been added to the index, it is staged. And if it was changed since it was checked out but has not been staged, it is modified.

2.3.3 Directed Acyclic Graphs

In order to plan, or visualize the history of a repository structure, a *Directed Acyclic Graph* (DAG), or commit graph, can be used. The name of the graph is derived from the fact that the flow of commits happens along the arrows of the graph (directed), and there is no way you can form a closed circle of commits by following the arrows (it is acyclic). We show an example in Figure 2.3, and will employ this graphic aid to help you visualize the state and the history of the kinds of commits we show.

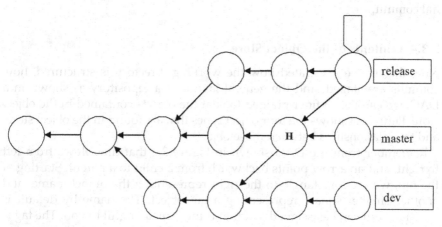

FIGURE 2.3
Example of DAG.

In Figure 2.3, the circles represent commits, and arrows point from a commit to its parent(s). Time does flow from left to right in a DAG, although there is no precise correlation in terms of a time or date stamp on any of the commits. There is just the implication that commits to the left happened earlier than commits to the right in the graph. But the arrows point from right to left! For most people, this is counterintuitive; usually we see the arrow pointing from something that happened first to its successor. In the DAG, arrows point *backward* toward a parent from a child. The first commit has no parents and is called a root commit; it was the initial commit in this repository's history. Most commits have a single parent, indicating that they evolved in a linear way from a single previous state of the project, usually incorporating a set of related changes or edits. A commit that has multiple parents is called a *merge commit*. This indicates that the commit incorporates the changes made on one branch of the commit graph into a commit on another branch of the graph.

There are two other important features of a DAG shown in Figure 2.3. The last commit on the "release" branch has a tag at the top of it, which could contain a descriptive abbreviation of the name of that commit – perhaps "Version 1.0," or something like that, denoting that this is the first release of the software project. Also, the letter "H" represents the position of HEAD, or the currently checked-out commit on the master branch.

Note
We will omit the arrowheads in such diagrams from now on.

The labels on the right side of this picture – release, master, and dev – are the named branches. The branch name refers to the latest commit on that branch. Such a commit is called the tip of the branch. The branch itself is defined as the collection of all commits in the graph that are reachable from the tip by following the parent arrows backward along the history to the initial commit.

2.3.4 Contents of the Object Store

Now that we've illustrated how the working directory is structured, how commits are staged, and the general layout of a repository as shown in a DAG, we can take a finer-grained look at the objects contained in the object store. Figure 2.4 shows the four object types that are found in the object store, and the relationships between those objects.

Remember from the DAG shown in Figure 2.3 that time flows from left to right, and an arrow points backward, from a child to a parent. Starting at the top, we see a rectangle to the right representing the branch name, and another smaller square representing a tag object. The name by default is "master," but can be assigned text that is more meaningful to you. The tag is a shorthand label that might represent the initial release number, or version

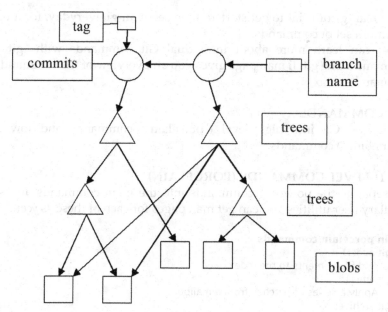

FIGURE 2.4
Contents of the object store.

of the software code. The circles represent commits. So this diagram shows two commits. The triangles represent tree objects, which can be thought of as directory, or linking information, between commits and blobs. Finally, at the bottom are a number of blobs, shown linked to the trees that point to them.

In the next section, we discuss a few examples involving Git and GitHub. Before discussing these examples, we give a brief description of the **git** command, taken from the man page on our Raspberry Pi system.

NAME
    git - the stupid content tracker

SYNOPSIS
    git [--version] [--help] [-C <path>] [-c <name>=<value>]
      [--exec-path[=<path>]] [--html-path] [--man-path] [--info-path]
      [-p|--paginate|-P|--no-pager] [--no-replace-objects] [--bare]
      [--git-dir=<path>] [--work-tree=<path>] [--namespace=<name>]
      [--super-prefix=<path>]
      <command> [<args>]

DESCRIPTION
Git is a fast, scalable, distributed revision control system with an unusually rich command set that provides both high-level operations and full access to internals.

See **man gittutorial** to get started, then see **man giteveryday**, for a useful minimum set of commands.

You can learn more about individual Git commands with "git help command". The **gitcli** man page gives you an overview of the command-line command syntax.

GIT COMMANDS
We divide Git into high level ("porcelain") commands and low level ("plumbing") commands.

HIGH-LEVEL COMMANDS (PORCELAIN)
We separate the porcelain commands into the main commands and some ancillary user utilities. You can get man pages for each of these as well.

Main porcelain commands
git-add(1)
>   Add file contents to the index.

git-am(1)
>   Apply a series of patches from a mailbox.

git-archive(1)
>   Create an archive of files from a named tree.

git-bisect(1)
>   Use binary search to find the commit that introduced a bug.

git-branch(1)
>   List, create, or delete branches.

git-bundle(1)
>   Move objects and refs by archive.

git-checkout(1)
>   Switch branches or restore working tree files.

git-cherry-pick(1)
>   Apply the changes introduced by some existing commits.

git-citool(1)
>   Graphical alternative to git-commit.

git-clean(1)
>   Remove untracked files from the working tree.

git-clone(1)
>   Clone a repository into a new directory.

git-commit(1)
>   Record changes to the repository.

git-describe(1)
>   Give an object a human readable name based on an available ref.

git-diff(1)
>   Show changes between commits, commit and working tree, etc.

git-fetch(1)
>   Download objects and refs from another repository.

git-format-patch(1)
>   Prepare patches for e-mail submission.

git-gc(1)
>   Cleanup unnecessary files and optimize the local repository.

git-grep(1)
Print lines matching a pattern.
git-gui(1)
A portable graphical interface to Git.
git-init(1)
Create an empty Git repository or reinitialize an existing one.
git-log(1)
Show commit logs.
git-maintenance(1)
Run tasks to optimize Git repository data.
git-merge(1)
Join two or more development histories together.
git-rerere(1)
Reuse recorded resolution of conflicted merges.
git-show-branch(1)
Show branches and their commits.
git-verify-commit(1)
Check the GPG signature of commits.
git-verify-tag(1)
Check the GPG signature of tags.
git-whatchanged(1)
Show logs with difference each commit introduces.
gitweb(1)
Git web interface (web frontend to Git repositories).

2.4 Examples of Using Git and GitHub

We show a few examples in this section describing how to make use of Git and GitHub.

Each example consists of the following:

1. Topic covered
2. Objectives
3. Introductory material for understanding the contents
4. Git commands referenced and used
5. Prerequisites
6. Detailed procedures
7. Conclusions.

Example 2.1: A Short Introduction to Git

Objectives: To briefly illustrate the Git staging model, and how to see differences between the various states of the parts of the repository.

Introduction: As shown previously, the workflow in Git basically follows a pattern of:

Add--> Edit--> Modify--> Stage--> Commit

This is the *staging model*. In this example, we show the essential Git commands that allow you to do that, repetitively if necessary. As you do more commits, you add, in a linear fashion, more nodes on the branch named master downstream, after you create the first node in this example. Earlier commits are called upstream commits. The history of the repository flows downstream from the initial commit to the latest commit. Similar to the **diff** command, the four basic forms of the **git diff** command allow you to examine and compare the files and directories present during different states the repository has gone through.

Git Commands Referenced

Table 2.1 shows the Git commands, and a brief description of each, that are used in this example. It is arranged in the order presented. Any argument enclosed in < > is a string of text. In order to get a more complete description

TABLE 2.1

Git Commands Referenced

Command	Description
git config --global user.name "<name>"	Sets the author of commits in this repository
git config --global user. Email <email_address>	Sets the email address of the author of commits in this repository
git init	Creates the .git directory in the working directory, initializing the data structures and objects necessary for a repository to exist
git status	Reports the on the differences between files in the working directory and the index, and what files are untracked.
git add <file>	Stages a file to the index
git commit	Takes a snapshot of the index, both files and directories
git diff	Shows the difference between two project states, in this form meaning your working directory and the index
git diff <commit_identifier>	Shows the differences between your working tree and a specifically identified commit
git diff –cached <commit_identfier>	Shows the differences between staged files in the index and a specifically identified commit
git diff <commit_id_1> <commit_id_2>	Shows the difference between two project states, in this form between commits commit_id_1 and commit_id_2
git log –oneline	Shows history of commits in an abbreviated format

of all the commands in the table, you can look at the man page for a particular command. For example, man git-status gives you a complete man page for the git status command.

Prerequisites

The following are the prerequisites for carrying out this example:

1. Having Git installed on your Raspberry Pi system.

2. Reading through and doing the In-Chapter Exercises shown in the previous subsections.

3. Anything you type on the command line is shown in **bold type**, and is always followed by pressing the **<Enter>** key.

Procedures

Do the following steps, in order, to meet the objectives of this example:

1. Create a working directory within which your Git repository will exist, and make that the current working directory.

   ```
   % mkdir short-git
   % cd short-git
   %
   ```

2. Do an initial configuration of Git, in our case for the user "bob."

   ```
   % git config --global user.name bob
   % git config --global bob.email "bob's_email_address"
   %
   ```

The last two lines above assume that you want to have a user name of "bob" (as shown in the first line), and will use the actual email address of bob in the second line.

If you give the **git config –global --edit** command to check this, you will see the following as output:

```
% git config --global --edit
[user]
      name = bob
[bob]
      email = bob's_email_address
```

Make sure you quit the default editor without changing anything!

3. Initialize a repository in the current working directory.

```
% git init
hint: Using 'master' as the name for the initial branch. This default branch name
hint: is subject to change. To configure the initial branch name to use in all
hint: of your new repositories, which will suppress this warning, call:
hint:
hint:  git config --global init.defaultBranch <name>
hint:
hint: Names commonly chosen instead of 'master' are 'main', 'trunk' and
hint: 'development'. The just-created branch can be renamed via this command:
hint:
hint:  git branch -m <name>
Initialized empty Git repository in /home/bob/short-git/.git/
%
```

The above command initializes an empty Git repository in /usr/home/bob/
short-git/.git/.

4. Create and save a short C program, named **hello.c**, in the current
    working directory, as shown:

    ```
    % cat > hello.c
    #include <stdio.h>
    int main() {
      // printf() displays the string inside quotation
      printf("Hello, World!");
      return 0;
    }
    <Ctrl> C
    %
    ```

5. Use Geany from the Raspberry Pi menu > Programming, to compile
    hello.c, and build it, then list the files in the current working direc-
    tory. You should have hello.c, hello.o, and hello in the directory.

6. Use the git status command to examine the status of the repository at
    this point. It will show you that you are on the branch named master,
    you can do your initial commit, the untracked files are hello.o and
    hello.c, and you can stage those files by using git add.

    ```
    % git status
    On branch master

    Initial commit

    Untracked files:
        (use "git add <file>..." to include in what will be committed)

        hello
        hello.c
        hello.o

    nothing added to commit but untracked files present (use "git add" to track)
    %
    ```

7. Stage only the source code file hello.c with the **git add** command.

```
% git add hello.c
%
```

8. Now do your initial commit, and in the editor (nano for us) that opens, add a message to go along with this commit.

```
% git commit
[master (root-commit) 0a93b9e] Hello, World!
1 file changed, 6 insertions(+)
create mode 100644 hello.c
```

9. Look at the status of the repository.

```
% git status
On branch master
Untracked files:
    (use "git add <file>..." to include in what will be committed)
        hello
        hello.o
nothing added to commit but untracked files present (use "git add" to track)
%
```

10. Now let's make a change in the file hello.c, and track the changes with some of the forms of the **git diff** command. First, edit the file with your favorite text editor, and on the fourth line, change the text as shown in the following command output:

```
% nano hello.c
#include <stdio.h>
int main() {
    // printf() displays the string inside quotation
    printf("Hello, Raspberry Pi Administrator!");
    return 0;
}
%
```

11. Examine the status of the repository. The output shows that the file has been changed since the last commit, but has not been staged for a new commit yet!

```
% git status
On branch master
Changes not staged for commit:
    (use "git add <file>..." to update what will be committed)
    (use "git restore <file>..." to discard changes in working directory)
        modified:   hello.c
```

```
Untracked files:
   (use "git add <file>..." to include in what will be committed)
      hello
      hello.o

no changes added to commit (use "git add" and/or "git commit -a")
%
```

12. Now we use the **git diff** command to see the difference between what is in the working directory and the index.

```
% git diff
diff --git a/hello.c b/hello.c
index 34d86c4..cf6bae2 100644
--- a/hello.c
+++ b/hello.c
@@ -1,6 +1,6 @@
#include <stdio.h>
int main() {
     // printf() displays the string inside quotation
-    printf("Hello, World!");
+    printf("Hello, Raspberry Pi Administrator!");
return 0;
}
%
```

13. Now stage the file hello.c in preparation for a new commit.

```
% git add hello.c
%
```

14. If you execute **git diff,** since there are no differences between what is in the working directory and the index, you get no output!

```
% git diff
%
```

15. Now use another form of the command: **git diff –cached commit,** to see the differences between the files staged in the index and any given commit. If you omit the commit argument, HEAD is used as the default commit. Remember from the glossary that HEAD is a reference to the current commit. The output should be exactly the same as from step 12. That's because what is in the working directory is the current commit as seen in the object store: HEAD, the current last commit.

```
% git diff --cached
diff --git a/hello.c b/hello.c
index 34d86c4..cf6bae2 100644
--- a/hello.c
+++ b/hello.c
@@ -1,6 +1,6 @@
#include <stdio.h>
int main() {
    // printf() displays the string inside quotation
-   printf("Hello, World!");
+   printf("Hello, Raspberry Pi Administrator!");
    return 0;
}
%
```

16. Now commit the changes, in the editor, add a message line to describe the new commit.

```
% git commit
[master 6112bd0] Added Raspberry Pi Administrator to the message.
1 file changed, 1 insertion(+), 1 deletion(-)
%
```

17. Examine the history of commits with the **git log** command in an abbreviated format with the **--oneline** option.

```
% git log --oneline
6112bd0 (HEAD -> master) Added Raspberry Pi Administrator to the message.
0a93b9e Hello, World!
%
```

18. See the differences between the two commits we have done so far by using **git diff commit1 commit2**, where **commit1** can be referred to as 0a93b9e, and **commit2** can be referred to as 6112bd0. These references are seen in the git log –oneline command output in step 17.

```
% git diff 0a93b9e 6112bd0
diff --git a/hello.c b/hello.c
index 34d86c4..cf6bae2 100644
--- a/hello.c
+++ b/hello.c
@@ -1,6 +1,6 @@
#include <stdio.h>
int main() {
    // printf() displays the string inside quotation
-   printf("Hello, World!");
+   printf("Hello, Raspberry Pi Administrator!");
    return 0;
}
%
```

Notice the changes are compared one after the other, and in different colors as well.

19. Examine with **git diff** the differences in only commit 0a93b9e.

```
% git diff 0a93b9e
diff --git a/hello.c b/hello.c
index 34d86c4..cf6bae2 100644
--- a/hello.c
+++ b/hello.c
@@ -1,6 +1,6 @@
#include <stdio.h>
int main() {
    // printf() displays the string inside quotation
-   printf("Hello, World!");
+   printf("Hello, Raspberry Pi Administrator!");
    return 0;
}
%
```

20. Repeat steps 4–19 as many times as you want to, each time creating or modifying new or existing files in the working directory. Also, it would be helpful to repeat this entire example several times, in several new directories with newly created repositories to gain practice. Each time, you stage the files with **git add** and then commit the additions or modifications with **git commit**. Then examine the differences as shown with **git diff** and the variations we've shown above. As you do more commits, you are adding, in a linear fashion, more and more nodes downstream on the branch named master.

Conclusions: This short example illustrated the staging model in Git. It introduced a small set of Git commands that allowed you to implement the model, once or repetitively, and see the differences between commits.

In-Chapter Exercise

2.4 The **git diff** command is similar to what other Linux command?

Example 2.2: Creating, Editing, and Branching a Git Repository

Objectives: To introduce the Git commands that create, edit, and allow you to develop a C source code project along different branches in a Git repository. To show how different branches may be merged.

Introduction: In order to appreciate, and effectively utilize the Git concepts shown in the previous example, we present another complete Git example showing repository creation, editing, branching, and merging. Maintaining source code files and their history was, and primarily still is, the objective of deploying Git. In the following steps, we create C source code files as needed, with a text editor in the directory that has a Git repository in it. This method of introducing the files into the working directory does not preclude placing those files in that directory by any other viable means, for example by copying them from another directory, or even another file system. We then edit those files to change their content and commit those changes. Finally, we show how to create branches along which different lines of development of the source code can proceed, and how to merge different branches. We try to emphasize the staging model, or the edit-stage-commit workflow model, as detailed in the previous example, throughout the current example.

Note
We have purposefully not done commits and merges of branches that would produce merge conflicts. The mechanisms and strategies for resolving content conflicts are more usefully covered in other Git reference sources beyond the scope of this example, just as the mechanisms and strategies for resolving context conflicts are.

Git Commands Referenced: Table 2.2 shows the Git commands, and a brief description of each, that are used in this example. It is arranged in the order presented. Any argument enclosed in < > is a string of text. In order to get a more complete description of all the commands in the table, you can look at the man page for a particular command. For example, **man git-status** gives you a complete man page for the **git-status** command.

Prerequisites: The following are the prerequisites for carrying out this example:

1. A recent version of Git available on your system, executable by an ordinary user from the command line. On our Raspberry Pi 4B and 400, Git was preinstalled.
2. Being able to use a text editor, such as nano, vi, vim, or emacs, to create C program source code files.
3. Having reviewed and done the In-Chapter Exercises above on Git concepts. This not only gives you a conceptual, top-down view of Git, but also shows you how to obtain Git help and use the man pages on the system for Git commands.
4. Completion of Example 2.1.

Procedures: Do the steps shown, in the order presented, to meet the objectives of this example. This is a long and detailed example. If you make mistakes,

TABLE 2.2

Git Commands Referenced

Command	Description
git init	Creates a Git repository in the current directory
git status	Views the status of each file in a repository
git add <file>	Stages a file for the next commit
git commit	Commits the staged files with a descriptive message
git log	Views a repository's commit history
git config --global user.name "<name>"	Defines the author name to be used in all repositories
git config --global user. Email <email>	Defines the author email to be used in all repositories
git checkout <commit-id>	Moves a previous commit into the working directory
git tag -a <tag-name> -m "<description>"	Creates an annotated tag pointing to the most recent commit
git revert <commit-id>	Undoes the specified commit by applying a new commit
git reset –hard	Resets tracked files to match the most recent commit
git clean –f	Removes untracked files
git reset --hard / git clean –f	Permanently undoes uncommitted changes
git branch	List all branches
git branch <branch-name>	Create a new branch using the working directory as its base
git checkout <branch-name>	Makes the working directory and HEAD match the specified branch
git merge <branch-name>	Merges a branch into the checked-out branch
git branch -d <branch-name>	Deletes a branch
git rm <file>	Removes a file from the working directory (if applicable) and stop tracking that file

which for a beginner not familiar with the commands is understandable (they are irrevocable,) simply start over again in a new directory that has another name than the one shown in step 1!

1. The first step in creating a repository to retain a history of your source code project files is to create a directory within which the repository can exist. We name this directory **first-git**. Then you can do a very elementary configuration of Git to identify yourself to the system. In our case, we do this for the user "bob".

If you have indeed done Example 2.1, you don't have to type in the third and fourth commands!

```
% mkdir first-git
% cd first-git
% git config --global user.name bob
% git config --global bob.email "bob's_email_address"
%
```

The last two lines above assume that you want to have a user named "bob" (as shown in the first line), and will use bob's email address in the second line. Of course, you can substitute your name and email address in place of those shown.

If you give the **git config –global --edit** command to check this, you will see the following as output:

```
% git config --global --edit
[user]
        name = bob
[bob]
        email = bob's_email_address
```

Make sure you quit the default editor without changing anything!

2. Create a C source code file named **first.c** with the text editor of your choice. Save it in the current working directory, which should be first-git.

3. The next command initializes the repository, which enables the Git program in the current working directory. There is now a .git subdirectory in first-git that stores all the tracking data for our repository. The .git folder is the only difference between a Git repository and an ordinary folder, so deleting it will turn your project back into a collection of files that are not version-controlled.

    ```
    % git init
    hint: Using 'master' as the name for the initial branch. This default branch name
    hint: is subject to change. To configure the initial branch name to use in all
    hint: of your new repositories, which will suppress this warning, call:
    hint:
    hint:   git config --global init.defaultBranch <name>
    hint:
    hint: Names commonly chosen instead of 'master' are 'main', 'trunk' and
    hint: 'development'. The just-created branch can be renamed via this command:
    hint:
    hint:   git branch -m <name>
    Initialized empty Git repository in /home/bob/first-git/.git/
    %
    ```

4. Before we try to start creating revisions, view the status of our new repository. Execute the following command:

```
% git status
On branch master

No commits yet

Untracked files:
(use "git add <file>..." to include in what will be committed)
      first.c

nothing added to commit but untracked files present (use "git add" to track)
%
```

This status message tells you that we are about to make our initial commit, and that we have nothing to commit but untracked files. An untracked file is one that is not under version control. Git doesn't automatically track files, because there are often project files that we don't want to keep under version, revision control. These might be binaries created by a C program, compiled Python modules (.pyc files), or any other unnecessary files. To keep a project small and efficient, you should only track source files, and omit anything that can be generated from those files. This latter content is part of the build process (compilation), *not revision control*.

5. The next step stages the file first.c in preparation for doing the first commit.

```
% git add first.c
%
```

We added first.c to the snapshot of the index for the next commit. Git's term for creating a snapshot is called *staging* because we can add or remove multiple files before actually committing it to the project history. The index holds a snapshot of the content of the working tree, and it is this snapshot that is taken as the contents of the next commit. Thus, after making any changes to the working directory and before running the commit command, you must use the **add** command to add any new or modified files to the index.

6. Now we examine the repository status with the git status command.

```
% git status
On branch master

No commits yet

Changes to be committed:
(use "git rm --cached <file>..." to unstage)
      new file:   first.c
%
```

Now, instead of first.c being an untracked file, it is shown as being staged to be committed.

7. We are ready to commit.

```
% git commit
%
```

The first part of committing is to use the default text editor you are put into by Git to add the text on the first line as "The initial commit." Then save and quit the editor.

```
[master (root-commit) ddd2dff] The initial commit
1 file changed, 0 insertions(+), 0 deletions(-)
create mode 100644 first.c
%
```

8. We need a new command, **git log**, to view the project revision history. When you execute this command, Git will output information about our first commit:

```
% git log
commit ddd2dff8ae8aeb6ebb3715d57ad2fea96d0334c8 (HEAD -> master)
Author: bob <bobk48@gmail.com>
Date:   Sun Jul 9 19:10:46 2023 -0700

    The initial commit
%
```

9. We continue to add new C source code files to our working directory. Create two C source code files named **second.c** and **third.c** with the text editor of your choice. Save them in the current working directory, which should be first-git.

10. We now need to stage those two new files, in preparation for committing them to our repository.

```
% git add second.c third.c
%
```

11. Take a look at the status of the repository.

```
% git status
On branch master
Changes to be committed:
    (use "git restore --staged <file>..." to unstage)
        new file:   second.c
        new file:   third.c
%
```

12. Take a look at the history of the repository.

```
% git log
commit 74088f645993f3df16f27565628ea38c271357e0
Author: bob <your_email_address>
Date:   Mon Nov 10 18:59:44 2014 -0800

    The initial commit
%
```

13. Commit the two new files.

```
% git commit
```

Use the text editor that automatically launches to add second.c and third.c added as the first line in the file. Then save the file and quit the text editor.

```
[master 138b11c] second.c and third.c added
2 files changed, 0 insertions(+), 0 deletions(-)
create mode 100644 second.c
create mode 100644 third.c
%
```

14. The **git add** command is used to stage new files. It can also be used to stage modified files. So, use a text editor to modify the previously created C source code files first.c, second.c, and third.c.

15. Then take a look at the status of the repository. Git lists the tracked files as being modified.

```
% git status
On branch master
Changes not staged for commit:
(use "git add <file>..." to update what will be committed)
(use "git restore <file>..." to discard changes in working directory)
      modified:   first.c
      modified:   second.c
      modified:   third.c

no changes added to commit (use "git add" and/or "git commit -a")
%
```

16. Stage those modified files.

```
% git add first.c second.c third.c
%
```

17. Now commit the modified, staged files. In the text editor, add a description that you feel is appropriate for this commit.

```
% git commit
[master dd57a94] Modified all three C files.
3 files changed, 3 insertions(+)
%
```

18. Our history can now be shown as follows:

```
% git log --oneline
dd57a94 (HEAD -> master) Modified all three C files.
138b11c second.c and third.c added
ddd2dff The initial commit
%
```

The **git log** command comes with formatting options. We use the **--oneline** flag, **git log --oneline**.

19. Condensing output to a single line is one way to get an overview of a repository. Another way is to pass a filename to **git log**:

```
% git log --oneline second.c
dd57a94 (HEAD -> master) Modified all three C files.
138b11c second.c and third.c added
%
```

20. Let's take a little break here to see what we've accomplished in this example so far. We've recorded different versions of a project into a Git repository. Maintaining these copies has provided us with backups. Critically, we can have independent versions of the state of the project that can be used for the purposes of creating multiple lines, tracks, or "branches" of code development. Our next objective will be to view the previous states of a project, revert back to them, and reset uncommitted changes if necessary. First, let's return to the state of the repository at the commit "138b11c second.c and third.c added"(step 18). The HEAD is now at dd57a94.

The **git checkout** command will position HEAD at any commit we desire, going all the way back to the initial commit!

```
% git checkout dd57a94
Note: switching to 'dd57a94'.
```

You are in 'detached HEAD' state. You can look around, make experimental changes and commit them, and you can discard any commits you make in this state without impacting any branches by switching back to a branch.

If you want to create a new branch to retain commits you create, you may do so (now or later) by using -c with the switch command. Example:

```
git switch -c <new-branch-name>
```

Or undo this operation with:

```
git switch -
```

Turn off this advice by setting config variable advice.detachedHead to false

HEAD is now at dd57a94 Modified all three C files.
%

As the Git messaging has told you, you are in the detached HEAD state. You can look around, make experimental changes and commit them, and you can discard any commits you make in this state without impacting any branches by performing another checkout.

Optional: If you want to create a new branch to retain new commits you want to create, you can (now or later) by using **-b** with the **checkout** command again. For example:

```
% git checkout -b new_branch_name
```

21. Let's go back to the initial commit.

    ```
    % git checkout ddd2dff
    Previous HEAD position was dd57a94 Modified all three C files.
    HEAD is now at ddd2dff The initial commit
    %
    ```

22. We can check the status of the repository at this point.

    ```
    % git status
    HEAD detached at ddd2dff
    nothing to commit, working tree clean
    %
    ```

23. In all previous steps, we worked on the master branch, where our second and third commits reside. To retrieve our complete history, we just have to check out this entire branch. This is a very brief introduction to branches, but it's all we need to know to navigate between commits. The following command makes Git update our working directory to reflect the state of the master branch's snapshot. It recreates the second.c and third.c files for us, and the content of first.c is updated as well. We're now back to the current state of the entire commits history of the project.

    ```
    % git checkout master
    Previous HEAD position was ddd2dff The initial commit
    Switched to branch 'master'
    %
    ```

24. Tags are references to milestones, or releases in a software project. They let developers easily browse and check out important revisions. For example, we can now use a tag named "v1.0" as a label referring to the third commit instead of its random number ID. To view a list of existing tags, execute the **git tag** command without any arguments. We can label this a stable version of the C program modules, if indeed it is one!. The **-a** option tells Git to create an annotated tag, which lets us record our name, the date, and a descriptive message, specified via the **-m** option. We can finalize it by tagging the most recent commit with a version number as follows:

```
% git tag -a v1.0 -m "Stable version of the software"
%
```

25. Now we can add C modules to the working directory that allow us to experiment, without committing those modules. Use the text editor of your choice to create an experimental C source code file named **experiment.c**, and save it in the current working directory.

26. Then stage that file.

```
% git add experiment.c
%
```

27. Now, let's check on the status of the repository.

```
% git status
On branch master
Changes to be committed:
    (use "git restore --staged <file>..." to unstage)
        new file:   experiment.c
%
```

28. Commit that file, and in the editor, add the label "Add an experimental C program."

```
% git commit
[master 0301d6a] Add an experimental C program
1 file changed, 0 insertions(+), 0 deletions(-)
create mode 100644 experiment.c
%
```

29. Now let's look at a history of commits to this repository.

```
% git log
commit 0301d6a443bb08a44621093fd443bb8e027ef1d9 (HEAD -> master)
Author: bob <bobk48@gmail.com>
Date:   Mon Jul 10 09:32:30 2023 -0700
```

```
        Add an experimental C program
    commit dd57a94ebf3514bb4cbcb8fcb307f1fe92ba8ce9 (tag: v1.0)
    Author: bob <bobk48@gmail.com>
    Date:   Mon Jul 10 06:37:40 2023 -0700

        Modified all three C files.

    commit 138b11c389046249ef16e7176ee68c1dc7d70995
    Author: bob <bobk48@gmail.com>
    Date:   Mon Jul 10 06:27:44 2023 -0700

        second.c and third.c added

    commit ddd2dff8ae8aeb6ebb3715d57ad2fea96d0334c8
    Author: bob <bobk48@gmail.com>
    Date:   Sun Jul 9 19:10:46 2023 -0700

        The initial commit

    %
```

30. Let's go back to our stable revision. Remember that the v1.0 tag is now
    a shortcut to the third commit's ID.

    % git checkout v1.0
    Note: switching to 'v1.0'.

You are in 'detached HEAD' state. You can look around, make experimental
changes, and commit them, and you can discard any commits you make
in this state without impacting any branches by switching back to a branch.
    If you want to create a new branch to retain commits you create, you may
do so (now or later) by using -c with the switch command. Example:

    git switch -c <new-branch-name>

Or undo this operation with:

    git switch -

Turn off this advice by setting config variable advice.detachedHead to false

HEAD is now at dd57a94 Modified all three C files.
%

As the Git message states:"You are in detached HEAD state. You can look
around, make experimental changes and commit them, and you can discard any commits you make in this state without impacting any branches by
performing another checkout,"
    and,

Optional: If you want to create a new branch to retain commits you create, you may do so (now or later) by using -b with the checkout command again. For example:

% git checkout -b new_branch_name

31. After seeing the stable version of the repository, you decide to scrap the C code experiment you started in step 25. But, before you undo the changes to the repository, you need to return to the master branch. If you didn't, all of your updates would be on some nonexistent branch. *You should never make changes directly to a previous revision!*

    % git checkout master
    Previous HEAD position was dd57a94 Modified all three C files.
    Switched to branch 'master'
    %

32. Now you can again examine the history of your repository with the **git log** command. This yields the shorthand name of the last commit we executed entitled, "Add an experimental C program."

    % git log --oneline
    0301d6a (HEAD -> master) Add an experimental C program
    dd57a94 (tag: v1.0) Modified all three C files.
    138b11c second.c and third.c added
    ddd2dff The initial commit
    %

33. Now you want to restore your stable release by removing the most recent commit.

Note
Make sure to change 0301d6a to the ID supplied by your system's Git for the experimental C code commit before running the next command. Also, the command we use, **git revert**, undoes the commit we specify as its argument.

% git revert 0301d6a

You are put into the default text editor, which allows you to change the title of the reverted commit. Leave the commit title the same, save the file and quit the editor.

Removing experiment.c
[master 290ec3e] Revert "Add an experimental C program"
 1 file changed, 0 insertions(+), 0 deletions(-)
 delete mode 100644 experiment.c
%

34. Look at what files are in the working directory, and also see a history of your commits.

```
% ls
first.c  second.c third.c
```

```
% git log --oneline
290ec3e (HEAD -> master) Revert "Add an experimental C program"
0301d6a Add an experimental C program
dd57a94 (tag: v1.0) Modified all three C files.
138b11c second.c and third.c added
ddd2dff The initial commit
%
```

Instead of deleting the "Add an experimental C program commit," Git undoes the changes it contains, then adds an additional commit showing the reversion. So, your fifth and fourth commits represent the exact same snapshot! *Git is designed to never lose history*: the fourth snapshot is still accessible, just in case you want to continue developing it.

35. Now you can try to add a file that we definitely will want to get rid of completely. Use your text editor to create a file named **dumbc.c**, and then edit first.c to make a small change in it. Now look at the status of the repository.

```
% git status
On branch master
Changes not staged for commit:
  (use "git add <file>..." to update what will be committed)
  (use "git restore <file>..." to discard changes in working directory)
        modified:   first.c

Untracked files:
  (use "git add <file>..." to include in what will be committed)
        dumb.c

no changes added to commit (use "git add" and/or "git commit -a")
%
```

36. You now have a tracked file, and an untracked file, that need to be changed. First, you'll take care of the tracked first.c.

```
% git reset --hard
HEAD is now at 290ec3e Revert "Add an experimental C program"
%
```

This changed all tracked files to match the most recent commit. You can also pass a filename to this command to reset only that file. For example, **git reset --hard first.c**. The **--hard** flag is what actually updates the file. Running git reset first.c without any flags will simply destage the file, leaving its contents as is. In either case, **git reset** only operates on the working directory and the staging area, so our **git log** history remains unchanged.

37. Now remove the dumb.c file. Of course, we could manually delete it, but using Git to reset changes eliminates human errors when working with several files in large teams. Run the following command:

```
% git clean -f
Removing dumbc.c
%
```

This will remove all untracked files. With dumb.c gone, **git status** should now tell you that you have a "clean" working directory, meaning our project repository matches the most recent commit.

Note
Be careful with **git reset** and **git clean**. Both operate on the working directory, not on the committed snapshots. Unlike **git revert**, they permanently undo changes, so make sure you really want to delete what you're working on before you use them!

38. To begin creating and using branches, list what branches exist at this point.

```
% git branch
* master
%
```

This command displays the only current branch, named *** master**. The master branch is Git's default branch, and the asterisk next to it means that it is currently checked out. This means that the most recent snapshot in the master branch resides in the working directory. There is only one working directory for each project, and additionally, only one branch can be checked out at a time.

39. Look at some previous commits before you begin creating a new branch. First get a shorthand list of the repository commit history.

```
% git log --oneline
290ec3e (HEAD -> master) Revert "Add an experimental C program"
0301d6a Add an experimental C program
dd57a94 (tag: v1.0) Modified all three C files.
138b11c second.c and third.c added
ddd2dff The initial commit
%
```

40. Then checkout the "Add an experimental C program" commit.

    ```
    % git checkout 0301d6a
    Note: switching to '0301d6a'.
    ```

You are in 'detached HEAD' state. You can look around, make experimental changes and commit them, and you can discard any commits you make in this state without impacting any branches by switching back to a branch.

If you want to create a new branch to retain commits you create, you may do so (now or later) by using -c with the switch command. Example:

```
git switch -c <new-branch-name>
```

Or undo this operation with:

```
git switch -
```

Turn off this advice by setting config variable advice.detachedHead to false

```
HEAD is now at 0301d6a Add an experimental C program
%
```

The HEAD normally is on the tip of a development branch, meaning you are on that branch. But when we checked out the previous commit, the HEAD moved to the middle of the branch. We are no longer on the master branch, since it contains more recent snapshots than the HEAD. This is reflected in the Git branch output from the previous command, which tells us that we're currently *not* on a branch.

41. You can now create a branch from this commit. Name it "test."

    ```
    % git branch test
    %
    ```

42. To be able to add commits to the new branch, move onto that branch by checking it out.

    ```
    % git checkout test
    Switched to branch 'test'
    %
    ```

43. Use your favorite text editor to make minor changes to the file experiment.c, so that we can begin development along this branch. Be sure to save the modified experiment.c!

44. Now stage the modified experiment.c.

```
% git add experiment.c
% git status
On branch test
Changes to be committed:
    (use "git restore --staged <file>..." to unstage)
            modified:   experiment.c
%
```

45. The following commit will create a fork in our project repository, as shown in Figure 2.5. Label the commit in the editor "Modified experiment.c."

```
% git commit
[test ef75671] Modified experiment.c
1 file changed, 1 insertion(+)
%
```

46. Now take a look at the history of your commits, in abbreviated form, with the following command:

```
% git log --oneline
ef75671 (HEAD -> test) Modified experiment.c
0301d6a Add an experimental C program
dd57a94 (tag: v1.0) Modified all three C files.
138b11c second.c and third.c added
ddd2dff The initial commit
%
```

The history before the fork is shown as part of the new branch. Since we are on the branch test, the test history spans all the way back to the first commit. The project repository has a complex history, but each individual branch still has a linear history. Snapshots and commits occur one after another in a

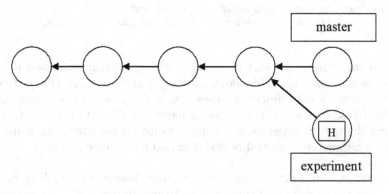

FIGURE 2.5
Forked project repository.

linearly evolving fashion. This means that we can work within branches in the same way we did in steps 1–37.

47. Add one more snapshot to the test branch. Use the **mv** command to rename experiment.c to experiment2.c, then use the following Git commands to update the repository.

```
% mv experiment.c experiment2.c
% git status
On branch test
Changes not staged for commit:
  (use "git add/rm <file>..." to update what will be committed)
  (use "git restore <file>..." to discard changes in working directory)
        deleted:    experiment.c

Untracked files:
  (use "git add <file>..." to include in what will be committed)
        experiment2.c

no changes added to commit (use "git add" and/or "git commit -a")

% git rm experiment.c
rm 'experiment.c'
% git status
On branch test
Changes to be committed:
  (use "git restore --staged <file>..." to unstage)
        deleted:    experiment.c

Untracked files:
  (use "git add <file>..." to include in what will be committed)
        experiment2.c
% git add experiment2.c
% git status
On branch test
Changes to be committed:
  (use "git restore --staged <file>..." to unstage)
        renamed:    experiment.c -> experiment2.c
%
```

The **git rm** command tells Git to stop tracking experiment.c (and delete it if necessary), and **git add** starts tracking experiment2.c. The "renamed: experiment.c -> experiment2.c" message in the final status output shows us that Git knows when we are just renaming a file. You could have made editing changes to experiment.c to justify moving the branch forward with another commit. Your snapshot is staged and ready to be committed.

48. We now do a new commit along the new branch. In the editor, provide the label "Renamed experiment.c to experiment2.c."

```
% git commit
[test 326fed6] Renamed experiment.c to experiment2.c
1 file changed, 0 insertions(+), 0 deletions(-)
rename experiment.c => experiment2.c (100%)
%
```

49. Look at the history of commits along this branch. Your project reposi- tory should now now look as shown in Figure 2.6.

```
% git log --oneline
326fed6 (HEAD -> test) Renamed experiment.c to experiment2.c
ef75671 Modified experiment.c
0301d6a Add an experimental C program
dd57a94 (tag: v1.0) Modified all three C files.
138b11c second.c and third.c added
ddd2dff The initial commit
%
```

50. Now fork another branch off the master branch. In preparation for doing this, return the HEAD to the master branch by using the **git checkout** command.

```
% git checkout master
Switched to branch 'master'
%
```

51. Now that you are back on the master branch, list the branches in this repository.

```
% git branch
* master
test
```

```
% git log --oneline
290ec3e (HEAD -> master) Revert "Add an experimental C program"
0301d6a Add an experimental C program
```

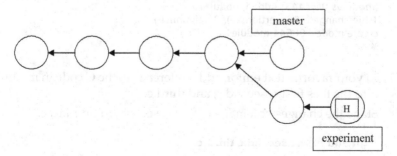

FIGURE 2.6
DAG of project repository.

```
dd57a94 (tag: v1.0) Modified all three C files.
138b11c second.c and third.c added
ddd2dff The initial commit
%
```

52. You will now create a new branch, forked off the master branch, and named "modules."

```
% git branch modules
%
```

53. Make the modules branch the current branch.

```
% git checkout modules
Switched to branch 'modules'
%
```

54. In your favorite text editor, create a C program file named "module1.c." Then stage module1.c.

```
% git add module1.c
%
```

55. Check the status of the repository.

```
% git status
On branch modules
Changes to be committed:
    (use "git restore --staged <file>..." to unstage)
          new file:   module1.c
%
```

56. Now commit module1.c, and in the editor, label the commit "Added module1.c."

```
% git commit
[modules 0aec443] Added module1.c
1 file changed, 0 insertions(+), 0 deletions(-)
create mode 100644 module1.c
%
```

57. In your favorite text editor, add a reference to the C code in module1.c into the files first.c, second.c, and third.c.

58. Stage the changes you made in first.c, second.c, and third.c.

```
% git add first.c second.c third.c
%
```

59. Check the status of the project repository.

% git status
On branch modules
Changes to be committed:
(use "git restore --staged <file>..." to unstage)
        modified: first.c
        modified: second.c
        modified: third.c
%

60. Commit the changes to the files first.c, second.c, and third.c, and in the editor, label this commit "Add references to module1.c."

% git commit
[modules 4321414] Added references to module1.c
3 files changed, 3 insertions(+)
%

61. Now examine the history of commits along this branch.

% git log --oneline
4321414 (HEAD -> modules) Added references to module1.c
0aec443 Added module1.c
290ec3e (master) Revert "Add an experimental C program"
0301d6a Add an experimental C program
dd57a94 (tag: v1.0) Modified all three C files.
138b11c second.c and third.c added
ddd2dff The initial commit
%

A DAG of your project repository at this point is shown in Figure 2.7.

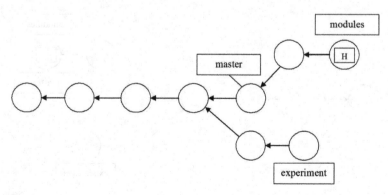

FIGURE 2.7
DAG of repository with three branches.

62. In preparation for merging the modules branch with the master branch, do the following. First, switch to the master branch, then check the files in the working directory, and finally look at the commit history of the repository as seen along the master branch.

```
% git checkout master
Switched to branch 'master'
```

```
% ls
first.c  second.c third.c
```

```
% git log --oneline
290ec3e (HEAD -> master) Revert "Add an experimental C program"
0301d6a Add an experimental C program
dd57a94 (tag: v1.0) Modified all three C files.
138b11c second.c and third.c added
ddd2dff The initial commit
%
```

63. You will now merge the modules branch with the master branch. This command always merges into the current branch. *The modules branch is unchanged.* Check the history of commits with **git log --oneline** to make sure that modules' history of commits has been added to master's history of commits. The DAG representing the final state of the repository is shown in Figure 2.8.

```
% git merge modules
Updating 290ec3e..4321414
Fast-forward
first.c  | 1 +
module1.c | 0
second.c | 1 +
```

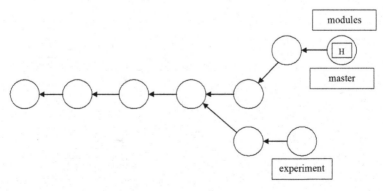

FIGURE 2.8
DAG of final state of project repository.

```
third.c  | 1 +
4 files changed, 3 insertions(+)
create mode 100644 module1.c
```

% git log --oneline
```
4321414 (HEAD -> master, modules) Added references to module1.c
0aec443 Added module1.c
290ec3e Revert "Add an experimental C program"
0301d6a Add an experimental C program
dd57a94 (tag: v1.0) Modified all three C files.
138b11c second.c and third.c added
ddd2dff The initial commit
%
```

Conclusions: In this example, we created C source code files as needed with a text editor in the directory that has the Git repository in it. We then edited those files to change their content and committed those changes. Finally, we showed how to create branches along which different lines of development of the source code can proceed, and how to merge different branches. We emphasized the staging model, or edit-stage-commit workflow model, as detailed in the previous example, throughout this example.

In-Chapter Exercises

2.5   Under what circumstances would you want to track, or stage, other kinds of files in a Git repository related to the C program development and build process?

2.6   If, after step 63, you were to create a new text file in the working directory, but not stage and commit, would that file still be in the working directory after you do a checkout of the initial commit? Why/why not?

2.5 GitHub as a Remote Repository

GitHub is a popular remote repository where you can easily and securely work together with a team to do the development and maintenance of a software project. We first provide some background information on Git URLs and *refspecs*. Then, in this section's examples, we show the basics of how to take files from a local repository and put them on a GitHub repository using the command line in a terminal window. We also show how to take files from GitHub and retrieve them back onto a local repository. The basis and groundwork for these operations are expedited on the command line with the Git commands we have illustrated thus far.

Therefore, having completed the previous subsections on Git is necessary to your understanding of the GitHub interactions shown here. We also introduce new Git commands to allow you to work with a GitHub remote repository.

We do not show how to get an account on GitHub, or how to create a new repository using the web-based GUI interface of GitHub. It is assumed in all of the examples that you can do those two basic steps via a Web browser at www.github.com, and can navigate to the URL we show. The repository on your system is called the local, or current repository, and a repository created and stored at GitHub is called the remote repository.

You can easily and expediently use the **git remote** command and its options and arguments to create, remove, manipulate, and view a remote repository at GitHub. For example, to add a remote reference specification, or *refspec*, to the current local repository, you can use the **git remote add** command with the proper options and arguments. You can also look at what has been defined as a remote repository in the .git/config file. All the remote repositories you added are recorded in the .git/config file, and can be manipulated using the **git config** command, and its options and arguments.

The basic Git commands that refer to remote repositories are the following:

git clone	Transfers a remote repository into the local repository
git fetch	Retrieves objects and their related data structures from a remote repository
git pull	Merges changes from a remote repository into a corresponding local branch
git push	Copies objects and their related data structures to a remote repository
git ls-remote	Lists references in a given remote repository

2.5.1 Git URLs

With the **git remote** command, Git names the argument forms of reference to the remote repository as Uniform Resource Locators (URLs). A Git URL that refers to a repository on a local file system can be:

/pathname/repo.git
file:///pathname/repo.git

The first reference form uses hard links within the Raspberry Pi file system to directly share exactly the same objects between the current and remote repository. The second, and preferred form, copies the data instead of sharing it via links.

A Git URL that refers to a repository on a remote system can take several forms. These forms include http, https, ssh, scp, rsync, and ftp. The primary and preferred ways of designating a remote repository using http or https, and which we use in the examples, are as follows:

```
http://github.com/pathname/repository_name
https://github.com/pathname/repository_name
```

where **pathname** is a username on GitHub, and **repository_name** is a specific named repository for that user. The named repository does *not* have to end in with a .git suffix. These two URL forms are most favored by GitHub.

Server firewalls usually allow the http port 80 and https port 443 to remain open, and by default on the Raspberry Pi, port 22 is for ssh.

For a remote repository whose data must be retrieved across a wide area network, such as the Internet, you can also use the Git native protocol, which refers to the custom protocol used internally by Git to transfer data. Examples of a native protocol URL include:

```
git://example.com/pathname/repo.git
git://example.com/~user/pathname/repo.git
```

These forms are used by Git to publish repositories for anonymous read. You can both clone and fetch using these URL forms.

The Git native protocol can be tunneled over an ssh connection using the following URL specification:

```
ssh://[user@]github.com[:port]/pathname/repo.git
```

where **user@** is the client-side ssh username on the local system, **port** is the optional designation of a port on the client other than the default port 22, **pathname** is the username on GitHub, and **repo.git** is the name of the specific repository on GitHub.

Git also supports a URL form with scp-like syntax. It is identical to the ssh forms, but there is no way to specify a port parameter:

```
[user@]example.com:/pathname/repo.git
```

For a more complete list and explanation of the remote URL specifications, use the command man git-clone. Then, you should page down to the URL specifications section of that man page.

2.5.2 Understanding Remote Pull and Push Operations

Git and GitHub workflow techniques, branching tactics and strategies, and particularly the resolution of merge conflicts when working with those techniques and strategies, can be very complicated. Those things are also as varied as the different kinds of software development and maintenance people work on, the size of the development teams, and their experience and goals. For the basic Git commands that allow you to work with remote repositories, it is helpful for a beginner to know some background material for those commands discussed in the previous sections. Since most of your workflow as a beginner involves using the **git push** and **git pull** commands, it is very helpful to know what the underlying assumptions and bases for those commands are.

After you have cloned a remote repository to a local one, the commands **git pull** and **git push** keep the two repositories synchronized as far as their local content is concerned. The most important thing to remember about keeping repositories synchronized is that, with regard to content, a repository consists of two things: an object store and a set of references, or refs – in other words, a commit graph and a set of branch names and tags that designate commits. When you clone a repository, such as with the command **git clone URL/ repository**, Git does the following things in the order shown:

1. Creates a new local repository that is essentially a replica of the remote repository

2. Adds a remote named origin to refer to the repository being cloned in .git/config:

    [remote "origin"]
    fetch = +refs/heads/*:refs/remotes/origin/*
    url = URL/repository

The line in the config file with fetch in it is the refspec, an assignment statement that specifies a correspondence between sets of refs in the two repositories: the pattern on the left side of the colon names refs in the remote, associated with the pattern on the right side of the colon, which are the corresponding refs in the local repository.

3. Runs the command **git fetch origin**, which updates our local refs for the remote's branches (creating them in this case), and asks the remote to send any objects we need to complete the history for those refs (in the case of this new repository, all of them).

4. Checks out the remote repository's current branch (its HEAD ref), giving you a working directory, and .git directory in it –that is, a replicated local repository cloned from the remote repository.

So now you can execute the **git show-ref** command as follows and view the local repository refs:

```
% git show-ref --abbrev master
b5216a81 refs/heads/master
%
```

When you use the **git pull** command, Git first executes a fetch on the remote for the current branch, updating the remote's local tracking refs and obtaining any new objects needed to complete the history of those refs – that is, all commits, tags, trees, and blobs reachable from the new branch tips. Then it tries to update the current local branch to match the corresponding branch in the remote. If only one side has added content to the branch, then this will succeed, and is called a fast-forward update since one ref is simply moved forward along the branch to catch up with the other.

If both sides have committed to the branch, however, then Git has to do something to incorporate both versions of the branch history into one shared version. By default, this is a merge: Git merges the remote branch into the local one, producing a new commit that refers to both sides of the history via its parent pointers. And this would most likely lead to merge conflicts.

When you use the *git push* command, Git updates the corresponding branch in the remote with your local repository branch contents, sending any objects the remote needs to complete the new state of the remote repository. This will fail if the update is non-fast-forward, and Git will suggest that you first git pull in order to resolve the differences between repositories.

Nothing in remote-tracking branches ties the things you do to your repository to the remote; the relationship is one way. Each remote-tracking branch is just a branch in your repository like any other branch, a ref pointing to a particular commit. They are only "remote" in the sense that they point to a remote repository. They track the state of corresponding branches in the remote, and you can update them using the command **git pull**.

A repository can have many remotes, set up at any time; see the **git remote add** command in Example 2.3. If the original repository you cloned from is no longer available, you can fix its URL by editing the .git/config file for a particular local repository. You can remove a remote reference entirely with **git remote rm**. This command will remove the remote-tracking branches for that remote repository too.

2.6 GitHub Examples

The following section illustrates your basic interaction with GitHub as a remote repository, using Git commands typed at the Raspberry Pi command line, and the web interface to GitHUb accessed through your Raspberry Pi web browser.

A brief description of each of the six examples in this section is as follows:

Example 2.3 illustrates how to set up a personal access token (PAT) at GitHub so that you can log into your account there with it. In the illustrative command line interactions we show, we create a local repository, named **RpiVols**, so that we can push content to it.

Example 2.4 illustrates how to create a new local repository, named **githubtest**, and push its initial content to GitHub. Then you modify the local content of that repository, and update it at GitHub.

Example 2.5 illustrates how to "clone" the GitHub repository **githubtest** you created in the previous example, into a new local repository named **github_clone**, into a subdirectory of the local repository **githubtest**.

Example 2.6 illustrates how to "pull" the contents of the GitHub repository for this book into a local repository named **RPibook**, similar to using the **git clone** command from the previous example.

Example 2.7 illustrates how to use the GitHUb web interface, via your Raspberry Pi web browser, to create and manipulate a new repository at GitHUb that has no local equivalent Git repository.

Note
In all of the examples in this section, we use local pathnames and repository names at GitHub that are pertinent to our Raspberry Pi filesystem, and the repositories we maintain at GitHub. You will use different paths and repositories, with different names, pertinent to your system, and your account at GitHub. Of course, with the exception of the URL to this book's repository at GitHub, used in Example 2.6.

Example 2.3 Setting Up a Personal Access Token at GitHub

Objectives: To obtain a Personal Access Token, or code, for your GitHub account, and use it to authenticate yourself to GitHub, log in, and do some basic operations there.

Prerequites

1. Having an account at Gihub that you can log into from a web browser.
2. Having gone through the above section to familiarize yourself with Git commands and operations.
3. Having a local repository that you've constructed with Git commands.

Procedures: Do the following steps, in the order presented, to complete the objectives of this example.

Note
Starting from August 13, 2021, GitHub no longer supports the use of passwords when authenticating Git operations, originating on the Raspberry

Pi command line, over HTTPS, which is basically what you do when you use the command line to access GitHub in the following examples of this section. Instead, you need to use PATs for authentication. Here's how you can use the **git push** command on the command line to push code to GitHub, using a PAT:

1. Generate a PAT on GitHub, and Enabling Public Access to Repositories:
   a. Go to your GitHub account settings.
   b. Navigate to the "**<> Developer settings**" section.
   c. Select "Personal access tokens." (The choice has a picture of a key to it).
   d. Make the pull down menu choice **Tokens (classic)**.
   e. Click on the button labeled "**Generate new token> Generate new token (classic)**"
   f. Provide a meaningful name for the token.
   g. Put a check mark in the box labeled **public_repo**, under "Scopes define the access for personal tokens." This gives you permissions to push or pull from the repositories.
   h. Set a useful longevity for the token, such as 30 days, or no expiration date (our preference.)
   i. Click "**Generate token**."

GitHub will display the generated personal access token. **Make sure to copy it down somewhere, electronically on your Raspberry Pi, on paper, etc., because you won't be able to see it again.**

2. Configure Git to use the personal access token:
   a. Open your terminal, and navigate to the local repository directory which you want to push, or pull, files to or from GitHub.
   b. Run the following command, replacing **Your Personal Access Token** with the token you generated in the previous step:

   ```
   git config --global credential.helper store
   git config --global user.name "Your GitHub username"
   git config --global user.email "Your GitHub email"
   git config --global user.password "Your Personal Access Token"
   ```

3. "Pushing" code to GitHub:

   Commit your changes using the **git commit** command. Then use the **git push** command to push your code to GitHub, as follows:

   ```
   git push origin <branch-name>
   ```

   Replace **<branch-name>** with the name of the branch you want to push.

4. Enter your personal access token when prompted.

Git will prompt you to enter your username and password. Instead of your GitHub password, enter the personal access token you generated in step 1.

That's it! Your code should now be pushed to GitHub using the **git push** command with a personal access token for authentication. Remember to keep your personal access token secure, and avoid sharing it with others, as it provides access to your GitHub account.

5. Following is the actual code (executed on the Raspberry Pi command line) we used, which accomplishes the above steps. In our code, the name of the local repository is **RpiVols**, which has not yet been initialized with the **git init** command:

```
~ $ mkdir RPiVols
~ $ cd RPiVols
~/RPiVols $ git config --global credential.helper store
~/RPiVols $ git config --global user.name "bobk48"
~/RPiVols $ git config --global user.email "bobk48@gmail.com"
~/RPiVols $ git config --global user.password "Your Personal Access Token"
~/RPiVols $ git init
hint: Using 'master' as the name for the initial branch. This default branch name
hint: is subject to change. To configure the initial branch name to use in all
hint: of your new repositories, which will suppress this warning, call:
hint:
hint:   git config --global init.defaultBranch <name>
hint:
hint: Names commonly chosen instead of 'master' are 'main', 'trunk' and
hint: 'development'. The just-created branch can be renamed via this command:
hint:
hint:   git branch -m <name>
Initialized empty Git repository in /home/bob/RPiVols/.git/
~/RPiVols $ nano README.md
~/RPiVols $ chmod u+x README.md
~/RPiVols $ git add README.md
~/RPiVols $ git commit -m "First commit."
[master (root-commit) 512c895] First commit.
1 file changed, 1 insertion(+)
create mode 100755 README.md
~/RPiVols $ git remote add origin https://github.com/bobk48/Raspberry
PiOS
~/RPiVols $ git push -u origin master
Username for 'https://github.com': bobk48
Password for 'https://bobk48@github.com': "Your Personal Access Token"
Enumerating objects: 3, done.
Counting objects: 100% (3/3), done.
Writing objects: 100% (3/3), 226 bytes | 226.00 KiB/s, done.
Total 3 (delta 0), reused 0 (delta 0), pack-reused 0
To https://github.com/bobk48/RaspberryPiOS
 * [new branch]      master -> master
Branch 'master' set up to track remote branch 'master' from 'origin'.
~/RPiVols $
```

Note

Our repository at GitHub, named **RaspberryPiOS** in Step 5., had no branch named **master** at this point. In Git's feedback to the **git push -u origin master** command on the Raspberry Pi command line, that branch was listed as "* [new branch] master -> master."

In the command line entries, wherever **"Your Personal Access Token"** is shown, type in your personal access token.

Example 2.4 Basic GitHub Operations

Objectives: To create a new repository in your existing account at GitHub, and transmit, or push, files to the new GitHub repository from a local repository.

Prerequisites: The following are the prerequisites for carrying out this example:

1. Having an account at www.github.com.

   Note

   Skip ahead to the steps of the Procedures in Example 2.7 for a more complete description of how to log on to your account at GitHub.

   Also, our authentication procedure at GitHub, from the command line, involved having an access code sent to our cell phone via SMS messaging, and we've found that method of authentication to be the quickest, and easiest means of credentialing and verifying ourselves to GitHub.

2. Having completed the previous subsections that familiarize you with Git commands executed on the command line.

3. Having an Internet connection and a suitable Web browser installed and operating on your Raspberry Pi system.

4. Local and remote GitHub repositories with only one branch each on them.

5. Having completed Example 2.3.

In this example, we first create a working directory with a new Git repository in it. Then we add a file to this new local repository, and use the git push command to move that file up to a repository at GitHub.

Git Commands Referenced: Table 2.3 shows the Git commands, and a brief description of each, that are used in this example. It is arranged in the order that the commands are presented. Any argument enclosed in < > is a string of text. In order to get a more complete description of all the commands in the table, you can look at the man page for a particular command. For example, **man git-push** gives you a complete man page for the **git push** command.

TABLE 2.3

Git Commands Referenced

Command	Description
git init	Adds a Git repository in the current directory
git add <file>	Stages <file> for the next commit
git commit -m "Message"	Executes a commit with Message automatically added using the –m option.
git remote add origin <path>	Identifies the valid <path> as a Git remote repository reference
git push -u origin master	Transmits the branch named master to the current remote repository and add upstream tracking information
git remote –v	Lists the remotes defined for this repository

Procedures: Do the following steps, in the order presented, to meet the object-ives of this example.

1. Create the working directory and make it the current directory.

    ```
    % mkdir githubtest
    % cd githubtest
    %
    ```

2. Add a new file to the directory.

    ```
    % touch README.md
    %
    ```

3. Initialize Git in this new directory.

    ```
    % git init
    hint: Using 'master' as the name for the initial branch. This default branch name
    hint: is subject to change. To configure the initial branch name to use in all
    hint: of your new repositories, which will suppress this warning, call:
    hint:
    hint:   git config --global init.defaultBranch <name>
    hint:
    hint: Names commonly chosen instead of 'master' are 'main', 'trunk' and
    hint: 'development'. The just-created branch can be renamed via this command:
    hint:
    hint:   git branch -m <name>
    Initialized empty Git repository in /home/bob/githubtest/.git/
    %
    ```

4. Stage the file README.md, and do an initial commit to the repository.

    ```
    % git add README.md
    % git commit -m "First Commit"
    [master (root-commit) 60fa518] First Commit
    ```

```
1 file changed, 0 insertions(+), 0 deletions(-)
create mode 100644 README.md
%
```

5. In your Web browser, navigate to GitHub at www.github.com, log into your account there, and create a new repository in your GitHub account. Name that repository **githubtest**.

   Note

   Skip ahead to the steps of the Procedures in Example 2.7 for a more complete description of how to do this, if you don't already know how.

6. Use the **git remote** command to designate your GitHub repository **githubtest** as a remote repository for the local repository we created in steps 1–4. To find the URL to designate as the GitHub repository, look in the URL bar of your browser when you are in the GitHub repository named **githubtest** that you created in step 5.

   On our system, in our browser, the URL to this new repository on GitHub is **https://github.com/bobk48/githubtest**

   This will be different for you on your system, into your account at GitHub!

   ```
   % git remote add origin https://github.com/bobk48/githubtest.git
   %
   ```

7. Use the **git push** command to take the local repository and move it up to GitHub. Supply the username and password for the GitHub repository as needed.

   Note

   You may need to supply your username and Personal Access Token in the next command.

   ```
   % git push -u origin master
   Enumerating objects: 3, done.
   Counting objects: 100% (3/3), done.
   Writing objects: 100% (3/3), 207 bytes | 207.00 KiB/s, done.
   Total 3 (delta 0), reused 0 (delta 0), pack-reused 0
   To https://github.com/bobk48/githubtest.git
   * [new branch]      master -> master
   Branch 'master' set up to track remote branch 'master' from 'origin'.

   %
   ```

8. Check the names of the files in the local repository.

    ```
    % ls
    README.md
    %
    ```

In your browser, check the content of the repository test. The only file in your GitHub repository should be README.md and it should be labeled as a First Commit.

9. Use the **git remote** command to list the remote repositories for this local repository.

    ```
    % git remote -v
    origin  https://github.com/bobk48/githubtest.git (fetch)
    origin  https://github.com/bobk48/githubtest.git (push)
    %
    ```

What this output shows you is that you can transfer (using the **git push** command) new content to the remote repository, and get content from it (using the **git fetch** command).

10. To add a new file to the GitHub repository from the local repository, first create the file with your favorite text editor, and put some text in it.

    ```
    % nano newfile.txt
    ... Create and save a new textfile named newfile.txt ...
    newfile.txt: new file: 1 lines, 47 characters.
    %
    ```

11. List the files in your working directory.

    ```
    % ls
    README.md   newfile.txt
    %
    ```

12. Stage **newfile.txt**, and commit it.

    ```
    % git add newfile.txt
    % git commit -m "second new file added"
    [master 51b1949] second new file added
    1 file changed, 1 insertion(+)
    create mode 100644 newfile.txt
    %
    ```

13. Now use **git push** again to push the contents of the repository to your GitHub repository.

Note

You may need to supply your username and PAT in the next command.

```
% git push origin master
Enumerating objects: 4, done.
Counting objects: 100% (4/4), done.
Delta compression using up to 4 threads
Compressing objects: 100% (2/2), done.
Writing objects: 100% (3/3), 293 bytes | 293.00 KiB/s, done.
Total 3 (delta 0), reused 0 (delta 0), pack-reused 0
To https://github.com/bobk48/githubtest.git
   60fa518..51b1949  master -> master
%
```

In your browser, after refreshing your view of the repository **githubtest**, check its content. You should see the same files there that are in your local repository along the branch master. And if you examine the file **newfile.txt**, the text you created in it locally should now be in that file at GitHub as well.

Conclusions: By designating a GitHub repository as a remote repository reference using an HTTP URL, we accomplished moving files up from a local repository to a GitHub repository.

In-Chapter Exercises

2.7   What refspec URL and fetch assignments are listed for the repository test? What branch refspecs are listed? How did you find this out?

2.8   What Git command do you use locally to put an earlier, or upstream, commit into the working directory?

Example 2.5 Cloning a GitHub Repository

Objectives: To clone an existing remote GitHub repository into a new local repository.

In order to share the contents of an existing GitHub repository between members of a software development and maintenance team, it is a usual practice to clone, or copy, a complete repository from GitHub into a new local repository. In the previous example (Example 2.4), we first created a working directory and a new Git repository in it. Then we added a file to this new local repository and used the **git push** command to move that file up to an existing repository at GitHub. In this example, we will use the **git clone** command to create an entirely new local Git repository from an existing remote GitHub repository. Then we will add a new file to the local repository and use **git push** to transfer that file to the GitHub repository. To simplify things for the beginner, there is only one branch on the remote GitHub repository.

Table 2.4 shows the Git commands, and a brief description of each, that are used in this example. It is arranged in the order presented. Any argument

TABLE 2.4

Git Commands Referenced

Command	Description
git clone <remote_designation>	Transfers a complete repository from the remote designated into a local repository, maintaining the branch and file structure
git status	Shows the current state of the repository
git add <object(s)>	Stages the named object(s) to the index
git commit –m "Message"	Commits the contents of the staged files in the index
git push <remote_designation> master	Transfers the working directory to the remote designated on the branch master

enclosed in < > is a string of text. In order to get a more complete description of all the commands in the table, you can look at the man page for a particular command. For example, **man git-clone** gives you a complete descriptive man page for the **git clone** command.

Prerequisites: The following are the prerequisites for carrying out this example:

1. Having completed the previous subsections that familiarize you with Git commands executed on the Raspberry Pi command line

2. Having an Internet connection, and a suitable Web browser installed and operating on your Raspberry system

3. Having completed Example 2.4, and having your Web browser pointed at the **githubtest** repository created in that example so you can check on its contents using the web browser interface to GitHub.

4. Having access to an account on GitHub that has in it the existing repository githubtest created in Example 2.4.

Procedures: Perform the following steps, in the order presented, to meet the objectives of this example:

1. Create a new empty directory beneath your home directory on your Raspberry Pi system named **github_clone**, and make that directory the current working directory.

    ```
    % mkdir github_clone
    % cd github_clone
    %
    ```

This new directory will serve as the file system landing zone, within which the **git clone** command shown in the next step will replicate the entire remote GitHub repository.

2. Use the **git clone** command to transfer the contents of the remote GitHub repository into the current working directory. Remember that the URL we show in the command is different from the one that you will be seeing on your system, so make the appropriate changes. Remember that the URL for this repository is valid for our system and account at GitHub. Your URL and account will be different from the one shown here!

```
% git clone https://github.com/bobk48/githubtest
Cloning into 'githubtest'...
remote: Enumerating objects: 6, done.
remote: Counting objects: 100% (6/6), done.
remote: Compressing objects: 100% (3/3), done.
remote: Total 6 (delta 0), reused 6 (delta 0), pack-reused 0
Receiving objects: 100% (6/6), done.
%
```

3. List the contents of the working directory. It should contain, in a sub-directory of **github_clone** named **githubtest**, the complete repository from your GitHub repository in Example 2.4. The directory listed is the working directory for the cloned repository. If you descend into that subdirectory, everything that is in your GitHub repository is in the directory **githubtest**.

```
% cd githubtest
% ls
newfile.txt  README.md
%
```

The githubtest directory is now your working directory, in Git terminology.

4. With your favorite text editor, create a new file, with any contents you want in it, in the directory githubtest. Save the file, and exit the text editor.

```
% nano newfile2.txt

newfile2.txt: new file: 1 lines, 58 characters.
%
```

5. List the contents of directory githubtest.

```
% ls
README.md    newfile.txt newfile2.txt
%
```

6. Check the status of the local repository with the git status command.

    ```
    % git status
    On branch master
    Your branch is up to date with 'origin/master'.

    Untracked files:
    (use "git add <file>..." to include in what will be committed)
         newfile2.txt

    nothing added to commit but untracked files present (use "git add" to track)
    %
    ```

7. Stage and commit the new file to the local repository, in preparation
    for transferring it up to GitHub.

    ```
    % git add newfile2.txt
    % git commit -m "Added newfile2.txt to test"
    [master e14e502] Added newfile2.txt to test
    1 file changed, 1 insertion(+)
    create mode 100644 newfile2.txt
    %
    ```

8. Use **git push** to thransfer the new file up to the GitHub repository
    named **githubtest** on the branch master. Remember that the URL for
    this repository is valid for our system and account at GitHub. Your
    URL and account will be different from the one shown here!

    ```
    % git push https://github.com/bobk48/githubtest master
    ```

    Note
    You may have to supple your login name and PAT at this point!

    ```
    Enumerating objects: 4, done.
    Counting objects: 100% (4/4), done.
    Delta compression using up to 4 threads
    Compressing objects: 100% (2/2), done.
    Writing objects: 100% (3/3), 329 bytes | 329.00 KiB/s, done.
    Total 3 (delta 0), reused 0 (delta 0), pack-reused 0
    To https://github.com/bobk48/githubtest
       51b1949..e14e502  master -> master

    %
    ```

9. From your Web browser, examine the GitHub repository named
    githubtest. It should now contain the file you pushed to it in step 8.

Conclusions: The easiest way to create a local repository that is an exact copy
of a GitHub repository is to use the **git clone** command.

You can also *fork* a repository.
From the GitHub docs:

> A fork is a new repository that shares code and visibility settings with the original "upstream" repository. Forks are often used to iterate on ideas or changes before they are proposed back to the upstream repository, such as in open source projects or when a user does not have write access to the upstream repository.

In fact, some users of this book will prefer to fork the book's repository so that changes made to that GitHub repository are always updated on the user's local repository.

We pose a project at the end of this chapter that asks you to fork this book's repository at GitHub.

In-Chapter Exercises

2.9 What refspec URL and fetch assignments are listed for the repository test? What branch refspecs are listed? How did you find this out?

2.10 After having completed both Examples 2.4 and 2.5, what command(s) would enable you to update the repository githubtest from Example 2.4 with what is in your online GitHub repository named githubtest?

2.11 What Git command can you use to see the abbreviated list of commits in the current branch of a repository, and their commit comments?

Example 2.6 Pulling from a GitHub Repository

Objectives: To show the mechanics of taking content from a GitHub repository branch, and adding it to a local repository by merging it with a local repository branch.

The easiest way to share content from a GitHub repository is to use the **git pull** command. This command combines **git fetch** and **git merge**, so that the content of a GitHub repository branch can be duplicated on a branch of one of your local repositories. We create a new local working directory, and repository in it, to receive the content from a remote source on GitHub. We then use the GitHub repository:

https://github.com/bobk48/RaspberryPiOS,

which contains all of the source code examples for the book you are now reading, and other pertinent materials, as the remote source. This is the URL specified in the Preface.

Table 2.5 shows the Git commands, and a brief description of each, that are used in this example. It is arranged in the order presented. Any argument

TABLE 2.5

Git Commands Referenced

Command	Description
git init	Creates the .git directory in the working directory, initializing the data structures and objects necessary for a repository to exist
git status	Reports on the differences between files in the working directory and the index, and what files are untracked
git add <file>	Stages a file to the index
git commit -m "<Message>"	Takes a snapshot of the index, both files and directories, with <Message> automatically added
git pull <ref> master	Retrieves the branch named master from the remote <ref> designated into the current branch

enclosed in < > is a string of text. In order to get a more complete description of all the commands in the table, you can look at the man page for a particular command. For example, **man git-pull** gives you a complete man page for the **git pull** command.

Prerequisites: The following are the prerequisites for carrying out this example:

1. Knowing how to navigate to www.github.com using a Web browser GUI interface

2. Having completed the previous subsections that familiarize you with Git commands executed on the Raspberry Pi command line

3. Having an Internet connection and a suitable Web browser installed and operating on your Raspberry Pi system

4. Having completed Examples 2.4 and 2.5.

Procedures: Carry out the following steps, in the order presented, to meet the objectives of this example:

1. Begin by setting up a new local repository working directory and initializing it as a Git repository.

```
% mkdir RPibook
% cd RPibook
% git init
Initialized empty Git repository in /usr/home/bob/RPibook/.git/
%
```

2. Put a file in the new repository.

```
% touch Readme.txt
%
```

3. Examine the status of the new repository.

```
% git status
On branch master

Initial commit

Untracked files:
    (use "git add <file>..." to include in what will be committed)

    Readme.txt

nothing added to commit but untracked files present (use "git add" to track)
%
```

4. Stage the **Readme.txt** file, and make your initial commit into the new repository.

```
% git add Readme.txt
% git commit -m "first commit"
[master (root-commit) 57e0400] first commit
1 file changed, 0 insertions(+), 0 deletions(-)
create mode 100644 Readme.txt
%
```

5. Use the **git pull** command to fetch and merge the entire RaspberryPiOS repository from the branch named master.

```
% git pull https://github.com/bobk48/RaspberryPiOS master
From https://github.com/bobk48/RaspberryPiOS
%
```

You are placed in the default editor. Leave the first line, numbered 1, as is, and save and quit the file.

```
* branch          master   -> FETCH_HEAD
 1 Merge branch 'master' of https://github.com/bobk48/RaspberrPiOS
 2
 3 # Please enter a commit message to explain why this merge is necessary,
 4 # especially if it merges an updated upstream into a topic branch.
 5 #
 6 # Lines starting with '#' will be ignored, and an empty message aborts
 7 # the commit.
/usr/home/bob/RPibook/.git/MERGE_MSG: 7 lines, 295 characters.
```

```
Merge made by the 'recursive' strategy.
.gitattributes                    |  22 ++++++
.gitignore                        |  43 +++++++++++++
README.md                         |   4 ++
...
```

Output Truncated

6. Examine the contents of the working directory.

```
% ls
The current contents of the RaspberryPIOS repository will appear here.
%
```

Conclusion: Using the **git pull** command, you can take content from a GitHub repository branch and put it on a local repository branch.

In-Chapter Exercise

2.12 What refspec URL and fetch assignments are listed for the repository RaspberryPiOS? How did you find this out?

Example 2.7 Web Interface to GitHub

Objectives
To illustrate some of the important actions that you can take to create and manage a new repository in your personal account at GitHub, using a web browser interface, and not using any **git** commands in a local folder on your Raspberry Pi system.

    In this example, you will use graphical techniques to accomplish some of the actions that you performed in a text-based interface to GitHub in the previous examples, without having a local repository constructed and managed with any **git** commands.

Prerequisites

1. Completion of Examples 2.1 through 2.6.
2. Having a valid account at www.github.com, with a username and password.
3. That you have repositories already created at GitHub from the previous examples.
4. It's assumed here that you do not have two-factor authentication (2FA) enabled in your account at GitHub.

Procedures: Do the following steps, in the order presented, to complete the requirements of this example.

Signing On

To access your GitHub account through a web browser, follow these steps:

1. Open a Web Browser

Launch your preferred web browser (e.g., Chrome, Firefox, Safari, etc.) on your Raspberry Pi.

2. Visit GitHub Website

Type the GitHub website URL in the address bar and press **<Enter>**
    The GitHub website is https://github.com

3. Login to GitHub

On the GitHub home page, you will find a "Sign in" button in the top-right corner. Click on it.

4. Enter Your Credentials:

Enter your GitHub username (or email address associated with your account) and your password. If you've enabled 2FA, you'll need to complete that step as well.

5. Authenticate

After entering your credentials, click on the "Sign in" button to authenticate and access your GitHub account.

6. Access Your Account

Once authenticated, you'll be directed to your GitHub account dashboard, where you can access your repositories, explore projects, manage settings, and perform other actions related to your account.

Make sure you're using the correct username, email, and password associated with your GitHub account to successfully log in. If you forgot your password or are having trouble accessing your account, GitHub provides options to reset your password or recover your account.

Creating a New Repository

7. The most important icon in the toolbar at the top of the dashboard for this example is the **Create new...** icon (a plus sign (+) with a downward facing arrow to the right of it). If you click on that icon, you can make further choices that create a **New repository, Import**

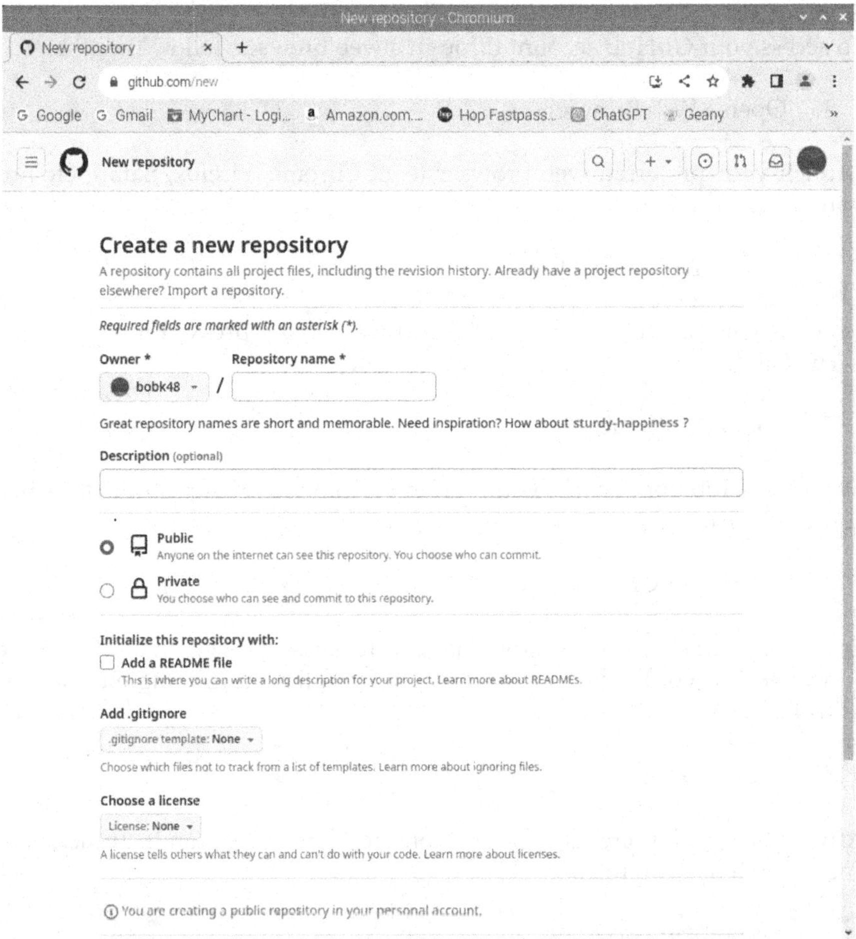

FIGURE 2.9
Create a new repository window.

repository, **New Codespace**, **New <gist>**, and **New organization**.
Click on **New repository**. A *Create a new repository* window appears,
as shown in Figure 2.9.

8. a. Add a Repository name
   b. Type in an optional description
   c. Keep the default setting of Public
   d. Add a README file
   e. Then scroll down to the bottom of the window, and click on the
      Create repository button.

You now have a new repository in your GitHub account.

Adding a New File by Dragging and Dropping

9.   Select the new repository. In the dashboard, click on the **Add file** button, and make the Upload files choice. An Upload files window appears. Drag and drop any local files you want into the "Drag files here to add them to your repository" pane of that window.

10. Make the **Commit changes** button choice at the bottom of this window when you've added the files you want to the repository.

In-Chapter Exercises

2.13

    a. Can you drag and drop a whole directory from the local filesystem on your Raspberry Pi to your new repository on GitHub, as is done in Step 9 of Example 2.7?

    b. If you've created a new repository at GitHub named **interactive**, and add files to it by dragging and dropping ordinary files into it from your local Raspberry Pi, how can you use **git** commands from the Raspberry Pi command line to manipulate the contents of that repository as it exists online? Why would you want to be able to do this, rather than use the facilities of the web browser interface to GitHub?

2.14 How do you delete files from a repository at GitHub, using the facilities of the web browser interface, if you've used the methods of Example 2.7 to create the repository?

2.15 How do you delete an entire repository from GitHub?

3

Virtualization Methodologies

3.0 Objectives

*   To give background information on operating system virtualization
*   To provide a description of the LXC/LXD virtualization methodology
*   To explicitly detail LXC/LXD installation on the Raspberry Pi OS
*   To illustrate LXC/LXD basic usage
*   To give command references for LXC/LXD
*   To give a set of complete worked examples of LXC/LXD usage
*   To list LXC/LXD best practices and provide examples of advanced LXC/ LXD usage
*   To illustrate Docker installation on the Raspberry Pi OS
*   To show how to run a Docker container and provide some useful Docker commands
*   To give various Docker utility commands
*   To illustrate how to run Nginx in a Docker container
*   To show how to expose Nginx ports on Docker containers
*   To detail how a Docker container's IP address is placed on the public network using iptables
*   To show how to build a web page for Nginx to use as content in a Docker container
*   To provide beginner help on managing content and Docker configuration files
*   To illustrate how to have ZFS as the backing store for Docker containers
*   To provide an abbreviated Docker command reference
*   To cover the commands and primitives:

    lxc, lxd, docker, iptables, zpool create

DOI: 10.1201/9781003455813-4

3.1 Introduction to Virtualization Methodologies and Background

Question: What does the word "virtual" mean?

Answer: As if

The three governing functions that the Linux kernel performs in order to maintain the system in a steady state are Virtualization, Concurrency, and Persistence. At a certain level of abstraction, the kernel itself, and its global resources, are virtualized by systemd, as shown in Volume 1, Chapter 2. In this chapter, namespaces, LXD, and Docker also do forms of "virtualizing."

Historically speaking, to perform the kernel functions of Virtualization and Concurrency, the multiprogramming paradigm was established. Multiprogramming is a computer system model where the computer hardware and software would be shared by several programs (and users) running and working on the system simultaneously. This led to the need for autonomy and sharing among programs. The needs of multiprogramming are closely tied to the concept of "virtual memory" in computers as well. In turn, this virtualization of memory is directly related to the virtualization of the entire operating system (OS) itself, as we describe it in this chapter.

Computer hardware virtualization is the simulation, to various degrees, of hardware platforms, parts of them, or only the functionality required to run one or more OSs. It abstracts and effectively "hides" the physical characteristics of the hardware from the users. Traditionally, the software that controlled virtualized machines was known as the "hypervisor." Currently, the hypervisor is often called a "virtual machine monitor" (VMM).

Platform virtualization is accomplished on any given hardware by host software (the hypervisor), which creates a simulated computer environment, a VM, for its guest software. The guest software can be as small as a single user application, or as large as a complete OS. The guest software executes *as if* it were running directly on the physical hardware.

Virtualization comes with some performance disadvantages, both in resources required to run the hypervisor and in reduced performance on the VM guest, compared with running applications on a non-virtualized host physical machine. A VM can be more easily controlled and inspected from outside than a physical one, and its configuration is more flexible. This is very useful in kernel development and for teaching OS courses. A new VM can be implemented as needed without the need for an up-front hardware purchase. A VM can easily be moved from one physical machine to another as needed. An unrecoverable fault inside a VM guest does not harm the host system, so there is no risk of crashing the host OS.

Examples of virtualization implementations are as follows:

* Running one or more applications that are not supported by the host OS: A VM running the required guest OS could allow the desired applications to be run, without altering the host OS.
* Evaluating an alternate OS: The new OS could be run within a VM, without altering the host OS.
* Server virtualization: Multiple virtual servers in containers could be run on a single physical server, to utilize more fully the hardware resources of the physical server. A cloud computing example of this is Amazon Web Services Elastic Cloud Computing (AWS EC2) virtual servers.
* Duplicating specific environments: A VM could, depending on the virtualization software used, be duplicated and installed on multiple hosts, or restored to a previously backed-up system state.
* Creating a protected environment: If a guest OS running on a VM becomes damaged in a way that is difficult to repair, such as may occur when testing, the VM can be discarded without harm to the host system, and a clean copy used next time.

Primary actual contemporary virtualization techniques are as follows:

* Full virtualization: In full virtualization, the VM simulates enough hardware to allow a complete "guest" OS, one designed for the same processor instruction set architecture (ISA) to be run in isolation. Examples for Linux systems running on X86 ISAs include VirtualBox, Parallels Workstation, Oracle VM, Virtual Server, Hyper-V, VMware Workstation, and VMware.
* Hardware-assisted virtualization: In hardware-assisted virtualization, the hardware provides architectural support that facilitates building a VMM and allows guest OSs to be run in isolation. Examples of virtualization platforms adapted to such hardware include KVM, VMware Workstation, VMware Fusion, Hyper-V, Xen, Oracle VM server for SPARC, and VirtualBox.
* Partial virtualization: In partial virtualization, including address space virtualization, the VM simulates multiple instances of much of an underlying hardware environment, particularly address spaces.
* Paravirtualization: In paravirtualization, the VM does not necessarily simulate hardware, but instead (or in addition) offers a special Application Programmer's Interface (API) that can only be used by modifying the "guest" OS. For this to be possible, the "guest" OS's source code must be available.

* OS-level virtualization: In OS-level virtualization, a physical server is virtualized at the OS level, enabling multiple isolated and secure virtualized servers to run on a single physical server. The "guest" OS environments share the same running instance of the OS as the host system. Thus, the same OS kernel is also used to implement the "guest" environments, and applications running in a given "guest" environment view it as a stand-alone system. In Linux, examples include LXC/LXD and their derivative management system, Docker. This chapter is based upon those systems. Similar proprietary derived techniques are used by AWS EC2, Google Cloud, and iCloud.

In this chapter, we provide examples of virtualization methodologies using the Raspberry Pi OS. Additionally, here in this chapter, we provide fully worked practical examples of LXC/LXD and Docker containerization using the Raspberry Pi OS.

We also provide OS-level/hardware-assisted virtualization examples with LXC/LXD and Docker. These techniques are very contemporary, popular, and important facilities for creating a virtual environment within which a Linux OS can work. What differentiates these facilities is that, in LXC/LXD, all virtual environments are running under the same kernel (implementing OS-level virtualization).

Practically speaking, an important application of these implementations, as already stated, is to provide a measure of system security, in addition to what we have already described. But that is not the only reason an ordinary user or system administrator would deploy the virtualization methods we demonstrate.

A user might want to take advantage of some of the facilities that an additional OS offers, above and beyond what is available via the Raspberry Pi OS into which the computer boots. Instead of shutting down the main OS and then booting into the additional OS, both can be run simultaneously using the virtualization method shown here. So if you run both OSs simultaneously, you can use both OS applications and facilities on the same physical machine. Of course, there are trade-offs in doing this, mainly in terms of performance speed and disk usage.

Also advantageous is the deployment of VMs to allow you to "test drive" a particular OS without devoting an entire hardware platform to it. This can also be achieved by running a "live" version of it from a DVD or a USB thumb drive, but the performance speed and persistence of data using these techniques is somewhat limited. In this chapter, we show examples of installing guest VMs on Linux, to allow you to "test drive" systems in a more fully functional way.

3.2 Raspberry Pi OS Containers with LXC/LXD

Question: Why would an ordinary Raspberry Pi user, who has the Raspberry Pi OS installed on her home desktop computer, need or want to use Linux containers?

Answer: Perhaps she wants to safely test one or many software applications (or even entire OSs!), and doesn't want them, through misbehavior, or for other reasons, destroying or significantly changing in any way her installed host system. Or perhaps she wants to securely run a web server on her machine, and via port forwarding on both the host system, and on her modem/router, publish pages and a website, on the Internet.

Both of these answers are very easily accommodated through the use of LXC/LXD containers.

In-Chapter Exercise

3.1 Why would you personally want to add a container system, and one or more containers, to your computer system? What "flavor" of container would you want to add, and why? What advantages would that give even an ordinary user on a single desktop or laptop computer? As you proceed through this chapter, compare adding a container system that we have shown in the following sections to VirtualBox and AWS EC2 (if you are familiar with those systems of virtualization). Relative to those types of virtualization, how do LXC/LXD containers compare, across all of the installation, maintenance, disk storage footprint, etc. profiles for your particular use case(s)?

The LXC/LXD container model uses a system programming feature, known as "namespaces," to implement isolated process environments within which LXD containers operate. We briefly mentioned namespaces in Volume 1 of this series, when we dealt with the forms and sites of Linux security. This programming feature and the namespaces API modules **clone()**, **unshare()**, and **setns()** provide another distinct form of virtualization in terms of the virtualization/concurrency of the Linux kernel.

The term "namespace," sometimes called a "name scope," is popularly defined as

"an abstract container or environment created to hold a logical grouping of unique identifiers or symbols (i.e. names). An identifier defined in a namespace is associated only with that namespace.*"

The concept and use of the term "namespace," as it is used in relation to the system programming API for Linux container virtualization, is analogous to several other applications of the same term in computer science and programming. We give these analogies here to help make the higher-level abstraction more clear to the ordinary user.

One obvious similarity of the application of this term is to locally scoped versus globally scoped variables. We show a brief example of this in Chapter 2 on GitHub, with Python variables. A namespace is like a locally scoped Python variable. In non-OOP Python programming, an identifier, or "name" is equated to some expression, or object, that gives that name a value. So the "namespace" of a locally scoped variable is the module that fully contains, limits, or encapsulates this equation of identifier to object.

Another analogy can be drawn to the use of the term in Python OOP program constructs. For example, OOP itself has the fundamental features of multiple representation, encapsulation, subtyping, inheritance, and open recursion, which hide the objects, their classes, and methods in namespace environments. The representation of an object is hidden from view outside of the object's definition: only the object's own methods can directly inspect or manipulate its fields. **

* Wikipedia, namespaces.

** Pierce, *Types and Programming Languages*, 2002.

Other OOP-capable languages, such as XML (Extensible Markup Language), also use the term to describe isolated environments. XML collects elements and attributes in a definition, in a style sheet for example, to limit the scope of an identifier.

There are currently six types of Linux namespace: mount, UTS, IPC, PID, network, and user, each of which provides a context within which a process can "virtualize" the global system resources, such as filesystem mounting, Interprocess Communication, Process Identification, networking, and isolated user spaces. A particular user namespace can, for example, also overlap with any of the other contexts as well.

Relative to namespaces, it is "as if" a user's process or processes were the only program(s) running on the hardware. We encourage you to read the man pages for **namespaces** and **user_namespaces** on your system, not only to gain some insight into the namespaces higher-level abstraction, but also to appreciate the complexity of its lower-level details. In our exposition of LXC/LXD, we do not make any references to the internals of namespaces, or to how LXC/LXD works in conjunction with these details. In this chapter, we have smaller fish to fry and take a bottoms-up approach to virtualization.

The current premier OS-level virtualization software in Linux is LXD (pronounced "lex-dee"). It is a combination of an older command line "client" utility named LXC (pronounced "lex-cee"), and a newer controlling container management daemon named LXD. Working with LXD involves using a combination of LXC and LXD commands, as we show throughout this section.

We first cover the installation and basic usage of LXC/LXD, and then give some extended examples of creating, running, and managing LXC/LXD containers.

In particular, we do some of these tasks by creating our containers with a ZFS filesystem on the Raspberry Pi OS, which is a downstream Debian-family release. The details of working with ZFS are detailed in Volume 1 of this series.

In-Chapter Exercise

    3.2 What advantages do you see in using ZFS as the storage filesystem for LXD containers?

3.2.1 Introduction to LXC/LXD

LXD (pronounced lex-dee) is the lightervisor, or lightweight container hypervisor. While this claim has been controversial, it has been quite well justified based on the original academic paper. It also nicely distinguishes LXD from LXC.

LXC is a program that creates and administers "containers" on a local system. It also provides an API to allow higher-level managers, such as LXD, to administer containers. In a sense, one could compare LXC to QEMU, while comparing LXD to libvirt.

The LXC API deals with a 'container'. The LXD API deals with 'remotes', which serve images and containers. This extends the LXC functionality over the network and allows concise management of tasks like container migration and container image publishing.

LXD uses LXC under the covers for some container management tasks. However, it keeps its own container configuration information and has its own conventions, so that it is best not to use classic LXC commands by hand with LXD containers. This document will focus on how to configure and administer LXD on Ubuntu systems.

Note

At the time of the writing of this book, the Debian-family of Linux systems (including the Raspberry Pi OS) were the only Linux systems that we could reliably and easily install LXC and LXD on. Many of the examples below reflect this, particularly the LXD/ZFS-based ones.

LXD is the latest version of LXC, a Linux container system that uses OS-level virtualization. It incorporates newer and more useful features for the creation, provisioning, management, and deployment of containers on host systems.

For our purposes, "provisioning" means configuring a container to have a set of features, which may be easily duplicated, or cloned, into as many containers as necessary. An example of that, which we show below, would be downloading and installing an Ubuntu OS image in the container. The container and the image it is built from by LXC/LXD are synonymous.

It is important to differentiate the host system from the container(s) running on the host. Different OS images can be downloaded and installed in containers, even though the host is running a particular OS.

3.2.1.1 Getting Help on LXC and LXD

The best documentation you can get for LXC and LXD on your installation on the Raspberry Pi OS is at the following URLs:

https://linuxcontainers.org/lxc/manpages/

Or, as an alternative, the following URL:

https://man7.org/linux/man-pages/man7/lxc.7.html

We encourage you to refer to these man pages for further explanations, and a summary overview of the options and the sub-commands that can be used with each.

There are man pages at the above URL as well for the sub-commands. For example, to see a man page for the **execute** sub-command of the **lxc** command view the **execute** entry. Table 3.1 lists those sub-commands, which gives a brief description of what each of them do.

In-Chapter Exercise

    3.3 Use the above two URLs to review all of the man pages for lxc and lxd that contain the sub-commands listed in Table 3.1. Then, make a preliminary list of which sub-commands you think are the most important and critical to the operation of LXC/LXD for your particular use case(s).

3.2.2 LXD and LXC Installation and Basic Commands for the Raspberry Pi OS

This section details some basic commands, such as how to download and install LXD and LXC, how to create and start a new container, and how to get information about images at your default repository, and on your machine.

TABLE 3.1

LXC/LXD "Sub-Commands" Listing and What They Do

Sub-Command	Description
attach	Starts a process inside a running container
autostart	Starts/stops/kills auto-started containers
checkconfig	Checks the current kernel for lxc support
checkpoint	Checkpoints a container
config	Manages configuration
console	Launches a console in the specified container
copy	Copies containers within or in between lxd instances
create	Creates a new container
delete	Deletes containers or container snapshots
destroy	Destroys a container
device	Manages devices of running containers
execute	Executes the specified command in a container
file	Manages files on a container
freeze	Freezes the containers processes
help	Presents details on how to use LXD
image	Manipulates container images
info	Lists information on LXD servers and containers
launch	Launches a container from a particular image
list	Lists the available resources
ls	Lists the containers that exist on the system
monitor	Monitors container state
move	Moves containers within or in between lxd instances
profile	Manages configuration profiles
publish	Publishes containers as images
remote	Manages remote LXD servers.
restart	Changes state of one or more containers to restart
restore	Sets the current state of a resource back to a snapshot
snapshot	Creates a read-only snapshot of a container
start	Changes state of one or more containers to start
stop	Changes state of one or more containers to stop
top	Monitors container statistics
unfreeze	Thaws all container's processes
unshare	Runs a task in a new set of namespaces
user-nic	Creates and attach a nic to another network namespace
usernet	Unpriveleged user network administration file
usernsexec	Runs a task as root in a new user namespace
version	Prints the version number of this client tool
wait	Waits for a specific container state

Example 3.1 Using a Raspberry PI as a Virtualization Server

Objectives:

To install LXC/LXD on a Raspberry Pi system, and to customize its profile to achieve container launching and networking amenable to beginners.

Prerequisites:

1. Doing the following on a Raspberry Pi 4, or 400, with 4 GB minimum of RAM, but it can work on older models. This example was done on a Raspberry Pi model 4b with 4 GB of main memory.

2. The system/boot medium is an SD card. We recommend one of at least 64 GB of capacity or bigger. But an external hard drive/thumb drive/network drive may also be used, and it will have to be permanently connected.

3. A wired ethernet connection. It is *not* possible at this time to use the Wi-Fi interface of the Raspberry Pi to create a network bridge, as we do below, to expose the containers via public-facing IP addresses. We disabled or turned off Wi-Fi with the command **sudo rfkill block Wi-Fi**. We want to create a network bridge so that the LXC/LXD containers can have public-facing IP addresses.

4. A DHCP server on your network which assigns IP addresses when new devices request them. Any common home network has a DHCP server activated by default.

5. ZFS is installed on your version of the Raspberry Pi OS. We predict that installation of ZFS will be a standard operation at the time this book is published.

Note
If you are limited to use only your Wi-Fi connection, OS containers can connect to the network via Network Address Translation (NAT), and can be accessed from the network using a proxy device. In such a case, forget about point number 4 above, and skip all the bridge-related materials presented below.

Note
All the commands below need to be executed as root, so execute the following command first!

```
# sudo su -
Wi-Fi is currently blocked by rfkill.
Use raspi-config to set the country before use.

root@raspberrypi:~#
```

Procedures:

1. You first create the network bridge. In order to do that, you must install the **bridge-utils** package:

```
root@raspberrypi:~# apt-get -y update
Output truncated ...
root@raspberrypi:~# apt-get -y install bridge-utils
Output truncated ...
```

2. Next, you need to actually create the network bridge, and you'll attach
    your wired network interface to it. You will achieve this by creating
    a dedicated network interface file, using nano, with the following
    command:

    root@raspberrypi:~# **nano /etc/network/interfaces.d/br0**

    That file has to have with the following contents:

    iface eth0 inet manual
    auto br0
    iface br0 inet dhcp
    bridge_ports eth0

    Save and exit nano after you've added the above lines to the file.

3. The Raspberry Pi OS uses the dhcpcd daemon to get IP addresses from
    the DHCP server on the network. You must exclude eth0 from getting
    any IP address from now on (since it will receive that address via the
    bridge). For that, we must edit the dhcpcd configuration file with the
    following command:

    root@raspberrypi:~# **nano /etc/dhcpcd.conf**
    And then, you can add the following line at the end of the file:

    denyinterfaces eth0

Note
Since we did *not* configure the Wi-Fi interface, there's no need to explicitly
disable the wlan0 interface neither in /etc/network/interfaces.d/br0 nor in
/etc/dhcpcd.conf.

**At this point, you should reboot your system in order to all changes take
effect.**

Once the system has restarted, you should see something like this when executing the **ip a** command. Notice in the output for the following command that
eth0 no longer has an IP address, but it is the bridge interface br0 that does. When
we executed this command on our Raspberry Pi 400, we got the following result:

root@raspberrypi:~# **ip a**
1: lo: <LOOPBACK,UP,LOWER_UP> mtu 65536 qdisc noqueue state UNKNOWN group
default qlen 1000
    link/loopback 00:00:00:00:00:00 brd 00:00:00:00:00:00
    inet 127.0.0.1/8 scope host lo
      valid_lft forever preferred_lft forever
    inet6 ::1/128 scope host
      valid_lft forever preferred_lft forever

```
2: eth0: <BROADCAST,MULTICAST,UP,LOWER_UP> mtu 1500 qdisc mq master br0 state
UP group default qlen 1000
    link/ether dc:a6:32:18:3f:bf brd ff:ff:ff:ff:ff:ff
3: wlan0: <BROADCAST,MULTICAST> mtu 1500 qdisc noop state DOWN group default
qlen 1000
    link/ether dc:a6:32:18:3f:c0 brd ff:ff:ff:ff:ff:ff
4: br0: <BROADCAST,MULTICAST,UP,LOWER_UP> mtu 1500 qdisc noqueue state UP
group default qlen 1000
    link/ether dc:a6:32:18:3f:bf brd ff:ff:ff:ff:ff:ff
    inet 192.168.1.15/24 brd 192.168.1.255 scope global dynamic br0
        valid_lft 86166sec preferred_lft 86166sec
    inet6 fe80::dea6:32ff:fe18:3fbf/64 scope link
        valid_lft forever preferred_lft forever

root@raspberrypi:~#
```

4. You can now Install LXD using **snap**.

"snap" refers to Snappy, a package management system and application deployment system developed by Canonical for Linux distributions. Snaps are a form of software package designed to work across a range of Linux distributions, allowing software developers to distribute their applications to a broader audience with fewer compatibility concerns. It is very similar to the APT package manager.

The main features of snaps include:

Cross-Distribution Support: Snaps are designed to work on various Linux distributions, so developers can create a single snap package that runs on multiple platforms.

Sandboxing: Snaps are isolated from the rest of the system, which enhances security by reducing the potential impact of software vulnerabilities.

Atomic Updates: Snaps are installed in a way that ensures atomic updates, meaning the package is either fully updated or remains unchanged.

Auto-Updates: By default, snaps are set to update automatically, ensuring users have the latest version of the software.

Dependency Management: Snaps include their dependencies, reducing potential conflicts with other software on the system.

Version Rollback: Snaps support version rollback, allowing users to revert to a previous version if needed.

To use snaps on a Linux distribution that supports them, like the Rasppberry Pi OS, you'll need to install the **snapd** package, which provides the snap runtime and tools for managing snaps. Once installed, you can use the command line interface to search for, install, and manage snap packages.

LXD is a system container manager used to manage LXC, an operating-system-level virtualization technique. LXD provides higher-level administration methods than LXC. LXD was not available as a Debian package for the Raspberry Pi OS at the time this book was written, but it could be installed with the **snap** facility.

You can install **snap** by executing the following commands:

Note
Currently, **snap** developers recommend a system restart of the root session, so that the new files placed by **snapd** (the daemon controlling snap module installations) in the directory /etc/profile.d/ are correctly reloaded, and the LXD binary is available along that path.

You can safely execute **snap** commands to install LXD, as follows:

```
root@raspberrypi:~# apt-get -y install snapd
Output truncated ...
root@raspberrypi:~# reboot
```

Wait until the system reboots.

```
root@raspberrypi:~# snap install core
2023-07-30T10:48:19-07:00 INFO Waiting for automatic snapd restart...
Output truncated ...
core 16-2.59.5 from Canonical✓ installed
root@raspberrypi:~# snap install lxd
```

```
Output truncated ...
```

```
lxd 5.15-002fa0f from Canonical✓ installed
root@raspberrypi:~#
```

5. Once LXD has been installed, it must be initialized. LXD is initialized via an interactive set of questions. We recommend you just select the default answers (press <Enter> on the keyboard), with the exception of the size in GB of the new loop device: that will be the maximum size you'll be able to use for your containers in total. The default size below varies depending on the size of the system/boot media used (in the example below, we ran the Raspberry Pi OS from a nominally 500 GB solid-state drive [SSD] on the USB3 bus). LXD is initialized by executing the following command:

Note
With the settings achieved in the following command, you'll give access to LXD containers to the "public" network via a specific profile. This allows you to have both "private" and "public" facing containers. If you want to create only "public" containers by default by directly attaching them to the br0 bridge, answer the following questions in the **lxd init** dialog below as follows:

Would you like to create a new local network bridge? (yes/no) [default= yes]: **no**

What should the new bridge be called? [default=lxdbr0]: **br0**

root@raspberrypi:~# **lxd init**
Would you like to use LXD clustering? (yes/no) [default=no]:
Do you want to configure a new storage pool? (yes/no) [default=yes]:
Name of the new storage pool [default=default]:
Name of the storage backend to use (dir, lvm, zfs, btrfs, ceph) [default=zfs]:
Create a new ZFS pool? (yes/no) [default=yes]:
Would you like to use an existing empty block device (e.g. a disk or partition)? (yes/no) [default=no]:
Size in GiB of the new loop device (1 GiB minimum) [default=30GiB]: **8GiB**
Would you like to connect to a MAAS server? (yes/no) [default=no]:
Would you like to create a new local network bridge? (yes/no) [default=yes]:
What should the new bridge be called? [default=lxdbr0]:
What IPv4 address should be used? (CIDR subnet notation, "auto" or "none") [default=auto]:
What IPv6 address should be used? (CIDR subnet notation, "auto" or "none") [default=auto]:
Would you like the LXD server to be available over the network? (yes/no) [default=no]:
Would you like stale cached images to be updated automatically? (yes/no) [default=yes]:
Would you like a YAML "lxd init" preseed to be printed? (yes/no) [default=no]:
root@raspberrypi:~#

Note
LXD uses a loop-based ZFS pool as the default storage backend when you initialize containers with a ZFS backing store. This loop-based pool is created on your host system, and uses a loop device (sometimes referred to as a *virtual block device*) to store the ZFS datasets on. This setup allows LXD to work with ZFS even if you don't have direct access to dedicated physical block devices or partitions that are separate from the boot/system medium. This is exactly the same as the files we created as VDEVs in Volume 2, Section 1.9, to illustrate many of our ZFS examples in that section.

LXD is running. We now want to create a network bridge so that OS-level containers will act as virtual computers, with their own IP addresses, directly connected to your home network. That's the easiest way for a beginner to utilize those virtual machines, in terms of communicating with them, as you shall see in subsequent sections and examples.

6. In this step, you will create an LXC profile to connect any containers you create later to the public network via the bridge. When we initialized LXD, we created a default profile with an "internal" network not visible from outside our LXD installation. From a beginner system administrator's perspective, that doesn't seem very useful to us, although for security purposes in commercial system administration, that is perhaps very critical and important.

To see what containers are running, use the following LXC command:

```
root@raspberrypi:~# lxc list
To start your first container, try: lxc launch ubuntu:22.04
Or for a virtual machine: lxc launch ubuntu:22.04 --vm

+------+-------+------+------+------+-----------+
| NAME | STATE | IPV4 | IPV6 | TYPE | SNAPSHOTS |
+------+-------+------+------+------+-----------+
root@raspberrypi:~#
```

At this point, no containers are running, as seen in the output of the above command.

The following commands that create a new container are only presented here to illustrate what this "internal" network looks like. At the time of the writing of this book, Ubuntu 22.04 was a readily available and stable container image to initially start up.

```
root@raspberrypi:~# lxc launch ubuntu:22.04 test
Creating test
Retrieving image: rootfs: 84% (8.92MB/s) ...
Starting Test
root@raspberrypi:~#
```

After creating the container image, you can see that the image has been assigned a private IP address in a network different from our public network (10.24.214.79):

```
root@raspberrypi:~# lxc list
+------+---------+---------------------+----------------------------+-----------+-----------------+
| NAME | STATE   |        IPV4         |            IPV6            |   TYPE    | SNAPSHOTS       |
+------+---------+---------------------+----------------------------+-----------+-----------------+
| test | RUNNING | 10.24.214.79 (eth0) | fd42:... (eth0)            | CONTAINER
| 0                |
+------+---------+---------------------+----------------------------+-----------+-----------------+
```

Optionally at this point, we could delete this test container with the following commands, but we chose *not* to

```
root@raspberrypi:~#
root@raspberrypi:~# lxc stop test
root@raspberrypi:~# lxc delete test
root@raspberrypi:~# lxc list
+------+-------+------+------+------+-----------+
| NAME | STATE | IPV4 | IPV6 | TYPE | SNAPSHOTS |
+------+-------+------+------+------+-----------+
root@raspberrypi:~#
```

From the output of the last command, we can see that there are no containers defined.

As a beginner, you want containers to be attached to your public-facing network, so we need a specific kind of LXC profile to achieve this. You will create a profile named **bridged** with the following commands:

```
root@raspberrypi:~# lxc profile create bridged
Profile bridged created
root@raspberrypi:~#
```

7. You have to edit the LXC bridged profile. On our Raspberry Pi system, the default editor was set to nano.

You can configure the bridged profile to deploy your newly created **br0** bridge with whatever your preferred editor is, with the following command:

```
root@raspberrypi:~# lxc profile edit bridged
```

On our system, nano opened the Yet Another Markup Language (YAML) file, and we created the following contents:

Note
There are a few important things to notice about this file. First, the lines with the ### are comment lines, and in the file already present, they suggest a sample profile you could construct. Second, the character spacing on a YAML line is *very important*. So, in the file we have constructed below, there is a space character between each colon (:) on a line, and the next character present, such as between the colon after the word **name**, and the character **e** in eth0, and so forth.

```
### This is a YAML representation of the profile.
### Any line starting with a '# will be ignored.
###
### A profile consists of a set of configuration items followed by a set of
### devices.
###
### An example would look like:
### name: onenic
### config:
###   raw.lxc: lxc.aa_profile=unconfined
### devices:
###   eth0:
###     nictype: bridged
###     parent: lxdbr0
###     type: nic
###
### Note that the name is shown but cannot be changed
```

```
config: {}
description: bridged connection
devices:
   eth0:
     name: eth0
     nictype: bridged
     parent: br0
     type: nic
name: bridged
used_by: []
```

Save the file after adding the changes we show above in the editor, and close the file. If you make syntax errors in the YAML, you will be given a chance to correct them. Containers with both the default and bridged profiles will be available on the network *as independent computers with their own public-facing IP addresses.*

8.   You will now create a container, another Ubuntu 22.04 virtual machine, that will use the bridged profile.

```
root@raspberrypi:~# lxc -p default -p bridged launch ubuntu:22.04 permanent
Output truncated...
Creating permanent
Starting permanent
root@raspberrypi :~# lxc list
+-----------+---------+---------------------+----------------------------------------------------+-----------+-----------+
| NAME   | STATE |    IPV4    |              IPV6              | TYPE  | SNAPSHOTS |
+-----------+---------+---------------------+----------------------------------------------------+-----------+-----------+
| permanent | RUNNING | 192.168.1.43 (eth0) |                                | CONTAINER | 0    |
+-----------+---------+---------------------+----------------------------------------------------+-----------+-----------+
| test    | RUNNING | 10.24.214.79 (eth0) | fd42:a712:aa5a:14d2:216:3eff:fe7b:975d
(eth0) | CONTAINER | 0    |
+-----------+---------+---------------------+----------------------------------------------------+-----------+-----------+
root@raspberrypi:~#
```

In the above **lxc launch** command, it is important to specify first the default profile, and second the bridged profile. This is because the bridged profile overwrites the network settings of the default profile.

Notice that in the output of the **lxc list** command above, you see that the new container is directly attached to our public-facing network.

Now, both of these demo containers should be stopped and deleted with the following commands, to prepare for subsequent examples below:

```
root@raspberrypi:~# lxc stop test permanent
root@raspberrypi:~# lxc delete test permanent
```

9. Verify the deletion of the two containers with the following command:

```
root@raspberrypi:~# lxc list
+------+-------+------+------+------+-----------+
| NAME | STATE | IPV4 | IPV6 | TYPE | SNAPSHOTS |
+------+-------+------+------+------+-----------+
root@raspberrypi:~#
```

Conclusion:
You installed LXC/LXD on a Raspberry Pi system, and customized its profile
to achieve container launching and networking amenable to beginners.

3.2.3 Container Management Commands
Now that you have LXC/LXD installed, and know how to launch a container with some specific characteristics, the following are the most
important commands that a beginner needs to know to actually manage
that container.

On the host system, you should first execute the following command to
become root:

```
bob@raspberrypi:~ $ sudo su -
root@raspberrypi:~#
```

To start a container, named "containerx," use the following command:

```
root@raspberrypi:~# lxc start containerx
```

To stop a container named "containery," or to force it to stop, use the following
commands:

```
root@raspberrypi:~# lxc stop containery
root@raspberrypi:~# lxc stop containery --force
```

To restart a container named "containerz," and force it to restart, use the
following commands:

```
root@raspberrypi:~# lxc restart containerz
root@raspberrypi:~# lxc restart containerz --force
```

To delete a container named "containerq," and force it to be deleted if it is still
running, use the following commands:

```
root@raspberrypi:~# lxc delete containerq
root@raspberrypi:~# lxc delete container --force
```

3.2.4 Internal Container Management Commands
Executed from the Host

The most useful and practical thing that you can do to manage containers is to be able to work inside of the container OS environment itself. This allows you to do tasks such as user file and container OS maintenance, install software in the container, create users and groups, monitor container performance, etc.

There are a few equivalent ways to do this. One of them is to start a shell, such as bash, inside the container and operate in that shell. Another is to ssh into the container, as we show in Section 3.2.6. There are also LXC commands available on the host to execute Linux commands in a container, and put or get files into/from a running container. As we show in Section 3.2.6, the container's filesystem is mounted on the host, and is accessible from the host OS as well. We show some of these techniques in this section.

On the host system, you should first execute the following command to become root:

```
bob@raspberrypi:~ $ sudo su -
root@raspberrypi:~#
```

To start a bash shell inside a container name "ztest2," use the following command:

```
root@raspberrypi:~# lxc exec ztest2 bash
root@ztest2:~#
```

To terminate the bash shell in container ztest2, type **exit**.

To execute a Linux command inside the running ztest2 container from the host, you can use the following syntax:

```
root@raspberrypi:~# lxc exec ztest2 -- ls -la /
```

Notice the syntax that partitions the command sent to ztest2, the two hypens(- -) and the /, with a space character before and after the command and its options.

To put a file into ztest2 from the host directory /home/bob, use the following command:

```
root@raspberrypi:/home/bob# lxc file push /home/bob/.ssh/id_rsa.pub \
ztest2/home/bob/.ssh/authorized_keys/
```

Notice that the above command assumes there is a directory in container ztest2 /*home*/bob

To get filexyz from ztest2, that is in the directory /home/bob on that container, and "pull" it to the host into a specific destination, use the following command:

```
root@raspberrypi:/home/bob# sudo lxc file pull \
ztest2/home/bob/filexyz /home/bob/
```

3.2.5 Container Backups, Snapshots, and Cloning

Certainly one of the most important tasks for the system administrator, or for that matter, the individual user that may be working and managing her own home computer, is filesystem backup. For LXD, backup strategies follow two distinct paths. You must not only backup the containers, and their filesystems, but also the "machinery" of LXD itself on the host computer you are running it on.

The backup of containers, and the data that supports each individually, is done with the **lxc snapshot** command. Restoring a container from it's backup snapshots is done with the **lxc restore** command. It is important to note here that LXD snapshots are more inclusive, and particularly in the examples we show in Section 3.2.6, are not the same thing as using **zfs snapshot** and **zfs rollback** on a container filesystems that is using ZFS.

The backup and restoration of LXD "machinery" is something we address in a problem at the end of this chapter.

To take a snapshot of a container, named "containera", use the following command:

root@raspberrypi:~# **lxc snapshot containera**

The name of the snapshot will be snap_number, where snap_number is an incrementing integer number, starting at zero(0).

To create a snapshot of containera with a distinct name that you choose, use the following command:

root@raspberrypi:~# **lxc snapshot containera containera_snapshot_2**

The number of snapshots that have been taken on a container is shown in the **lxc list** command, for example:

root@raspberrypi:~# **lxc list containera**
```
| NAME       | STATE   | IPV4               | IPV6 | TYPE      | SNAPSHOTS |
| containera |RUNNING |  192.168.1.22 (eth0) |      | CONTAINER | 0         |
```

To rename a snapshot, use the **lxc move** command as follows:

root@raspberrypi:~# **lxc move containera/containera_snapshot_2 \
containera/containera_snapshot_3**

The lxc move command can also be used to rename a stopped container, retaining its IP address according to our methodology of bridged adapter network address assignment, using the following syntax:

root@raspberrypi:~# **lxc move <old name> <new name>**

To restore a snapshot, use the following command, and be aware that the snapshot, in this case named **containera_snapshot_2**, is restored into the container that it is a snapshot of: in this case, containera.

That brings up an interesting similarity between LXD snapshots, and ZFS dataset snapshot and rollback: Once you restore, or rollback, you have lost the version of the container (or in the case of ZFS, the dataset) as it perhaps evolved since the snapshot was taken. Contrast and compare this to using the **git** command, where you can "rollback" to a previous commit, and then roll forward again to the latest commit along any branch.

root@raspberrypi:~# **lxc restore containera containera_snapshot_3**

To escape the snapshot/rollback dilemma presented by the previous command, you can create a new container which is identical to another container's snapshot.

root@raspberrypi:~# **lxc copy containera/containera_snapshot_ 3 containerb**

So following from all the commands presented in this section, a list of the containers and snapshots you have is as follows:

1. snap0 (the first automatically named snapshot),
2. containera (not the originary container, but the one overwritten by containera_snapshot_3),
3. containera_snapshot_3 (the renamed snapshot, which was containera_snapshot_2), and
4. containerb.

To delete a snapshot, do the following:

root@raspberrypi:~# **lxc delete containera/containera_snapshot_3**

In container management, it is often necessary to use one container as a master "template" for provisioning and creating several other containers. To make a copy of a container and then effectively "clone" it into a new container, use the following command:

root@raspberrypi:~# **lxc copy <source container> <destination container>**

3.2.6 Extended LXD Installation and Container Management Examples

In this section, we show specific extended examples of the installation, execution and creation of LXD containers, ZFS, and bridge-utils on a Raspberry Pi host system. These examples should be done consecutively, as they build upon each other to achieve the goals of this section. A very useful technique we employ here is using ZFS as the backing store for LXD containers, to configure a ZFS zpool on a vdev that is a physical block device. Furthermore, in the primary example, we implement a bridged networking setup, so individual LXD containers provisioned by LXD can be automatically assigned an IP address via the DHCP server on your network.

These examples execute tasks that achieve a few system management objectives for us, as follows:

1. Integrates our ZFS system management paradigm and knowledge with a contemporary OS-level virtualization model.

2. Uses a realistic way of working with ZFS, deploying a physical block device to build a zpool on. We also pose a problem at the end of the chapter that allows you to use a physical block device as a vdev for ZFS/LXD installation.

3. Expose the LXD containers with their own "public-facing" network addresses, rather than on a private subnet such as 10.0.0X. This method uses the **iptables** command to expose containers as ports on the host computer. We find that this "public-facing" IP address method is simpler and more useful for a novice user trying to learn about LXD containers and the networking of these containers on their own home network, than the traditional way of networking the containers.

4. Gets your hands dirty with LXD.

The examples in this section make these assumptions:

* You are working on a Raspberry Pi host that has at least 4 GB of memory, is a 64-bit machine, with the latest Raspberry Pi OS and Linux kernel installed on it.

* You have enough space on the medium you're running your system from to accommodate not only the installation of ZFS, LXD, and bridge-utils packages, but also that you can add an adequately sized USB-mounted external medium to the system.

* You have superuser privileges on your computer system.

* In the primary example we download and install an Ubuntu 22.04 image, and create our first container with it. The fundamental reason for doing this is you can work with either that LTS version, or the latest available stable release of Ubuntu in the container without having to relearn any new commands or facilities, such as working with another package management system to download and install software in the container.

Example 3.2 Running Containers with a ZFS Filesystem Backing Store

Objective:
Exploring LXD containers, and their utilization of ZFS.

Prerequisites:

1. Completion of Example 3.1.
2. Knowledge of basic Linux commands.
3. Optional completion of Volume 4, Chapter 1 on ZFS.

Background:
This primary example follows up on the installation, initialization, creation, and deletion of the two LXD containers as described in Example 3.1. It also allows you to further experiment with ZFS and bridged network adapters. It also assumes that you will be working in your home account on your Raspberry Pi computer system.

Procedures:

1. Launch a new container, named **ztest**, with the following command:

   root@raspberrypi:~# **lxc -p default -p bridged launch ubuntu:22.04 ztest**

   This will allow you to experiment with, and view, some of the ZFS backing store characteristics of an LXD container.

2. Once the container is created and started, use the following command to view the zpools on the system:

   root@raspberrypi:~# **zpool list**
   NAME SIZE ALLOC FREE   CKPOINT EXPANDSZ FRAG CAP DEDUP   HEALTH
   ALTROOT
   default 7.50G 743M 6.77G   -   -   0%   9% 1.00x ONLINE -
   root@raspberrypi:~#

3. Use the following command to list the ZFS filesystems that exist on your system:

   root@raspberrypi:~# **zfs list**
   NAME   USED AVAIL   REFER MOUNTPOINT
   default   743M 6.54G   24K legacy
   default/buckets   24K 6.54G   24K legacy
   default/containers   126M 6.54G   24K legacy
   default/containers/ztest 126M 6.54G   726M legacy
   default/custom   24K 6.54G   24K legacy
   default/deleted   144K 6.54G   24K legacy

```
default/deleted/buckets              24K   6.54G    24K  legacy
default/deleted/containers           24K   6.54G    24K  legacy
default/deleted/custom               24K   6.54G    24K  legacy
default/deleted/images               24K   6.54G    24K  legacy
default/deleted/virtual-machines     24K   6.54G    24K  legacy
default/images                       616M  6.54G    24K  legacy
default/images/e59722a2...           616M  6.54G    616M legacy
default/virtual-machines             24K   6.54G    24K  legacy
root@raspberrypi:~#
```

We see that the default zpool takes up 7.50 G bytes of storage.

4. Now we can get LXD configuration information using the command line interface known as lxc. Type the following command:

```
root@raspberrypi:~# lxc info
config: {}
api_extensions:
- storage_zfs_remove_snapshots
- container_host_shutdown_timeout
- container_stop_priority
- container_syscall_filtering
- auth_pki
- container_last_used_at
Output truncated...
server_version: "5.15"
    storage: zfs
    storage_version: 2.1.11-1~bpo11+1~rpt1
Output truncated...
```

What we can see in the output of the above command is that LXD is using ZFS for storage of container information, and the name of the zpool for that storage is **default**.

5. At this point, it would also be prudent to examine the LXD **bridged** profile, using the following command:

```
root@raspberrypi:~# lxc profile show bridged
config: {}
description: bridged connection
devices:
  eth0:
   name: eth0
   nictype: bridged
   parent: br0
   type: nic
name: bridged
used_by:
- /1.0/instances/ztest
root@raspberrypi:~#
```

From this command output, you can see that the bridged adapter **br0** is being used by containers that you have created so far.

6.   We can now open a bash shell into the container ztest, do some file explorations, and then exit the container, with the following commands:

```
root@raspberrypi:~# lxc shell ztest
root@ztest:~# ls -la
total 10
drwx------    5 root root     8      Aug  1   20:31   .
drwxr-xr-x   18 root root    21      Jul 29   07:35   ..
-rw-------    1 root root    754     Aug  2   02:01   .bash_history
-rw-r--r--    1 root root    3106    Oct 15   2021    .bashrc
drwxr-xr-x    3 root root     3      Aug  1   20:31   .local
-rw-r--r--    1 root root    161     Jul 9    2019    .profile
drwx------    2 root root     5      Aug  1   20:35   .ssh
drwx------    3 root root     3      Aug  1   19:36   snap
root@ztest:~# pwd
/root
root@ztest:~# exit
logout
root@raspberrypi:~#
```

Example 3.3 Creating an LXC Container on a Physical Block Device vdev

Objectives:
To create a new container, with a ZFS backing store, on a physical device.

Prerequisties:

1.   Completion of Examples 3.1 and 3.2.

2.   Optional completion of Volume 2, Chapter 1, Section 1.9 on ZFS.

3.   Having a usable, sacrificial USB thumbdrive, or other medium that can mount, and be recognized on your Raspberry Pi system.

Background:
The previous examples mapped containers onto loop devices, which were essentially files constructed by LXC in lieu of using physical, block devices.

Note
A zpool *cannot* be created on a block device that has another filesystem mounted on it, such as the boot/root filesystem of the Raspberry Pi OS. LXC creates loop device zpools, essentially on files, because of this fact.

Here, we use a physical device, a USB-mounted thumbdrive, to construct our LXC container on. The essential command presented here is

lxc storage create name zfs source=zpoolname

where **name** is the name of the pool which will hold any container(s) you want to map to it, and **source=zpoolname** designates, for our purposes here, the name of the zpool you've created with the **zpool create** command on a physical block device. When you launch a container onto that device, the **--storage name** option of the **lxc launch** command specifies that named zpool.

Procedures:

1. Insert the USB medium in one of your Raspberry Pi system's available connectors. Use one of the USB3 connectors if available. It's device name will appear in /dev, such as /*dev*/sdb, with perhaps a single partition on it named /*dev*/sdb1. If it doesn't appear there after insertion, select another sacrificial USB thumbdrive that properly mounts in /dev. We used a Kingston 8 GB device, pre-formatted to FAT32 in this example. But in later examples, we used a SATA SSD mounted in an external USB3 enclosure.

2. Unmount the thumbdrive from Step 1 with the following command:

   ```
   root@raspberrypi:~# umount /dev/sdb1
   root@raspberrypi:~#
   ```

3. Create a zpool on the thumbdrive with the following command:

   ```
   root@raspberrypi:~# zpool create -f test27 /dev/sdb1
   root@raspberrypi:~#
   ```

4. List the zpools on your system with the following command:

   ```
   root@raspberrypi:~# zpool list
   NAME    SIZE   ALLOC  FREE   CKPOINT  EXPANDSZ  FRAG  CAP  DEDUP
   HEALTH  ALTROOT
   default  7.50G  743M  6.77G    -         -       0%   9%  1.00x
   ONLINE -
   test27  7G     104K   7.00G    -         -       0%   0%  1.00x
   ONLINE -
   root@raspberrypi:~#
   ```

5. Create a new storage backend on this block device, named **prod**, with the following command. This will take some time, depending upon the capacity of your block device.

```
root@raspberrypi:~# lxc storage create prod zfs source=test27
storage pool prod created
root@raspberrypi:~#
```

6. List the LXC storage pools now on the system with the following command:

```
root@raspberrypi:~# lxc storage ls
```

NAME	DRIVER	SOURCE	DESCRIPTION	USED BY	STATE
default	zfs	/var/snap/lxd/common/lxd/disks/default.img		3	CREATED
prod	zfs	test27		0	CREATED

7. Create a new container in that storage pool with the following command. This will take a while, depending on the size of your block device.

```
root@raspberrypi:~# lxc -p default -p bridged launch --storage prod
ubuntu:22.04 ztest2
Creating ztest2
Remapping container filesystem
Starting ztest2
root@raspberrypi:~#
```

Conclusion:

We launched a container on a physical device, separate from the Raspberry Pi OS boot/root medium, and specified a ZFS filesystem on the host to hold that container's data and files. Note carefully here, the zpool, and ZFS exists as a filesystem on the host, not as an installed filesystem in the container. This is a more realistic and useful methodology for system administration, particularly since you can deploy the advantages that ZFS gives you in terms of file integrity, and backup strategies via mirroring, with physical block devices. In server-class ZFS systems, Error Correction Code (ECC) memory is used to ensure data integrity. If instead of using a USB thumbdrive as we do in this example, you used an externally mounted SSD, or USB3 PCIe M2 card to create the zpool on, those devices have ECC capability built into them for data integrity.

In-Chapter Exercise

3.4 What does the **zfs list** command show now?

Example 3.4 Viewing the Contents of a Container from the Host

Objectives:
To enter the filesystem of a running LXC container from the host Raspberry Pi system, and to do file maintenance and exploration in the container.

Prerequisites:

1. Completion of Examples 3.1 through 3.3.

Background:
After you've launched an LXD container, such as the ones we started above in Examples 3.1 through 3.3, you are able to enter a container via the commands **lxc shell**, **lxc exec**, or **lxc console** to do file creation, maintenance, or simply to view or modify the files in that container. This example shows you how to access the filesystem of the container from the host Raspberry Pi.

As you did in Example 3.1, the snap package installed LXD and created a default location for containers you would subsequently launch.

But remember we created a location named **prod** for our containers. LXD mounts the filesystems for those containers in a subdirectory under /var/snap/lxd/common/lxd/storage-pools/prod/containers/. If you use the following commands on the host to examine the files in the container ztest2 you created in Example 3.2, you'll enter that container. Each container is found in a subdirectory of the previous pathname, and that subdirectory is named after each container name.

```
$ sudo su -

root@raspberrypi:~# ls -l /var/snap/lxd/common/lxd/storage-pools/prod\
containers/ztest2
total 0
root@raspberrypi:~#
```

The question is "Why is the container directory empty?"

Assuming the container is running, the contents show as empty, and for a good reason.

LXD uses a facility we covered in the previous volumes of this book – Linux namespaces. You need to enter the namespace of the LXD service for you to view the container files from the host. The critical command here is the **nsenter** command. With the -t option, you can specify the target namespace, and the process ID of the LXD service. With the -m option, you can specify that you want to enter the *mount namespace* of this process. You can view more detailed information about the **nsenter** command in its manpage on your host Raspberry Pi system.

Procedures:

1. Enter the namespace of the LXD service.

   ```
   root@raspberrypi:~# nsenter -t $(cat /var/snap/lxd/common/lxd.pid) -m

   -bash-5.1#
   ```

2. You'll be looking at the container you created in Example 3.3, named **ztest2**.

   ```
   -bash-5.1# cd /var/snap/lxd/common/lxd/storage-pools/prod\
   containers
   -bash-5.1# ls -l ztest2
   total 8
   -r--------    1   root   root          3851   Aug 2 13:49  backup.yaml
   -rw-r--r--    1   root   root           297   Jul 29 01:10  metadata.yaml
   drwxr-xr-x   18   1000000 1000000        21   Jul 29 00:35  rootfs
   drwxr-xr-x    2   root   root             3   Jul 29 01:10  templates
   -bash-5.1#
   ```

3. You can now look at the files of this container in detail.

These files are important if you lose your LXD database somehow.

The **metadata.yaml** file, along with the **templates** directory, is the description of how the container was parametarized. In an Ubuntu 22.04 container, the defaults are used, except for networking. And last in the listing is **rootfs**, which is where the filesystem of the container resides.

The **rootfs** directory has UID/GID of 100000/100000. The files inside the root filesystem of container **ztest2** have IDs that are shifted by 100000 from the typical range 0–65534. The files inside the container will have IDs that range from 100000 to 165534. The root account in the container will have real UID 100000, but will appear as 0 in the container. Here is the list of the root directory of the container, as viewed from the host.

```
-bash-5.1# cd ztest2/rootfs
-bash-5.1# ls -la
total 34
drwxr-xr-x   18 1000000 1000000      21  Jul 29 00:35   .
d--x------    4 1000000 root          6  Aug  2 13:47   ..
lrwxrwxrwx    1 1000000 1000000       7  Jul 29 00:22   bin -> usr/bin
drwxr-xr-x    2 1000000 1000000       2  Jul 29 00:35   boot
drwxr-xr-x    4 1000000 1000000      16  Jul 29 00:30   dev
drwxr-xr-x   90 1000000 1000000     178  Aug  2 13:51   etc
drwxr-xr-x    3 1000000 1000000       3  Aug  2 13:50   home
lrwxrwxrwx    1 1000000 1000000       7  Jul 29 00:22   lib -> usr/lib
drwxr-xr-x    2 1000000 1000000       2  Jul 29 00:23   media
drwxr-xr-x    2 1000000 1000000       2  Jul 29 00:23   mnt
drwxr-xr-x    2 1000000 1000000       2  Jul 29 00:23   opt
```

```
drwxr-xr-x       2 1000000 1000000        2   Apr 18  2022    proc
drwx------       4 1000000 1000000        7   Aug  3 05:51    root
drwxr-xr-x       4 1000000 1000000        4   Jul 29 00:31    run
lrwxrwxrwx       1 1000000 1000000        8   Jul 29 00:22    sbin -> usr/sbin
drwxr-xr-x       6 1000000 1000000        7   Jul 29 00:31    snap
drwxr-xr-x       2 1000000 1000000        2   Jul 29 00:23    srv
drwxr-xr-x       2 1000000 1000000        2   Apr 18  2022    sys
drwxrwxrwt      10 1000000 1000000       10   Aug  3 08:54    tmp
drwxr-xr-x      11 1000000 1000000       11   Jul 29 00:23    usr
drwxr-xr-x      13 1000000 1000000       15   Jul 29 00:30    var
-bash-5.1#
```

4. At this point, we have not added any users to the system. But, you can now create a file in the container's rootfs from the host, in the default **ubuntu** user in that container's home subdirectory, and see what it will look like from within the container. To achieve this, open a Bash shell into the container.

```
-bash-5.1# cd home/ubuntu
-bash-5.1# touch test_file
-bash-5.1#
```

5. From another terminal on the host, run the following commands:

```
root@raspberrypi:~# lxc shell ztest2
root@ztest2:~# cd /home/ubuntu
root@ztest2:/home/ubuntu# ls -la
total 10
drwxr-x---  3  ubuntu ubuntu    7     Aug 5 13:07  .
drwxr-xr-x  3  root   root      3     Aug 5 13:06  ..
-rw-r--r--  1  ubuntu ubuntu    220   Jan 6 2022   .bash_logout
-rw-r--r--  1  ubuntu ubuntu    3771  Jan 6 2022   .bashrc
-rw-r--r--  1  ubuntu ubuntu    807   Jan 6 2022   .profile
drwx------  2  ubuntu ubuntu    3     Aug 5 13:06  .ssh
-rw-r--r--  1  nobody nogroup   0     Aug 5 13:07  test_file
root@ztest2:/home/ubuntu#
```

Conclusion:
We have seen how to enter the mount namespace of the LXD service from the host Raspberry Pi system, and create and have a look at a file in the default home directory on the Ubuntu 22.04 container. We also opened a Bash shell in the container and examined that file from within the container.

Example 3.5 Using ssh to Log into an LXD Container

Objective:
Allow ssh login from another Raspberry Pi on the network, into an LXD container.

Prerequisites:

1. Completion of Example 3.1 through 3.4.

Background:
This example is a follow-up to Example 3.4, and allows you ssh into an LXD container from another Raspberry Pi on your local intranet, or from the host running the container itself.

Note
On our Ubuntu 22.04 container, sshd was already installed, as it was on our host.

Procedures:

1. For the purposes of this example, you will add a new user with the same name as the user on the host, to the container named ztest2, and then exit to the host using the following commands:

    ```
    bob@raspberrypi:~ $ sudo su -

    root@raspberrypi:~#
    root@raspberrypi:~# lxc shell ztest2
    root@ztest2:~#
    root@ztest2:~# adduser bob
    Adding user `bob' ...
    Adding new group `bob' (1001) ...
    Adding new user `bob' (1001) with group `bob' ...
    Creating home directory `/home/bob' ...
    Copying files from `/etc/skel' ...
    New password:
    Retype new password:
    passwd: password updated successfully
    Changing the user information for bob
    Enter the new value, or press ENTER for the default
        Full Name []: bob
        Room Number []:
        Work Phone []:
        Home Phone []:
        Other []:
    Is the information correct? [Y/n] Y
    root@ztest2:~# exit
    logout
    root@raspberrypi:~#
    ```

2. Now back on the host, check the automatically generated IP address of the container named **container1**:

```
root@raspberrypi:~# lxc list
+----------+---------+--------------------+------+----------+------------------+------------+
| NAME | STATE |       IPV4         | IPV6 | TYPE     | SNAPSHOTS |
+----------+---------+--------------------+------+----------+------------------+
| ztest | RUNNING | 192.168.1.37 (eth0) |      | CONTAINER | 0        |         |
+----------+---------+--------------------+------+----------+------------------+
| ztest2 | RUNNING | 192.168.1.45 (eth0) |      | CONTAINER | 0        |         |
+----------+---------+--------------------+------+----------+------------------+
root@raspberrypi:~#
```

3. By default, all Ubuntu LXD images for containers are set up with **PasswordAuthentication no** in their SSH configuration.

Therefore, in the container ztest2, you must edit the config file for sshd as root, and do the following:

```
root@raspberrypi:~# lxc shell ztest2
root@ztest2:~# nano /etc/ssh/sshd_config
```

Scroll down in nano to the line **PasswordAuthentication no** and change the **no** to **yes**, if necessary. If that line has a pound sign (#) in front of it, indicating it's commented out, delete the pound sign.
Save and exit the file */etc/*ssh/sshd_config

4. Restart the SSH service with the following command:

```
root@ztest2:~# systemctl restart ssh
root@ztest2:~#
```

5. You should now be able to ssh into the container from the host system. If you get the following message on the host

```
@@@@@@@@@@@@@@@@@@@@@@@@@@@@@@@@@@@@@@@@@@@@@@@@@@@@@@@@@
@   WARNING: REMOTE HOST IDENTIFICATION HAS CHANGED!    @
@@@@@@@@@@@@@@@@@@@@@@@@@@@@@@@@@@@@@@@@@@@@@@@@@@@@@@@@@
IT IS POSSIBLE THAT SOMEONE IS DOING SOMETHING NASTY!
Someone could be eavesdropping on you right now (man-in-the-middle attack)!
It is also possible that a host key has just been changed.
The fingerprint for the ECDSA key sent by the remote host is
SHA256:ff8e+evJbf4aCtfYbfMFxOwjZZ+NnkOFCy6QDmT84KQ.
Please contact your system administrator.
Add correct host key in /home/bob/.ssh/known_hosts to get rid of this message.
Offending ECDSA key in /home/bob/.ssh/known_hosts:35
  remove with:
  ssh-keygen -f "/home/bob/.ssh/known_hosts" -R "192.168.1.45"
ECDSA host key for 192.168.1.45 has changed and you have requested strict checking.
Host key verification failed.
```

Remove the offending key as indicated, and reattempt the following **ssh** command.

```
bob@raspberrypi:~ $ ssh bob@192.168.1.45
The authenticity of host '192.168.1.45 (192.168.1.45)' can't be established.
ECDSA key fingerprint is SHA256:ff8e+evJbf4aCtfYbfMFxOwjZZ+NnkOFCy6QDmT84KQ.
Are you sure you want to continue connecting (yes/no/[fingerprint])? yes
Warning: Permanently added '192.168.1.45' (ECDSA) to the list of known hosts.
bob@192.168.1.45's password: <The password you established in Step 1.>
Welcome to Ubuntu 22.04.2 LTS (GNU/Linux 6.1.21-v8+ aarch64)
```

* Documentation: https://help.ubuntu.com

* Management: https://landscape.canonical.com

* Support: https://ubuntu.com/advantage

```
System information as of Fri Aug  4 17:05:46 UTC 2023

System load:     1.02734375  Temperature:         34.1 C
Usage of /home:  unknown      Processes:           30
Memory usage:    71%          Users logged in:     0
Swap usage:      98%          IPv4 address for eth0: 192.168.1.45
```

* Strictly confined Kubernetes makes edge and IoT secure. Learn how MicroK8s just raised the bar for easy, resilient, and secure K8s cluster deployment.

```
https://ubuntu.com/engage/secure-kubernetes-at-the-edge
Output truncated...

bob@ztest2:~$
```

In-Chapter Exercise

3.5 Execute all of the steps of Example 3.5 on your own system, to provision and start a new LXD container so that you can ssh to it from another machine on your LAN, or from the Internet.

Example 3.6 Enabling the Nginx Web Server in an LXD Container

Objective:
Installation of the web server Nginx in an LXD container

Prerequisites:

1. Completion of Examples 3.1 through 3.5.

Background:
This example allows you to install a web server named **Nginx** in the container named "ztest," which you can then use to display web pages stored in the container, by using a web browser.

Procedures:

1. Open a bash shell on the container named **ztest** and check the status of the nginx service:

   ```
   bob@raspberrypi:~ $ sudo su ·
   root@ztest:~# systemctl status nginx
   Unit nginx.service could not be found.
   root@ztest:~#
   ```

   From the above output, you can see that Nginx is *not* installed.

2. To get the latest Nginx package, first update the Ubuntu package repository, and then install the Nginx service, using the following commands:

   ```
   root@ztest:~# apt-get update

   Output truncated...
   Fetched 10.7 MB in 39s (272 kB/s)
   Reading package lists... Done
   ```

   ```
   root@ztest:~# apt-get install nginx

   Output truncated...
   Scanning processes...
   ```

   No services need to be restarted.
   No containers need to be restarted.
   No user sessions are running outdated binaries.
   No VM guests are running outdated hypervisor (qemu) binaries on this host.
   root@ztest:~#

3. A firewall application name Uncomplicated Firewall (ufw) exists in the container. Check which applications are available to ufw and check the status of ufw to see if it is protecting those applications:

   ```
   root@ztest:~# ufw app list
   Available applications:
     Nginx Full
     Nginx HTTP
     Nginx HTTPS
     OpenSSH
   ```

```
root@ztest:~# ufw status
Status: inactive
root@ztest:~#
```

The above output shows that ufw is *not* active. If on your system, it is active, and firewall rules are in effect, you're going to have to disable ufw, and/or modifying its rules.

4. Check the status of the Nginx service:

```
root@ztest:~# systemctl status nginx
● nginx.service - A high performance web server and a reverse proxy server
  Loaded: loaded (/lib/systemd/system/nginx.service; enabled; vendor preset:>
  Active: active (running) since Sat 2023-08-05 16:24:40 UTC; 7min ago
    Docs: man:nginx(8)
Output truncated...
root@ztest:~#
```

What we see from the output of this command is that the installation of the Nginx service using **apt-get** not only installed it, but started it as well, and that the service is active and running.

5. You can now test the Nginx web server by pointing your web browser to the URL of the container ztest, which in our case is 192.168.1.37. You will see the Nginx Welcome page displayed, with the following content:

```
Welcome to nginx!
If you see this page, the nginx web server is successfully installed and
working. Further configuration is required.
```

For online documentation and support please refer to nginx.org.
   Commercial support is available at nginx.com.
   Thank you for using nginx.

6. Managing the Nginx process

Now that you have your web server up and running in the container, let's review some basic management commands you can use at the container command line.

```
To stop your web server, type:
sudo systemctl stop nginx
```

```
To start the web server when it is stopped, type:
sudo systemctl start nginx
```

```
To stop and then start the service again, type:
sudo systemctl restart nginx
```

If you are only making configuration changes, Nginx can often reload without dropping connections. To do this, type:
sudo systemctl reload nginx

By default, Nginx is configured to start automatically when the server boots. If this is not what you want, you can disable this behavior by typing:
sudo systemctl disable nginx

To re-enable the service to start up at boot, you can type:
sudo systemctl enable nginx

You have now learned a few basic management commands, and should be ready to configure the site to host more than one domain.

Conclusion:
You installed the Nginx web server in an LXC/LXD container.

In-Chapter Exercise

3.6 Execute all of the steps of Example 3.6 on your own computer system to provision and start a new LXD container, so that the web server Nginx is installed in it. Then do an initial test of the default Nginx web page, either from a browser on another machine on your LAN, or from the Internet.

3.3 Docker

Similar to, but more commercially utilized than LXC/LXD, Docker is a robust and widely used container management system that has revolutionized the world of software development and deployment.

Most notably, Docker provides a virtualization platform for developers to create, package, and distribute applications and their dependencies in lightweight, portable containers.

These containers encapsulate everything needed for an application to run, from the code and runtime environment to libraries and system tools, ensuring consistency and reliability across different environments. Docker's strength lies in its ability to simplify the software development lifecycle by allowing developers to build and test applications in isolated containers, making it easy and efficient to move these containers between the stages of development, testing, and production environments, ready for shipment to customers. Its efficiency, scalability, and compatibility have made it an essential tool in modern DevOps and cloud-native workflows, empowering organizations to develop, deploy, and scale applications faster and more efficiently.

In the following sections, we provide you with installation instructions for Docker on the Raspberry Pi OS, show its basic usage, the deployment of an Nginx Docker container with a public-facing IP address, and give a brief command reference for its essential commands. This presentation can be the fundamental basis for you to proceed with further Docker DevOps.

3.3.1 Docker Installation on the Raspberry Pi OS

As of the time this book was written, the easiest and simplest way of installing Docker on the Raspberry Pi OS is to use the following commands:

```
bob@raspberrypi:~ $ curl -fsSL https://get.docker.com -o get-docker.sh
bob@raspberrypi:~ $ sudo sh get-docker.sh
# Executing docker install script, commit: c2de0811708b6d9015ed1a2c80f02c9b70c
8ce7b
+ sh -c apt-get update -qq >/dev/null
+ sh -c DEBIAN_FRONTEND=noninteractive apt-get install -y -qq apt-transport-https
ca-certificates curl >/dev/null
+ sh -c install -m 0755 -d /etc/apt/keyrings
+ sh -c curl -fsSL "https://download.docker.com/linux/debian/gpg" | gpg --dearmor
--yes -o /etc/apt/keyrings/docker.gpg
+ sh -c chmod a+r /etc/apt/keyrings/docker.gpg
+ sh -c echo "deb [arch=arm64 signed-by=/etc/apt/keyrings/docker.gpg] https://down-
load.docker.com/linux/debian bullseye stable" > /etc/apt/sources.list.d/docker.list
+ sh -c apt-get update -qq >/dev/null
+ sh -c DEBIAN_FRONTEND=noninteractive apt-get install -y -qq docker-ce docker-ce-cli
containerd.io docker-compose-plugin docker-ce-rootless-extras docker-buildx-plugin >/
dev/null
+ sh -c docker version
Client: Docker Engine - Community
Version:            24.0.5
API version:        1.43
Go version:         go1.20.6
Git commit:         ced0996
Built               Fri Jul 21 20:35:38 2023
OS/Arch:            linux/arm64
Context:            default

Server: Docker Engine - Community
Engine:
Version:            24.0.5
API version:        1.43 (minimum version 1.12)
Go version:         go1.20.6
Git commit:         a61e2b4
Built:              Fri Jul 21 20:35:38 2023
OS/Arch:            linux/arm64
Experimental:       false
containerd:
Version:            1.6.22
```

```
GitCommit:            8165feabfdfe38c65b599c4993d227328c231fca
runc:
Version:              1.1.8
GitCommit:            v1.1.8-0-g82f18fe
docker-init:
Version:              0.19.0
GitCommit:            de40ad0
```
==

To run Docker as a non-privileged user, consider setting up the
Docker daemon in rootless mode for your user:

```
    dockerd-rootless-setuptool.sh install
```

Visit https://docs.docker.com/go/rootless/ to learn about rootless mode.

To run the Docker daemon as a fully privileged service, but granting non-root
users access, refer to https://docs.docker.com/go/daemon-access/

WARNING: Access to the remote API on a privileged Docker daemon is equivalent
        to root access on the host. Refer to the 'Docker daemon attack surface'
        documentation for details: https://docs.docker.com/go/attack-surface/

==

```
bob@raspberrypi:~ $
```

3.3.2 Adding a Non-Root User on the Docker Group and Checking the Docker Version

An essential operation for beginners is to add a non-root user to the Docker
group, as follows:

```
bob@raspberrypi:~ $ sudo usermod -aG docker bob
bob@raspberrypi:~ $ sudo docker version
Client: Docker Engine - Community
Version:  4.0.5
API version:    1.43
Go version:     go1.20.6
Git commit:     ced0996
Built:          Fri Jul 21 20:35:38 2023
OS/Arch:        linux/arm64
Context:        default

Server: Docker Engine - Community
Engine:
Version:        24.0.5
API version:    1.43 (minimum version 1.12)
Go version:     go1.20.6
Git commit:     a61e2b4
Built:          Fri Jul 21 20:35:38 2023
OS/Arch:        linux/arm64
```

```
Experimental:   false
containerd:
Version:        1.6.22
GitCommit:      8165feabfdfe38c65b599c4993d227328c231fca
runc:
Version:        1.1.8
GitCommit:      v1.1.8-0-g82f18fe
docker-init:
Version:        0.19.0
GitCommit:      de40ad0
```

3.3.3 Run the Sample "Hello World" Containers

The first test of Docker for a beginner is to "pull" and run the following container on your host system:

```
bob@raspberrypi:~ $ sudo docker run hello-world
Unable to find image 'hello-world:latest' locally
latest: Pulling from library/hello-world
70f5ac315c5a: Pull complete
Digest:     sha256:926fac19d22aa2d60f1a276b66a20eb765fbeea2db5dbdaafeb456ad
8ce81598
Status: Downloaded newer image for hello-world:latest

Hello from Docker!
This message shows that your installation appears to be working correctly.
```

To generate this message, Docker took the following steps:

1. The Docker client contacted the Docker daemon.

2. The Docker daemon pulled the "hello-world" image from the Docker Hub.

   (arm64v8)

3. The Docker daemon created a new container from that image which runs the executable that produces the output you are currently reading.

4. The Docker daemon streamed that output to the Docker client, which sent it to your terminal.

To try something more ambitious, you can run an Ubuntu container with

```
bob@raspberrypi:~ $ docker run -it ubuntu bash
Unable to find image 'ubuntu:latest' locally
latest: Pulling from library/ubuntu
5af00eab9784: Pull complete
Digest:     sha256:0bced47fffa3361afa981854fcabcd4577cd43cebbb808cea2b1f33a3d
d7f508
```

```
Status: Downloaded newer image for ubuntu:latest
root@2b96338f770f:/# exit
exit
bob@raspberrypi:~ $
```

3.4 Docker Optional Configurations

This section contains optional procedures for configuring your Raspberry Pi system, so that your work with Docker is more effective.

3.4.1 Running Docker without Root Privileges

The docker daemon binds to a Unix socket instead of a TCP port. By default that Unix socket is owned by the root user, and other users can access it with the **sudo** command. For this reason, the "docker daemon" always runs as the root user.

To avoid having to use **sudo** every time you use the **docker** command, create a group called **docker**, and add users to it. When the docker daemon starts, it makes the ownership of the socket read/writable by the docker group.

Note

Being in the docker group is equivalent to being the root user.

To verify that docker is running the container built above, use the following command:

```
bob@raspberrypi:~ $ docker ps -l
CONTAINER ID  IMAGE   COMMAND  CREATED      STATUS    PORTS  NAMES
2b96338f770f  ubuntu  "bash"   11 hours ago Exited (0)       trusting_shirley
bob@raspberrypi:~ $
```

3.4.2 Configuring UFW and Making Other Configuration Changes

If you use UFW on the same host as you run Docker, you may need to do additional configuration. Docker uses a bridge to manage container networking. By default, UFW drops all forwarding traffic. As a result, for Docker to run when UFW is enabled, you must set UFW's forwarding policy appropriately.

Also, UFW's default set of rules denies all incoming traffic. If you want to reach your containers from another host, allow incoming connections on the Docker port. The Docker port defaults to 2376 if TLS is enabled or 2375 when it is not. If TLS is not enabled, communication is unencrypted. By default, Docker runs without TLS enabled.

To view, and perhaps configure UFW to allow incoming connections on the Docker port, IF UFW IS ACTIVE, first use the following commands:

```
bob@raspberrypi:~ $ sudo ufw status
Status: inactive
bob@raspberrypi:~ $ cat /etc/default/ufw
# /etc/default/ufw
#

# Set to yes to apply rules to support IPv6 (no means only IPv6 on loopback
# accepted). You will need to 'disable' and then 'enable' the firewall for
# the changes to take affect.
IPV6=yes

# Set the default input policy to ACCEPT, DROP, or REJECT. Please note that if
# you change this you will most likely want to adjust your rules.
DEFAULT_INPUT_POLICY="DROP"

# Set the default output policy to ACCEPT, DROP, or REJECT. Please note that if
# you change this you will most likely want to adjust your rules.
DEFAULT_OUTPUT_POLICY="ACCEPT"

# Set the default forward policy to ACCEPT, DROP or REJECT. Please note that
# if you change this you will most likely want to adjust your rules
DEFAULT_FORWARD_POLICY="DROP"

# Set the default application policy to ACCEPT, DROP, REJECT or SKIP. Please
# note that setting this to ACCEPT may be a security risk. See 'man ufw' for
# details
DEFAULT_APPLICATION_POLICY="SKIP"

# By default, ufw only touches its own chains. Set this to 'yes' to have ufw
# manage the built-in chains too. Warning: setting this to 'yes' will break
# non-ufw managed firewall rules
MANAGE_BUILTINS=no

#
# IPT backend
#
# only enable if using iptables backend
IPT_SYSCTL=/etc/ufw/sysctl.conf

# Extra connection tracking modules to load. IPT_MODULES should typically be
# empty for new installations and modules added only as needed. See
# 'CONNECTION HELPERS' from 'man ufw-framework' for details. Complete list can
# be found in net/netfilter/Kconfig of your kernel source. Some common modules:
# nf_conntrack_irc, nf_nat_irc: DCC (Direct Client to Client) support
# nf_conntrack_netbios_ns: NetBIOS (samba) client support
# nf_conntrack_pptp, nf_nat_pptp: PPTP over stateful firewall/NAT
# nf_conntrack_ftp, nf_nat_ftp: active FTP support
# nf_conntrack_tftp, nf_nat_tftp: TFTP support (server side)
# nf_conntrack_sane: sane support
IPT_MODULES=""
bob@raspberrypi:~ $
```

If UFW is active, use nano to edit the /etc/default/ufw file.

```
bob@raspberrypi:~$ sudo nano /etc/default/ufw
```

Set the DEFAULT_FORWARD_POLICY policy ="ACCEPT"
Save and close the file.

Then, reload UFW to invoke the new setting.

```
bob@raspberrypi:~$ sudo ufw reload
bob@raspberrypi:~$
```

Finally, allow incoming tcp connections on the default Docker port.

```
bob@raspberrypi:~$ sudo ufw allow 2375/tcp
bob@raspberrypi:~$
```

To configure Docker to start on boot, you need to use systemd to modify the dockerd service. The Raspberry Pi OS uses systemd as its boot and service manager. To configure the docker daemon to start on boot, use the following command:

```
bob@raspberrypi:~ $ sudo systemctl enable docker
Synchronizing state of docker.service with SysV service script with /lib/systemd/
systemd-sysv-install.
Executing: /lib/systemd/systemd-sysv-install enable docker
bob@raspberrypi:~ $
```

3.5 Uninstallation of Docker

Sometimes, in the system administration of the Raspberry Pi OS, it becomes necessary to uninstall a service, for whatever reason. We only show the commands that achieve this below, but do not execute them on our Raspberry Pi Os.

To uninstall the Docker package:
```
$ sudo apt-get purge docker-engine
```

To uninstall the Docker package and dependencies that are no longer needed:
```
$ sudo apt-get autoremove --purge docker-engine
```

The above commands will *not* remove images, containers, volumes, or user-created configuration files on your host. If you wish to delete all images, containers, and volumes, use the following command:

```
$ rm -rf /var/lib/docker
```

You have to then delete your user created configuration files, if there are any, manually.

3.6 Running a Docker Container and Useful Docker Commands

This section assumes you have a working installation of Docker, as specified in Section 3.3.1. To verify Docker is installed, use the following command:

```
bob@raspberrypi:~ $ docker info
Client: Docker Engine - Community
Version:    24.0.5
Context:    default
Debug Mode: false
Plugins:
 buildx: Docker Buildx (Docker Inc.)
 Version: v0.11.2
 Path:    /usr/libexec/docker/cli-plugins/docker-buildx
 compose: Docker Compose (Docker Inc.)
 Version: v2.20.2
 Path:    /usr/libexec/docker/cli-plugins/docker-compose

Server:
 Containers: 2
  Running: 0
  Paused: 0
  Stopped: 2
 Images: 2
 Server Version: 24.0.5
 Storage Driver: overlay2
  Backing Filesystem: extfs
  Supports d_type: true
  Using metacopy: false
  Native Overlay Diff: true
  userxattr: false
 Logging Driver: json-file
 Cgroup Driver: systemd
 Cgroup Version: 2
 Plugins:
  Volume: local
  Network: bridge host ipvlan macvlan null overlay
  Log: awslogs fluentd gcplogs gelf journald json-file local logentries splunk syslog
 Swarm: inactive
 Runtimes: io.containerd.runc.v2 runc
 Default Runtime: runc
 Init Binary: docker-init
 containerd version: 8165feabfdfe38c65b599c4993d227328c231fca
 runc version: v1.1.8-0-g82f18fe
 init version: de40ad0
 Security Options:
  seccomp
  Profile: builtin
  cgroupns
 Kernel Version: 6.1.21-v8+
```

```
Operating System: Debian GNU/Linux 11 (bullseye)
OSType: linux
Architecture: aarch64
CPUs: 4
Total Memory: 3.704GiB
Name: raspberrypi
ID: d5f88ac0-1495-426f-b448-a44bd20089b2
Docker Root Dir: /var/lib/docker
Debug Mode: false
Experimental: false
Insecure Registries:
127.0.0.0/8
Live Restore Enabled: false

WARNING: No memory limit support
WARNING: No swap limit support
bob@raspberrypi:~ $
```

If the system responds- **docker: command not found**, or something like **/var/lib/docker/repositories: permission denied**, or you may have an incomplete Docker installation, or **insufficient privileges to access Docker** on your Raspberry Pi system. With the default installation of Docker, docker commands need to be run by a user that is in the docker group, or by a user with root privileges.

Depending on your Docker system configuration, you may be required to preface each docker command with **sudo**. One way to avoid having to use **sudo** with the docker commands is to create a group called "docker," and add users that will be entering docker commands to the "docker" group. We illustrated this procedure in Section 3.4.1.

3.6.1 Downloading a Pre-Built Docker Image

How do you find out what Docker images are available for download to your local machine? You can use your host's web browser, and at www.hub. docker.com, follow the link to

https://hub.docker.com/search?image%20filter=official&type=image

There you'll find a large collection of descriptive links to Docker images, a vast majority of which are "Docker Official Images."

On your Raspbeery Pi host, use the following commands to download a pre-built image of Oraclelinux:

```
bob@raspberrypi:~ $ docker pull oraclelinux:9
9: Pulling from library/oraclelinux
3a618052811d: Pull complete
Digest: sha256:103fdd36d9ff59713274481c980f72738198cf2bb87c50744632dd2c9
ec07dd6
Status: Downloaded newer image for oraclelinux:9
docker.io/library/oraclelinux:9
bob@raspberrypi:~ $
```

This will find the Oraclelinux:9 image by name on Docker Hub, and download it from Docker Hub to a local image cache. By default, it will be the latest image for Oraclelinux.

Note
When the image is successfully downloaded, you see a 12 character hash, 3a618052811d: Pull complete which is the short form of the image ID. These short image IDs are the first 12 characters of the full image ID – which can be found using the docker commands **docker inspect** or **docker images --no-trunc=true**.

3.6.2 Running an Interactive Shell

To run a short-lived container using an interactive shell in the Ubuntu image we pulled in the previous section, use the following command:

```
bob@raspberrypi:~ $ docker run -i -t oraclelinux:9 /bin/bash
[root@d13ccf512452 /]#
```

The **-i** option to the command starts an "interactive container." The **-t** option to the command creates a pseudo-TTY that attaches to stdin and stdout.

To list the files in the current working directory while in this Oraclelinux container, use the following command:

```
[root@d13ccf512452 /]# ls -la
```

To return to the host's command line, type **exit**.

To detach the tty without exiting the shell, use the escape sequence **<Ctrl-p> + <Ctrl-q>**. The container will continue to exist in a stopped state once exited. To list all containers on the host, stopped and running, use the **docker ps -a** command.

3.6.3 Starting Continually Running Processes in a Container

We now present commands that allow you to start a continually running process in a container. You start by running a container based on the Oracle Linux image, open a shell in that container, and then execute a command that will continue to run and give output.

```
bob@raspberrypi:~ $ JOB=$(docker run -d oraclelinux:9 /bin/sh -c \ "while true;
do echo Keep Going; sleep 1; done")
bob@raspberrypi:~ $
```

To view the output of the job at any point in time, use the following command:

```
bob@raspberrypi:~ $ docker logs $JOB
Keep Going
Keep Going
```

```
Keep Going
Keep Going
Keep Going
Keep Going
Output truncated...
```

To stop the process, type the following-
```
bob@raspberrypi:~ $ docker kill $JOB
d76c6d4b9b38396500a2e8d5a035179297a620fb3aa25a411bb1a7ea93a4d54f
bob@raspberrypi:~ $
```

Let's step through what the **docker run** command did.

1. First we specified the docker program code and the command we wanted to execute, run. The docker run combination runs containers.

2. We specified an image: ubuntu. This is the source of the container we ran. Docker calls this an image. In this case we used an Ubuntu OS image.

When you specify an image, Docker looks first for the image on your Docker host. If it can't find it then it downloads the image from the Docker Hub public image registry.

Next we told Docker what command to run inside our new container:

```
/bin/echo 'Hello world'
```

When our container was launched Docker created a new Oracle Linux environment and then executed the /bin/echo command inside it. We saw the result on the command line:

Hello world

So what happened to our container after that? Well Docker containers only run as long as the command you specify is active. Here, as soon as Hello world was echoed, the container stopped.

3.6.4 Various Docker Utility Commands

The following commands give you a list all running containers, all containers, and only the last container:

```
bob@raspberrypi:~ $ docker ps
bob@raspberrypi:~ $ docker ps -a
bob@raspberrypi:~ $ docker ps -l
```

The following commands show various ways of controlling containers:

To start a new container-

```
bob@raspberrypi:~ $ JOB=$(docker run -d ubuntu /bin/sh -c "while true; do echo Keep Going; sleep 1; done")
```

To stop that container-

```
bob@raspberrypi:~ $ docker stop $JOB
```

To again start that container-

```
bob@raspberrypi:~ $ docker start $JOB
```

To restart that container-

```
bob@raspberrypi:~ $ docker restart $JOB
```

To kill that container-

```
bob@raspberrypi:~ $ docker kill $JOB
```

To remove, or delete that container, after stopping it-

```
bob@raspberrypi:~ $ docker stop $JOB
bob@raspberrypi:~ $ docker rm $JOB
```

3.6.5 Committing (Saving) a Container State, Listing and Deleting Images

To save your container's state to an image, so that the state can be re-used later, you can use the **docker commit** command. When you "commit" your container, Docker only stores the diff (difference) between the original source image and the current state of the container's image. To list images you already have, use the **docker images** command.

The following command commits your container to a new named image:

```
bob@raspberrypi:~$ docker commit <container> <some_name>
```

The following command lists your Docker images:

```
bob@raspberrypi:~$ docker images
```

You now have an image state from which you can create new instances.
The following command removes an image named **ubuntu**:

```
bob@raspberrypi:~$ docker rmi ubuntu
```

3.7 Running an Important Web Application in a Docker Container

In the sections above, you achieved some primary objectives in Docker. You launched your first containers using the **docker run** command, you started an interactive container that ran in the foreground, and you also started a detached container that ran in the background. Particularly, you learned about several Docker commands, most importantly:

docker ps - Lists containers.
docker logs - Shows you the standard output of a running container.
docker stop - Stops running a container.

In the examples that follow, we will be running an important and ubiquitous web application program: Nginx. This will give you a very illustrious and informative view of what Docker containers can really, and practically, accomplish.

By containerizing Nginx, we cut down on our sysadmin overhead. We will no longer need to manage Nginx through a package manager or build it from source. The Docker container allows us to simply replace the whole container when a new version of Nginx is released. We only need to maintain the Nginx configuration file and our content.

Nginx describes itself as:

"nginx [engine x] is an HTTP and reverse proxy server, a mail proxy server, and a generic TCP proxy server – originally written by Igor Sysoev."

In practice many sysadmins use Nginx to serve web content, from flat-file websites to upstream APIs in NodeJS. In this tutorial we will serve a basic web page, so we can focus on configuring Nginx with a Docker container.

Docker containers are a popular form of a relatively old operations practice: containerization. Containerization differs from virtualization in that virtualization abstracts away the hardware, while containerization abstracts away the base OS, too. In practical terms this means we can take an application (or group of applications) and wrap them in a container (or containers) to make them modular, portable, composable, and lightweight.

This portability means you can install the Docker Engine (also referred to as Docker Core, and even just Docker) on a wide variety of OSs, and any functional container written by anyone will run on it.

If you want to learn more about Docker you can check out an introductory Docker tutorial.

3.8 Nginx and the Necessity of Exposing Ports

When a container is created using the commands **docker create** or **docker run**, by default it does not publish any of its ports to the outside world. In fact, it protects those ports heavily for security purposes.

In order to make a port available to services outside of Docker, or to Docker containers which are not connected to the container's network, we can use the **-P** or **-p** options and their arguments. These options create a protective rule, which associates, or maps a container port to a port on the Docker host, and therefore to the outside world.

The purposes of these options are as follows:

-p or **--publish list** : Publishes a container's port(s) to the host.
-P or **--publish-all** : Publishes all exposed ports to random ports.

We use the **curl** command in the sessions below to examine web output. The **curl** command in Linux is a powerful utility that allows you to interact with various types of servers and resources, using a wide range of protocols. The name "curl" stands for "Client URL."

The primary purpose of the curl command is to transfer data to or from a server using various protocols, including HTTP, HTTPS, FTP, FTPS, SCP, SFTP, LDAP, and more. It supports a wide range of options and features, making it a versatile tool for tasks such as downloading files, uploading files, making HTTP requests, testing APIs, and more.

Let's create a nginx container using Docker without any port mapping.

```
bob@raspberrypi:~ $ docker container run -d nginx
Unable to find image 'nginx:latest' locally
latest: Pulling from library/nginx
90524f7dc01b: Pull complete
14cea127239b: Pull complete
8a2be7a4590d: Pull complete
9dc7844e6774: Pull complete
a274c3e9974e: Pull complete
b24de7c2768b: Pull complete
49c25f2442ea: Pull complete
Digest: sha256:67f9a4f10d147a6e04629340e6493c9703300ca23a2f7f3aa56fe615d7
5d31ca
Status: Downloaded newer image for nginx:latest
2ca1c237c0a82f866f939f0879edbe81bcda014bb55e148e81608762a2efff2b
bob@raspberrypi:~ $
```

The above command will pull the nginx image from the Docker Hub and create a container for us.

Check the port for nginx container

```
bob@raspberrypi:~ $ docker container ls
CONTAINER ID   IMAGE  COMMAND              CREATED        STATUS       PORTS
NAMES
2ca1c237c0a8   nginx  "/docker-entrypoint. ..."  53 seconds ago  Up 51 seconds 80/tcp
exciting_zhukovsky
bob@raspberrypi:~ $
```

The above command describes the nginx container. We have assigned it by default a tcp port 80. However it is not yet "mapped," which is DockerSpeak for the establishment of an association between what's inside the container, and the outside host, particularly in terms of network connections.

Check if we get any response from localhost.

```
bob@raspberrypi:~ $ curl localhost
curl: (7) Failed to connect to localhost port 80: Connection refused
```

Connection refused because we don't have port mapping set for port 80.

Get the private IP of the container

```
bob@raspberrypi:~ $ docker container inspect 2ca1c237c0a8 | grep 'IPAddress'
            "SecondaryIPAddresses": null,
            "IPAddress": "172.17.0.2",
                    "IPAddress": "172.17.0.2",
bob@raspberrypi:~ $ curl 172.17.0.2
<!DOCTYPE html>
<html>
<head>
<title>Welcome to nginx!</title>
<style>
html { color-scheme: light dark; }
body { width: 35em; margin: 0 auto;
font-family: Tahoma, Verdana, Arial, sans-serif; }
</style>
</head>
<body>
<h1>Welcome to nginx!</h1>
<p>If you see this page, the nginx web server is successfully installed and
working. Further configuration is required.</p>

<p>For online documentation and support please refer to
<a href="http://nginx.org/">nginx.org</a>.<br/>
Commercial support is available at
<a href="http://nginx.com/">nginx.com</a>.</p>

<p><em>Thank you for using nginx.</em></p>
</body>
</html>
```

This is an HTML text representation of the content of Nginx home page.

Expose port 3000 on container. Once we expose the port, it means now this port is available to be mapped. We can re-map them using -p or -P flag.

```
bob@raspberrypi:~ $ docker container run -d --expose 3000 nginx
ac475e92dca831eeb3f52a667b574bbfb6de6bc2ff6af0ba64aa50a658369a9c
bob@raspberrypi:~ $
```

Verify if port 3000 is open

```
bob@raspberrypi:~ $ docker container ls
CONTAINER ID   IMAGE    COMMAND            CREATED        STATUS
PORTS                NAMES
ac475e92dca8   nginx    "/docker-entrypoint. ..."  35 seconds ago  Up 34 seconds
80/tcp, 3000/tcp   angry_proskuriakova
2ca1c237c0a8   nginx    "/docker-entrypoint. ..."  17 minutes ago  Up 17 minutes
80/tcp             exciting_zhukovsky
bob@raspberrypi:~ $
```

Alternatively we can expose and map the port at the same time:

```
bob@raspberrypi:~ $ docker container run -d --expose 3000 -p 80:8080 nginx
b99fd96ecd37781a123e04cad8151f962aa4f9ff5a5e84ab7f712a23d203c591
bob@raspberrypi:~ $
```

80: port that will be running on host machine.

8080: container is now port mapped with port 80.
```
bob@raspberrypi:~ $ docker ps
```

```
CONTAINER ID   IMAGE    COMMAND                 CREATED      STATUS
b99fd96ecd37   nginx    "/docker-entrypoint. ..."   A minute     Up About a minute
PORTS                        NAMES
nervous_euclid 80/tcp, 3000/tcp,  0.0.0.0:80->8080/tcp, :::80->8080/tcp
ac475e92dca8   nginx    "/docker-entrypoint. ..."   7 minutes    Up 7 minutes
80/tcp, 3000/tcp   angry_proskuriakova
2ca1c237c0a8   nginx    "/docker-entrypoint. ..."   25 minutes   Up 24 minutes
80/tcp             exciting_zhukovsky
```

```
bob@raspberrypi:~ $
bob@raspberrypi:~ $ docker container inspect b99fd96ecd37 | grep 'IPAddress'
    "SecondaryIPAddresses": null,
    "IPAddress": "172.17.0.4",
        "IPAddress": "172.17.0.4",
bob@raspberrypi:~ $
```

```
bob@raspberrypi:~ $ curl 172.17.0.4:80
<!DOCTYPE html>
<html>
<head>
<title>Welcome to nginx!</title>
<style>
html { color-scheme: light dark; }
body { width: 35em; margin: 0 auto;
```

```
font-family: Tahoma, Verdana, Arial, sans-serif; }
</style>
</head>
<body>
<h1>Welcome to nginx!</h1>
<p>If you see this page, the nginx web server is successfully installed and
working. Further configuration is required.</p>

<p>For online documentation and support please refer to
<a href="http://nginx.org/">nginx.org</a>.<br/>
Commercial support is available at
<a href="http://nginx.com/">nginx.com</a>.</p>

<p><em>Thank you for using nginx.</em></p>
</body>
</html>
bob@raspberrypi:~ $
```

Again, we see the HTML representation of the Nginx Welcome page.

We can see all the port mappings for specified container by using the following command on the host:

bob@raspberrypi:~ $ **docker container port b99fd96ecd37**
8080/tcp -> 0.0.0.0:80
8080/tcp -> [::]:80
bob@raspberrypi:~ $

In-Chapter Exercise

3.7 Is the IP address and port **172.17.0.4:80** of the above Nginx container a "public-facing" IP address and port number? For example, if you entered that URL and port number into a web browser *on another Raspberry Pi on your LAN*, would you see the Nginx Welcome page? Why, or why not?

3.8.1 Exposing a Container's IP Address on the Public Network Connected to the Host Using iptables

In order to circumvent the Docker strategy of isolating containers inside of private networks, as we illustrated and discovered above in Section 3.8, you need to map a Docker container's IP address to the host's IP address using the **iptables** command. That strategy originates in very important security concerns.

Note
You typically perform a NAT using port forwarding to achieve this.

This allows incoming, and by extension, outgoing traffic to a specific port on the host to be redirected to and from a specific port on the Docker container of interest. After all, it can be argued that the utility of having containers in the first place is to deploy them to communicate via a network with a LAN, or to other containers on the host, or to the Internet.

Here's the general process we illustrate to achieve this:

1. Find the Container's IP Address: Identify the IP address of the Docker container you want to map to the host.

2. Choose a Host Port: Decide on a port on the host that you want to use for accessing the container. For example, you might want to map host port 8080 to the container's port 80.

3. Use **iptables** command: Run the **iptables** command, with the proper options, option arguments, and command arguments, to set up the port forwarding, as follows generally:

   ```
   sudo iptables -t nat -A PREROUTING -p tcp --dport HOST_PORT -j
   DNAT --to-destination
   CONTAINER_IP:CONTAINER_PORT
   You replace HOST_PORT with the host port number you chose and CON-
   TAINER_IP and CONTAINER_PORT with the IP address and port number of the
   Docker container.
   ```

4. You enable IP forwarding (if necessary), and depending on your system's configuration, to enable IP forwarding and allow the redirection to work.

Here's how we achieved this on our Raspberry Pi system:

0. We run a Docker Nginx container mapped to a specific port on the host – port 80.

   ```
   bob@raspberrypi:~ $ docker run -p 80:80 -d nginx
   700146e28444b23b0bd6ebfd0986400a3d406d4daeeaf970d43486f6a6
   ced340
   ```

1. We examine the characteristics of that container.

   ```
   bob@raspberrypi:~ $ docker container ls
   CONTAINER ID   IMAGE COMMAND CREATED    STATUS     PORTS  NAMES
   700146e28444   nginx  "/docker-entrypoint. ..."    54 seconds
   ago      Up 53 seconds  0.0.0.0:80->80/tcp, :::80->80/tcp
   beautiful_visvesvaraya
   ```

2. We find out what the container's internal IP address is with the following command:

```
bob@raspberrypi:~ $ docker container inspect 700146e28444 | grep 'IPAddress'
        "SecondaryIPAddresses": null,
        "IPAddress": "172.17.0.2",
            "IPAddress": "172.17.0.2",
bob@raspberrypi:~ $
```

As in Section 3.8, now port 80 is exposed on the private network, at IP address 172.17.0.2. That is not a public-facing IP address! To prove that, try setting a URL in a web browser to that address. It's unreachable as a public-facing IP address on your LAN.

3. Now comes the critical command in our exposition! The **iptables** command we now deploy forwards the host's public-facing IP address and port 80 to the private network address, and port 80 of the Nginx container.

```
bob@raspberrypi:~ $ sudo iptables -t nat -A PREROUTING -p tcp -- \dport 80 -j DNAT --to-destination 172.17.0.2:80
```

4. Additionally, we make sure that on the host, port forwarding is allowed, using the following command:

```
bob@raspberrypi:~ $ sudo sysctl net.ipv4.ip_forward=1
net.ipv4.ip_forward = 1
bob@raspberrypi:~ $
```

To make this change permanent, you can edit the /etc/sysctl.conf file and set net.ipv4.ip_forward = 1.

Please note that using **iptables** directly can be a bit complex and may have limitations, especially when dealing with Docker containers that are frequently started, stopped, or have dynamically changing IP addresses. An alternative approach is to use Docker's built-in networking features to achieve similar results in a more manageable way.

5. So how do you test that our exposure of the container port 80 on your LAN actually works? Open a web browser, either on the host or on another Raspberry Pi on your LAN, and enter the URL 192.168.1.15:80. The Nginx Welcome screen appears, as follows:

Welcome to nginx!

If you see this page, the nginx web server is successfully installed and working. Further configuration is required.

For online documentation and support please refer to nginx.org.

Commercial support is available at nginx.com.

Thank you for using nginx.

In six easy steps, we exposed a port on a container we launched to a port on the host, using essentially a public IP address, rather than a private one.

3.9 Docker Nginx Review and Further Docker Examples

For the purposes of expanding our coverage of a useful container application, we will present more Nginx installations and provisioning in Docker containers. We also show how to use ZFS as the backing store for Docker.

3.9.1 Reviewing Container Basics: Run, List, Remove

As a useful review, this section shows how to run a basic container, and then remove it.

We've installed the Docker client as part of our Docker installation, so we have access to the command line tool that allows us to interact with our containers.

Run the following command to see the status of exiting containers:

```
bob@raspberrypi:~ $ sudo docker ps -a
CONTAINER ID  IMAGE      COMMAND          CREATED       STATUS        PORTS      NAMES
700146e28444  nginx      "/docker-entrypoint. ..."    24 hours ago  Up 24 hours
0.0.0.0:80->80/tcp, :::80->80/tcp   beautiful_visvesvaraya
01aa8c259b21  nginx      "/docker-entrypoint. ..."    27 hours ago  Created
vigilant_sinoussi
d76c6d4b9b38  oraclelinux:9    "/bin/sh -c 'while t..."  2 days ago    Exited (137)
2 days ago                     confident_gauss
d13ccf512452  oraclelinux:9    "/bin/bash"              2 days ago    Exited
(0) 2 days ago      vigorous_feistel
ea4e2a9baa72  2358e484cec7    "/bin/bash"             3 days ago    Exited (127)
3 days ago          eloquent_aryabhata
2b96338f770f  ubuntu        "bash"                   5 days ago    Exited
(0) 5 days ago                 trusting_shirley
57cc2ed20567  hello-world    "/hello"                6 days ago    Exited
(0) 6 days ago
relaxed_ardinghelli
bob@raspberrypi:~ $
```

We can see some basic information about the containers we've launched so far.

You see that they have nonsensical names, like vigilant_sinoussi; these names are generated automatically if you don't specify one when creating the container.

You can also see in that the hello-world example container was run 6 days ago, and exited 6 days ago.

If we run this container again with this command (replacing relaxed_ardinghelli with your own container name):

bob@raspberrypi:~ $ **docker start relaxed_ardinghelli**
relaxed_ardinghelli
bob@raspberrypi:~ $

And then run the command to list containers once more:

bob@raspberrypi:~ $ **docker ps -a**

You should now see that the container has run recently:

```
CONTAINER ID   IMAGE         COMMAND        CREATED        STATUS
PORTS          NAMES
Output truncated...
57cc2ed20567   hello-world   "/hello"       6 days ago     Exited (0)
2 minutes ago  relaxed_ardinghelli
```

By default, Docker containers run their assigned commands and then exit.

Some containers will be set up to run through a list of tasks and finish, while others will run indefinitely.

You've reviewed some Docker basics, so let's remove the hello-world image, because you won't be needing it again (remember to replace relaxed_ardinghelli with your container's name, or use your container ID, which in our case is 57cc2ed20567).

bob@raspberrypi:~ $ **docker rm relaxed_ardinghelli**
relaxed_ardinghelli
bob@raspberrypi:~ $

3.9.2 Building a Web Page for Nginx to Use as Content in a Container

It would be very useful at this point to be able to create a custom index page for a website in a container, since Nginx is running in one of our containers, and could be used to serve that page up for content-viewing on either a LAN or even the Internet. The procedures in this section allow you to have a persistent website content that's hosted by the container. Follow these basic steps:

0. stop, and then remove the Docker container we created above in Section 3.8.1 with the following commands:

    bob@raspberrypi:~ $ **docker stop beautiful_visvesvaraya**
    beautiful_visvesvaraya

```
bob@raspberrypi:~ $ docker rm beautiful_visvesvaraya
beautiful_visvesvaraya
bob@raspberrypi:~ $ docker ps
CONTAINER ID  IMAGE   COMMAND  CREATED  STATUS  PORTS   NAMES
bob@raspberrypi:~ $
```

1. You'll create a custom page for your website. This setup allows you to have persistent website content that's hosted outside the container.

    Create a new directory for your website content below your home directory and make that sub-directory the current working directory with the following commands:

    ```
    bob@raspberrypi:~ $ mkdir -p ~/docker-nginx/html
    bob@raspberrypi:~ $ cd ~/docker-nginx/html
    ```

2. Create an HTML file to serve content. The following example uses nano, but you can use your preferred text editor:

    ```
    bob@raspberrypi:~ $ nano index.html

    <html>
      <head>
        <title>Docker nginx Tutorial</title>
      </head>

      <body>
        <div class="container">
          <h1>Hello From My Website</h1>
          <p>This Nginx page is brought to you by Docker and Nginx</p>
        </div>
      </body>
    </html>
    ```

If you're using the nano text editor, exit and save this file by pressing <CTRL+X>, then Y, then <ENTER>.

You now have an index page that replaces the default Nginx Welcome page. Use the **chmod** command to give group and others **rwx** access privileges on the file index.html.

3. Linking the container to the local filesystem

You'll link Nginx to your container so that it is publicly accessible over port 80, and connect it to your website content on the host.

Docker allows you to link directories from your virtual machine's local filesystem to your container. Since you want to serve the new web page, you will need to give your container the files to render. By using Docker's *data volumes* feature, you can create a symbolic link between your host's filesystem and the container's filesystem. This allows you to edit your existing Index file, web page files, and maybe even add new ones into the host sub-directory you created above in Step 1. With a symbolic link, your container will have access to these files. If you want to read more about Docker and volumes check out the data volumes documentation.

Inside the Nginx container, it is set up by default to look for an index page at /usr/share/nginx/html. In a new Docker Nginx container, you will need to give that location access to the host directory **~/docker-nginx/html**.

To achieve this, you use the **-v** option of the **docker run** command, to link the ~/docker-nginx/html folder on your host to a relative path in the container **/usr/share/nginx/html**, with the following command:

```
bob@raspberrypi:~ $ docker run --name docker-nginx -p 80:80 -d -v \
~/docker-nginx/html:/usr/share/nginx/html nginx
```

A brief explanation of this command is as follows:

-v option specifies that you're linking a volume.
To the left of the **:** is the location of your directory on your server, **~/docker-nginx/ html**.
To the right of the **:** is the location that you are symbolically linking to your container **/usr/share/nginx/nginx/html**.

4. Repeat Steps 1 through 4 in Section 3.8.1, even if you've already done them in that section, where you exposed port 80 on the host to port 80 on this new container that's using Nginx to serve your own index. html page. Remember to use the proper container IP address in the **iptables** command.

5. Enter your host's IP address, and port 80, into a browser running on another Raspberry Pi on your LAN to view your new index.html page. Your new default page would now be displayed, instead of the Nginx Welcome page.

Alternatively, you could use **curl** to view the HTML of that index.html page on the Docker host itself, with the following command:

```
bob@raspberrypi:~/docker-nginx/html $ curl 172.17.0.2:80
```

```
<html>
  <head>
    <title>Docker nginx Tutorial</title>
  </head>

  <body>
    <div class="container">
      <h1>Hello From My Website</h1>
        <p>This Nginx page is brought to you by Docker and Nginx</p>
    </div>
```

```
  </body>
</html>
bob@raspberrypi:~/docker-nginx/html $
```

6. You can upload more content to the ~/docker-nginx/html/ directory, and it will be added to your website.

For example, if you modify your HTML file, and refresh your browser, it will be updated accordingly. You could also build a whole site out of HTML files this way. For instance, if you added a file named **another_page.html**, you could access it at **http://your_server_ip/another_page.html** without needing to interact with the container.

3.9.3 Working with the Nginx Docker Container in More Detail

You have a working Nginx Docker container that's displaying your own web page and has a public-facing IP address, (a) but how do you manage the web page content (such as adding links, or more pages), and (b) take more control of the Nginx configuration, and logging? The following section shows how to do that.

3.9.3.1 Managing Content and Configuration Files

You can create the content served by Nginx, as you saw in Section 3.9.2. And Nginx configuration files inside the container can also be edited. One way to achieve this in Nginx is to create your own Nginx configuration file. The following Docker commands and options achieve content and configuration editing for you – **docker run -v** and **docker cp**. We give a brief overview of them, taken from the Docker documentation, and online sources, in Section 3.10.

1. You're already in the directory where you're keeping your web page materials. Now you have to copy the Nginx configuration directory from the container that's running from Section 3.9.2 into the host web page directory with the following command:

```
bob@raspberrypi:~/docker-nginx/html $ docker cp \
docker-nginx:/etc/nginx/conf.d/default.conf default.conf
Successfully copied 3.07kB to /home/bob/docker-nginx/html/default.conf
bob@raspberrypi:~/docker-nginx/html $
```

2. Stop and remove the container from Section 3.9.2, so you can reuse the port forwarding from the host, with the following commands:

```
bob@raspberrypi:~/docker-nginx/html $ docker stop docker-nginx
docker-nginx
bob@raspberrypi:~/docker-nginx/html $ docker rm docker-nginx
docker-nginx
bob@raspberrypi:~/docker-nginx/html $
```

3. Maintaining content and configuration from the Docker host

As shown in Section 3.9.2, when you created an Nginx container, you associated, or mounted, a local directory on the Docker host to a directory in the container with the volume **-v** option of the **docker run** command. Additionally, the Nginx Docker image uses the default Nginx configuration, which deploys /usr/share/nginx/html inside the container as the container's root directory, and puts configuration files in /etc/nginx. For a Docker host with content in the local host directory ~/docker-nginx/html, and configuration files on the host in ~/docker-nginx/default.conf, run this command:

```
bob@raspberrypi:~/docker-nginx/html $ docker run --name docker-nginx -p 80:80\
-v ~/docker-nginx/html:/usr/share/nginx/html \
-v ~/docker-nginx/default.conf:/etc/nginx/conf.d/default.conf -d nginx
bob@raspberrypi:~/docker-nginx/html $
```

Any change you make to the files in the local directories ~/docker-nginx/ html and ~/docker-nginx/default.conf on the Docker host are reflected in the directories /usr/share/nginx/html and /etc/nginx/conf.d/default.conf in the container. The **:ro** option means these directors are read only *inside the container*.

3.9.4 Using ZFS as the Backing Store for Docker Containers

Similar to your using ZFS as the storage backend for LXC/LXD containers, shown as part of the initialization routine for LXC/LXD in Step 5 of Example 3.1, Docker can also assign ZFS as a backing store for containers. This section shows how to do that and also additionally allows you to create containers on an external medium, which must necessarily be different from the system/boot medium.

Note
Changing the storage driver makes any containers you have already created *inaccessible* on the local system. But you can use the **docker save** command to save already-pulled/run containers, and push existing images to Docker Hub, or a private repository, so that you do not need to re-create them later. You also must have ZFS installed on your Raspberry Pi system.

Prerequisites:

1. ZFS requires its datasets to be on one or more dedicated block devices, preferably SSDs, which incidentally incorporates a feature which is like ECC memory, and as noted, the block device *cannot* be the system/boot medium. There are two main types of devices in Linux systems, character and block devices. Character devices are those that don't use buffering, and block devices are those which use a cache to access them. Block devices are also random access devices, and most character devices are not. ZFS filesystems can be mounted on block devices, but also on files, which is what LXC/LXD does by default in its initialization process if you specify ZFS as the backing store for containers. An example of a block device is a USB-mounted SSD.

2. The /var/lib/docker/ directory in this section is mounted on a ZFS-formatted filesystem, which as we illustrate with the **zpool create** command in Step 5 of the following Procedures is achieved by ZFS, no matter what the previous filesystem format of the block device used here was at the start.

Procedures:

1. Insert a useable USB medium into one of the ports on your Raspberry Pi. In this example, we added a 1 TB SSD. Then use the **lsblk** command to find out its name. In our case, the 1 TB drive (listed with a capacity of 953.9 G) was /*dev*/sda, with a single partition on it named /*dev*/sda1.

    ```
    $ sudo su -
    root@raspberrypi:~# lsblk

    NAME     MAJ:MIN   RM   SIZE     RO   TYPE   MOUNTPOINT
    loop0    7:0       0    104.3M   1    loop   /snap/core/15515
    loop1    7:1       0    93.3M    1    loop   /snap/core/15930
    loop2    7:2       0    68.5M    1    loop   /snap/core22/861
    loop3    7:3       0    68.5M    1    loo    /snap/core22/867
    loop4    7:4       0    161.3M   1    loop   /snap/lxd/25116
    sda      8:0       0    953.9G   0    disk
    └─sda1   8:1       0    953.9G   0    part   /media/bob/E45F-158E
    sdb      8:16      0    476.9G   0    disk
    ├─sdb1   8:17      0    256M     0    part   /boot
    └─sdb2   8:18      0    476.7G   0    part   /
    ```

2. The critical step! Unmount the USB medium, using the following umount command:

    ```
    root@raspberrypi:~# umount /dev/sda1
    root@raspberrypi:~#
    ```

3. First stop Docker with the following command:

   root@raspberrypi:~# **systemctl stop docker**

4. Delete everything in */var*/lib/docker on the host.

   root@raspberrypi:~# **rm -rf /var/lib/docker/***

5. Create the zpool with an appropriate name (we named ours zpool-docker4).

   root@raspberrypi:~# **zpool create -f zpool-docker4 -m /var/lib/docker / dev/sdb**

6. List your ZFS filesystems.

   ```
   root@raspberrypi:~# zfs list
   NAME                               USED     AVAIL    REFER   MOUNTPOINT
   Default                            1.65M    7.26G    24K     legacy
   default/buckets                    24K      7.26G    24K     legacy
   default/containers                 24K      7.26G    24K     legacy
   default/custom                     24K      7.26G    24K     legacy
   default/deleted                    144K     7.26G    24K     legacy
   default/deleted/buckets            24K      7.26G    24K     legacy
   default/deleted/containers         24K      7.26G    24K     legacy
   default/deleted/custom             24K      7.26G    24K     legacy
   default/deleted/images             24K      7.26G    24K     legacy
   default/deleted/virtual-machines   24K      7.26G    24K     legacy
   default/images                     24K      7.26G    24K     legacy
   default/virtual-machines           24K      7.26G    24K     legacy
   zpool-docker4                      444K     922G     96K     /var/lib/docker
   ```

7. Edit the daemon.json file that holds configuration data for Docker and add the text shown.

   root@raspberrypi:~# **nano /etc/docker/daemon.json**

   ```
   {
       "storage-driver": "zfs"
   }
   ```

   Save and exit the .json file.

8. Start up Docker with the new ZFS storage driver for the storage backend.

   root@raspberrypi:~# **systemctl start docker**

9. Use the docker info command to get a view of Docker configuration settings.

```
root@raspberrypi:~# docker info
Client: Docker Engine - Community
 Version:   24.0.5
 Context:   default
 Debug Mode: false
 Plugins:
  buildx: Docker Buildx (Docker Inc.)
   Version: v0.11.2
   Path:    /usr/libexec/docker/cli-plugins/docker-buildx
  compose: Docker Compose (Docker Inc.)
   Version: v2.20.2
   Path:    /usr/libexec/docker/cli-plugins/docker-compose

Server:
 Containers: 0
 Running: 0
 Paused: 0
 Stopped: 0
 Images: 0
 Server Version: 24.0.5
 Storage Driver: zfs
 Zpool: zpool-docker4
 Zpool Health: ONLINE
 Parent Dataset: zpool-docker4
 Space Used By Parent: 524288
 Space Available: 990526308352

Output truncated...
```

10. Take a look at where Docker keeps its machinery.

```
root@raspberrypi:~# cd /var/lib/docker
root@raspberrypi:/var/lib/docker# ls
buildkit containers engine-id image network plugins runtimes swarm tmp
volumes zfs
root@raspberrypi:/var/lib/docker#
```

Any container you build now will be stored on the USB-mounted medium that is constructed on zpool-docker4 and will use ZFS as its backing store.

11. Let's build a container from an image and look into it.

```
root@raspberrypi:~# docker ps -a
CONTAINER ID  IMAGE   COMMAND  CREATED  STATUS  PORTS   NAMES

root@raspberrypi:~# docker pull oraclelinux:9
9: Pulling from library/oraclelinux
55f10f17cb98: Pull complete
Digest: sha256:a704f734a5745776d570fffe223013e1e3f626aa0e650352bfd2
e84ff307405b
Status: Downloaded newer image for oraclelinux:9
```

```
docker.io/library/oraclelinux:9
root@raspberrypi:~# docker run -i -t oraclelinux:9 /bin/bash
[root@129404adf287 /]# ls
afs bin boot dev etc home lib lib64 media mnt opt proc root run sbin
srv sys tmp usr var
```

At this point, you could do accountant creation, file maintenance, install software, etc., but you'll just exit at this point.

```
[root@129404adf287 /]# exit
exit
root@raspberrypi:~# docker ps -a
CONTAINER ID   IMAGE          COMMAND      CREATED      STATUS        PORTS    NAMES
129404adf287 oraclelinux:9 "/bin/bash"  3 minutes ago   Exited (0) 6 seconds ago
lucid_hamilton
root@raspberrypi:~#
root@raspberrypi:~#
```

In-Chapter Exercises

3.8 How do you know that the oraclelinux9 container is built on a ZFS filesystem?

3.9 How would you create a mirror of the Docker oraclelinux9 container?

3.10 What command in oraclelinux installs software into the container?

3.10 A Docker Reference

In this section, we first give you a listing of what can be obtained via help on the Raspberry Pi command line. Then we delve a little more deeply into specific commands, as they are organized in logical groupings, in an encyclopedia-like presentation.

If you type just plain **docker** on the command line, you get the following display:

$ docker

Usage: docker [OPTIONS] COMMAND

A self-sufficient runtime for containers

Common Commands:
run	Create and run a new container from an image
exec	Execute a command in a running container
ps	List containers
build	Build an image from a Dockerfile

pull	Download an image from a registry
push	Upload an image to a registry
images	List images
login	Log in to a registry
logout	Log out from a registry
search	Search Docker Hub for images
version	Show the Docker version information
info	Display system-wide information

Management Commands:

builder	Manage builds
buildx*	Docker Buildx (Docker Inc., v0.11.2)
compose*	Docker Compose (Docker Inc., v2.20.2)
container	Manage containers
context	Manage contexts
image	Manage images
manifest	Manage Docker image manifests and manifest lists
network	Manage networks
plugin	Manage plugins
system	Manage Docker
trust	Manage trust on Docker images
volume	Manage volumes

Swarm Commands:

| swarm | Manage Swarm |

Commands:

attach	Attach local standard input, output, and error streams to a running container
commit	Create a new image from a container's changes
cp	Copy files/folders between a container and the local filesystem
create	Create a new container
diff	Inspect changes to files or directories on a container's filesystem
events	Get real time events from the server
export	Export a container's filesystem as a tar archive
history	Show the history of an image
import	Import the contents from a tarball to create a filesystem image
inspect	Return low-level information on Docker objects
kill	Kill one or more running containers
load	Load an image from a tar archive or STDIN
logs	Fetch the logs of a container
pause	Pause all processes within one or more containers
port	List port mappings or a specific mapping for the container
rename	Rename a container

restart	Restart one or more containers
rm	Remove one or more containers
rmi	Remove one or more images
save	Save one or more images to a tar archive (streamed to STDOUT by default)
start	Start one or more stopped containers
stats	Display a live stream of container(s) resource usage statistics
stop	Stop one or more running containers
tag	Create a tag TARGET_IMAGE that refers to SOURCE_IMAGE
top	Display the running processes of a container
unpause	Unpause all processes within one or more containers
update	Update configuration of one or more containers
wait	Block until one or more containers stop, then print their exit codes

Global Options:

	--config string	Location of client config files (default "/home/bob/.docker")
-c,	--context string	Name of the context to use to connect to the daemon (overrides DOCKER_HOST env var and default context set with "docker context use")
-D,	--debug	Enable debug mode
-H,	--host list	Daemon socket to connect to
-l,	--log-level string	Set the logging level ("debug", "info", "warn", "error", "fatal") (default "info")
	--tls	Use TLS; implied by --tlsverify
	--tlscacert string	Trust certs signed only by this CA (default "/home/bob/.docker/ca.pem")
	--tlscert string	Path to TLS certificate file (default "/home/bob/.docker/cert.pem")
	--tlskey string	Path to TLS key file (default "/home/bob/.docker/key.pem")
	--tlsverify	Use TLS and verify the remote
-v,	--version	Print version information and quit

Run 'docker COMMAND --help' for more information on a command.

For more help on how to use Docker, head to https://docs.docker.com/go/guides/
$

If you want specific help on a command, for example, the **stop** command, type the following-

$ docker stop --help

Usage: docker stop [OPTIONS] CONTAINER [CONTAINER...]

Stop one or more running containers

Aliases:
docker container stop, docker stop

Options:
-s, --signal string   Signal to send to the container
-t, --time int   Seconds to wait before killing the container
$

Following is a listing, organized by major usage divisions, of many of the commands found in Section 3.9. The primary online source for complete descriptions of these commands is https://docs.docker.com/engine/reference/commandline/cli/

3.10.1 Container Management Commands
```
*************************************************************************************
```
docker ps

Usage :
docker ps [OPTIONS]

Description:
List containers
Options:
Option Short Default Description

Option	Short	Default	Description
--all	-a	false	Show all containers (default shows just running)
--filter	-f		Filter output based on conditions provided
--format			Format output using a custom template: 'table': Print output in table format with column headers (default) 'table TEMPLATE': Print output in table format using the given Go template 'json': Print in JSON format 'TEMPLATE': Print output using the given Go template. Refer to https://docs.docker.com/go/formatting/open_in_new for more information about formatting output with templates
--last	-n	-1	Show n last created containers (includes all states)
--latest	-l	false	Show the latest created container (includes all states)
--no-trunc		false	Don't truncate output
--quiet	-q	false	Only display container IDs
--size	-s	false	Display total file sizes

Examples:
Do not truncate output (--no-trunc)
Running docker ps --no-trunc showing 2 linked containers.

content_copy
$ docker ps –no-trunc

Show both running and stopped containers (-a, --all)
The docker ps command only shows running containers by default. To see all containers, use the --all (or -a) flag:

$ docker ps -a
docker ps groups exposed ports into a single range if possible. E.g., a container that exposes TCP ports 100, 101, 102 displays 100-102/tcp in the PORTS column.

```
*****************************************************************************************
```
docker create

Usage:

docker create [OPTIONS] IMAGE [COMMAND] [ARG...]

Description:
The docker container create (or shorthand: docker create) command creates a new container from the specified image, without starting it.

When creating a container, the docker daemon creates a writeable container layer over the specified image and prepares it for running the specified command. The container ID is then printed to STDOUT. This is similar to docker run -d except the container is never started. You can then use the docker container start (or shorthand: docker start) command to start the container at any point.

Options:

Option	Short	Default	Description
--add-host			Add a custom host-to-IP mapping (host:ip)
--annotation	map[]		API 1.43+ Add an annotation to the container (passed through to the OCI runtime)
--attach	-a		Attach to STDIN, STDOUT or STDERR
--mount			Attach a filesystem mount to the container
--name			Assign a name to the container
--net			Connect a container to a network
--rm		false	Automatically remove the container when it exits

Examples:
Create and start a container
The following example creates an interactive container with a pseudo-tty attached, then starts the container and attaches to it:

$ docker container create -i -t --name mycontainer alpine
6d8af538ec541dd581ebc2a24153a28329acb5268abe5ef868c1f1a261221752

$ docker container start --attach -i mycontainer
/ # echo hello world
hello world
The above is the equivalent of a docker run:

$ docker run -it --name mycontainer2 alpine
/ # echo hello world
hello world

****

docker rename
Usage:

docker rename CONTAINER NEW_NAME

Description:

The docker rename command renames a container.
Example:
$ **docker rename my_container my_new_container**

****

docker rm

Usage:

docker rm [OPTIONS] CONTAINER [CONTAINER...]

Description:
Remove one or more containers

Options:

Option	Short	Default	Description
--force	-f	false	Force the removal of a running container (uses SIGKILL)
--link	-l	false	Remove the specified link
--volumes	-v	false	Remove anonymous volumes associated with the container

Examples:
Remove a container
This removes the container referenced under the link /redis.

$ **docker rm /redis**

/redis

Remove a link specified with --link on the default bridge network (--link)
This removes the underlying link between /webapp and the /redis containers on the default bridge network, removing all network communication between the two containers. This does not apply when --link is used with user-specified networks.

$ docker rm --link /webapp/redis

/webapp/redis

Force-remove a running container (--force)
This command force-removes a running container.

$ docker rm --force redis

redis

The main process inside the container referenced under the link redis will receive SIGKILL, then the container will be removed.

****

docker logs

Usage:

docker logs [OPTIONS] CONTAINER

Description:
The docker logs command batch-retrieves logs present at the time of execution.

The docker logs --follow command will continue streaming the new output from the container's STDOUT and STDERR.

Passing a negative number or a non-integer to --tail is invalid and the value is set to all in that case.

The docker logs --timestamps command will add an RFC3339Nano timestampopen_in_new, for example 2014-09-16T06:17:46.000000000Z, to each log entry. To ensure that the timestamps are aligned the nano-second part of the timestamp will be padded with zero when necessary.

The docker logs --details command will add on extra attributes, such as environment variables and labels, provided to --log-opt when creating the container.

Options:

Option	Short	Default	Description
--details		false	Show extra details provided to logs
--follow	-f	false	Follow log output
--since			Show logs since timestamp (e.g. 2013-01-02T13:23:37Z) or relative (e.g. 42m for 42 minutes)
--tail	-n	all	Number of lines to show from the end of the logs

--timestamps -t   false   Show timestamps
--until   API 1.35+ Show logs before a timestamp
                                       (e.g. 2013-01-02T13:23:37Z) or relative (e.g.
                                       42m for 42 minutes)

Examples:
Retrieve logs until a specific point in time (--until)
In order to retrieve logs before a specific point in time, run:

```
$ docker run --name test -d busybox sh -c "while true; do $(echo date); sleep\
1; done"
$ date
Tue 14 Nov 2017 16:40:00 CET
$ docker logs -f --until=2s test
Tue 14 Nov 2017 16:40:00 CET
Tue 14 Nov 2017 16:40:01 CET
Tue 14 Nov 2017 16:40:02 CET
```

****

docker events

Usage:

docker events [OPTIONS]

Description:
Use docker events to get real-time events from the server. These events
differ per Docker object type. Different event types have different scopes.
Local scoped events are only seen on the node they take place on, and swarm
scoped events are seen on all managers.

Only the last 1000 log events are returned. You can use filters to further
limit the number of events returned.

Options:

Option	Short	Default	Description
--filter	-f		Filter output based on conditions provided
--format			Format the output using the given Go template
--since			Show all events created since timestamp
--until			Stream events until this timestamp

Examples:
Basic example
You'll need two shells for this example.

Shell 1: Listening for events:

$ docker events

Shell 2: Start and stop containers:

$ docker create --name test alpine:latest top
$ docker start test
$ docker stop test

Shell 1: (Again .. now showing events):

```
2017-01-05T00:35:58.859401177+08:00 container create 0fdb48addc82871eb34eb
23a847cfd033dedd1a0a37bef2e6d9eb3870fc7ff37 (image=alpine:latest, name=test)
Output truncated...
To exit the docker events command, use CTRL+C
```

****

docker update

Usage:
docker update [OPTIONS] CONTAINER [CONTAINER...]

Description:
The docker update command dynamically updates container configuration. You can use this command to prevent containers from consuming too many resources from their Docker host. With a single command, you can place limits on a single container or on many. To specify more than one container, provide space-separated list of container names or IDs.

Options:

Option	Short	Default	Description
--blkio-weight		0	Block IO (relative weight), between 10 and 1000, or 0 to disable (default 0)
--cpu-period		0	Limit CPU CFS (Completely Fair Scheduler) period
--cpu-quota		0	Limit CPU CFS (Completely Fair Scheduler) quota
--cpu-rt-period		0	API 1.25+ Limit the CPU real-time period in microseconds
--cpu-rt-runtime		0	API 1.25+ Limit the CPU real-time runtime in microseconds
--cpu-shares	-c	0	CPU shares (relative weight)
--cpus			API 1.29+ Number of CPUs
--cpuset-cpus			CPUs in which to allow execution (0-3, 0,1)

--cpuset-mems			MEMs in which to allow execution (0-3, 0,1)
--memory	-m	0	Memory limit
--memory-reservation		0	Memory soft limit
--memory-swap		0	Swap limit equal to memory plus swap: -1 to enable unlimited swap
--pids-limit		0	API 1.40+ Tune container pids limit (set -1 for unlimited)
--restart			Restart policy to apply when a container exits

Examples:

Update a container's cpu-shares (--cpu-shares)
To limit a container's cpu-shares to 512, first identify the container name or ID. You can use docker ps to find these values. You can also use the ID returned from the docker run command. Then, do the following:

$ docker update --cpu-shares 512 abebf7571666

****

docker port

Usage:
docker port CONTAINER [PRIVATE_PORT[/PROTO]]

Description:
List port mappings or a specific mapping for the container

Examples:
Show all mapped ports
   You can find out all the ports mapped by not specifying a PRIVATE_PORT, or just a specific mapping:

```
content_copy
$ docker ps
CONTAINER ID    IMAGE           COMMAND         CREATED         STATUS
PORTS                                           NAMES
b650456536c7    busybox:latest  t op            54 minutes ago  Up 54 minutes
0.0.0.0:1234->9876/tcp, 0.0.0.0:4321->7890/tcp  test
```

$ docker port test

```
7890/tcp -> 0.0.0.0:4321
9876/tcp -> 0.0.0.0:1234
```

****

3.10.2 Running a Container

****

docker run

Usage:
docker run [OPTIONS] IMAGE [COMMAND] [ARG...]

Description:
The docker run command runs a command in a new container, pulling the image if needed and starting the container.

You can restart a stopped container with all its previous changes intact using docker start. Use docker ps -a to view a list of all containers, including those that are stopped.

Options:

Option	Short	Default	Description
--add-host			Add a custom host-to-IP mapping (host:ip)
--annotation		map[]	API 1.43+ Add an annotation to the container (passed through to the OCI runtime)
--attach	-a		Attach to STDIN, STDOUT or STDERR

Examples:
Create, start, and provide a custom name for the container:

$ docker run --name [container-name] [image]

Establish a connection with a container by mapping a host port to a container port:

$ docker run -p [host-port]:[container-port] [image]

Run a container and remove it after it stops:

$ docker run --rm [image]

Run a detached (background) container:

$ docker run -d [image]

Start an interactive process, such as a shell, in a container:

$ docker run -it [image]

****

docker start

Usage:
docker start [OPTIONS] CONTAINER [CONTAINER...]

Description:
Start one or more stopped containers

Options:

Option	Short	Default	Description
--attach	-a	false	Attach STDOUT/STDERR and forward signals
--checkpoint			experimental (daemon) Restore from this checkpoint
--checkpoint-dir			experimental (daemon) Use a custom checkpoint storage directory
--detach-keys			Override the key sequence for detaching a container
--interactive	-i	False	Attach container's STDIN

Examples:

$ **docker start my_container**

****
docker stop

Usage:
docker stop [OPTIONS] CONTAINER [CONTAINER...]

Description:
The main process inside the container will receive SIGTERM, and after a grace period, SIGKILL. The first signal can be changed with the STOPSIGNAL instruction in the container's Dockerfile, or the --stop-signal option to docker run.

Options:

Option	Short	Default	Description
--signal	-s		Signal to send to the container
--time	-t	0	Seconds to wait before killing the container

Examples:

$ **docker stop my_container**

****

docker kill

Usage:
docker kill [OPTIONS] CONTAINER [CONTAINER...]

Description:
The docker kill subcommand kills one or more containers. The main process inside the container is sent SIGKILL signal (default), or the signal that is specified with the --signal option. You can reference a container by its ID, ID-prefix, or name.

The --signal flag sets the system call signal that is sent to the container. This signal can be a signal name in the format SIG<NAME>, for instance SIGINT, or an unsigned number that matches a position in the kernel's syscall table, for instance 2.

While the default (SIGKILL) signal will terminate the container, the signal set through --signal may be non-terminal, depending on the container's main process. For example, the SIGHUP signal in most cases will be non-terminal, and the container will continue running after receiving the signal.

Options:

Option	Short	Default	Description
--signal	-s		Signal to send to the container

Examples:
Send a KILL signal to a container
The following example sends the default SIGKILL signal to the container named **my_container**:

$ docker kill my_container

Send a custom signal to a container (--signal)
The following example sends a SIGHUP signal to the container named my_container:

$ docker kill --signal=SIGHUP my_container

You can specify a custom signal either by name or number. The SIG prefix is optional, so the following examples are equivalent:

$ docker kill --signal=SIGHUP my_container
$ docker kill --signal=HUP my_container
$ docker kill --signal=1 my_container

****

docker exec

Usage:
docker exec [OPTIONS] CONTAINER COMMAND [ARG...]

Description:
The docker exec command runs a new command in a running container.

The command started using docker exec only runs while the container's primary process (PID 1) is running, and it is not restarted if the container is restarted.

COMMAND runs in the default directory of the container. If the underlying image has a custom directory specified with the WORKDIR directive in its Dockerfile, this directory is used instead.

COMMAND must be an executable. A chained or a quoted command does not work. For example, docker exec -it my_container sh -c "echo a && echo b" does work, but docker exec -it my_container "echo a && echo b" does not.

Options:

Option	Short	Default	Description
--detach	-d	false	Detached mode: run command in the background
--detach-keys			Override the key sequence for detaching a container
--env	-e		API 1.25+ Set environment variables
--env-file			API 1.25+ Read in a file of environment variables
--interactive	-i	False	Keep STDIN open even if not attached
--privileged		False	Give extended privileges to the command
--tty	-t	False	Allocate a pseudo-TTY
--user	-u		Username or UID (format: <name | uid>[:<group | gid>])
--workdir	-w		API 1.35+ Working directory inside the container

Examples:
Run docker exec on a running container
First, start a container.

$ docker run --name mycontainer -d -i -t alpine /bin/sh

This creates and starts a container named mycontainer from an alpine image with an sh shell as its main process. The -d option (shorthand for --detach) sets the container to run in the background, in detached mode, with a pseudo-TTY attached (-t). The -i option is set to keep STDIN attached (-i), which prevents the sh process from exiting immediately.

Next, execute a command on the container.

$ docker exec -d mycontainer touch /tmp/execWorks
This creates a new file /tmp/execWorks inside the running container mycontainer, in the background.

Next, execute an interactive sh shell on the container.

$ docker exec -it mycontainer sh
This starts a new shell session in the container mycontainer

****

3.10.3 Docker Images

****

docker pull

Usage:
docker pull [OPTIONS] NAME[:TAG|@DIGEST]

Description:
Most of your images will be created on top of a base image from the Docker Hub registry.
Docker Hub contains many pre-built images that you can pull and try without needing to define and configure your own.
To download a particular image, or set of images (i.e., a repository), use docker pull.

Options:

Option	Short	Default	Description
--all-tags	-a	false	Download all tagged images in the repository
--disable-content-trust		true	Skip image verification
--platform			API 1.32+ Set platform if server is multi-platform capable
--quiet	-q	false	Suppress verbose output

Examples:

Pull an image from Docker Hub
To download a particular image, or set of images (i.e., a repository), use docker image pull (or the docker pull shorthand). If no tag is provided, Docker Engine uses the:latest tag as a default. This example pulls the debian:latest image:

$ docker image pull debian
Using default tag: latest
latest: Pulling from library/debian
e756f3fdd6a3: Pull complete
Digest: sha256:3f1d6c17773a45c97bd8f158d665c9709d7b29ed7917ac934086ad96
f92e4510
Status: Downloaded newer image for debian:latest
docker.io/library/debian:latest

Docker images can consist of multiple layers. In the example above, the image consists of a single layer: e756f3fdd6a3. Layers can be reused by images. For example, the debian:bullseye image shares its layer with the debian:latest. Pulling the debian:bullseye image therefore only pulls its metadata, but not its layers, because the layer is already present locally:

$ docker image pull debian:bullseye

****

docker commit

Usage:
docker commit [OPTIONS] CONTAINER [REPOSITORY[:TAG]]

Description:
It can be useful to commit a container's file changes or settings into a new image. This allows you to debug a container by running an interactive shell, or to export a working dataset to another server. Generally, it is better to use Dockerfiles to manage your images in a documented and maintainable way. Read more about valid image names and tags.

The commit operation will not include any data contained in volumes mounted inside the container.

Options:

Option	Short	Default	Description
--author	-a		Author (e.g., John Hannibal Smith <hannibal@a-team.com>)
--change	-c		Apply Dockerfile instruction to the created image
--message	-m		Commit message
--pause	-p	true	Pause container during commit

Examples:
Commit a container

$ docker commit c3f279d17e0a svendowideit/testimage:version3

f5283438590d

$ docker images

REPOSITORY	TAG	ID	CREATED	SIZE
svendowideit/testimage	version3	f5283438590d	16 seconds ago	335.7

****

docker images

Usage:
docker images [OPTIONS] [REPOSITORY[:TAG]]

Description:
The default docker images will show all top level images, their repository and tags, and their size.

Docker images have intermediate layers that increase reusability, decrease disk usage, and speed up docker build by allowing each step to be cached. These intermediate layers are not shown by default.

The SIZE is the cumulative space taken up by the image and all its parent images. This is also the disk space used by the contents of the Tar file created when your docker save an image.

An image will be listed more than once if it has multiple repository names or tags. This single image (identifiable by its matching IMAGE ID) uses up the SIZE listed only once.

Options:

Option	Short	Default	Description
--all	-a	false	Show all images (default hides intermediate images)
--digests		false	Show digests
--filter	-f		Filter output based on conditions provided
--format			Format output using a custom template: 'table'
--no-trunc	false		Don't truncate output
--quiet	-q	false	Only show image IDs

Examples:
List the most recently created images

$ docker images

REPOSITORY	TAG		IMAGE ID	CREATED	SIZE
<none>	<none>		77af4d6b9913	19 hours ago	1.089 GB
committ	latest		b6fa739cedf5	19 hours ago	1.089 GB
<none>	<none>		78a85c484f71	19 hours ago	1.089 GB
Docker	latest		30557a29d5ab	20 hours ago	1.089 GB
<none>	<none>		5ed6274db6ce	24 hours ago	1.089 GB
postgres		9	746b819f315e	4 days ago	213.4 MB
postgres		9.3	746b819f315e	4 days ago	213.4 MB
postgres		9.3.5	746b8 19f315e	4 days ago	213.4 MB
postgres		latest	746b819f315e	4 days ago	213.4 MB

****

docker rmi

Usage:
docker rmi [OPTIONS] IMAGE [IMAGE...]

Description:
Removes (and un-tags) one or more images from the host node. If an image has multiple tags, using this command with the tag as a parameter only removes the tag. If the tag is the only one for the image, both the image and the tag are removed.

This does not remove images from a registry. You cannot remove an image of a running container unless you use the -f option. To see all images on a host use the **docker image ls** command.

Options:

Option	Short	Default	Description
--force	-f	false	Force removal of the image
--no-prune		false	Do not delete untagged parents

Examples:
You can remove an image using its short or long ID, its tag, or its digest. If an image has one or more tags referencing it, you must remove all of them before the image is removed. Digest references are removed automatically when an image is removed by tag.

$ docker images

REPOSITORY	TAG	IMAGE ID	CREATED	SIZE
test1	latest	fd484f19954f	23 seconds ago	7 B (virtual 4.964 MB)
Test	latest	fd484f19954f	23 seconds ago	7 B (virtual 4.964 MB)
test2	latest	fd484f19954f	23 seconds ago	7 B (virtual 4.964 MB)

$ docker rmi fd484f19954f

Error: Conflict, cannot delete image fd484f19954f because it is tagged in multiple repositories, use -f to force

2013/12/11 05:47:16 Error: failed to remove one or more images

$ docker rmi test1:latest

Untagged: test1:latest

$ docker rmi test2:latest

Untagged: test2:latest

****

3.10.4 General Management Commands

****
docker inspect

Usage:
docker inspect [OPTIONS] NAME|ID [NAME|ID...]

Description:

Docker inspect provides detailed information on constructs controlled by Docker.
By default, docker inspect will render results in a JSON array.
Format the output (--format)
If a format is specified, the given template will be executed for each result.
Go's text/templateopen_in_new package describes all the details of the format.
Specify target type (--type)
--type container | image | node | network | secret | service | volume | task | plugin

The docker inspect command matches any type of object by either ID or name. In some cases multiple type of objects (for example, a container and a volume) exist with the same name, making the result ambiguous.
To restrict docker inspect to a specific type of object, use the --type option.

Options:

Option	Short	Default	Description
--format	-f		Format output using a custom template: 'json'.
--size	-s	false	Display total file sizes if the type is container
--type			Return JSON for specified type

Examples:
Get an instance's IP address
  For the most part, you can pick out any field from the JSON in a fairly
straightforward manner.

**$ docker inspect --format='{{range .NetworkSettings.Networks}}{{.IPAddress}}
{{end}}' $INSTANCE_ID**

Get an instance's MAC address
**$ docker inspect --format='{{range .NetworkSettings.Networks}}{{.MacAddress}}
{{end}}' $INSTANCE_ID**

Get an instance's log path
$ docker inspect --format='{{.LogPath}}' $INSTANCE_ID

****

docker version

Usage:
docker version [OPTIONS]

Description:
The version command prints the current version number for all independ-
ently versioned Docker components. Use the --format option to customize
the output.
  The version command (docker version) outputs the version numbers of
Docker components, while the --version flag (docker --version) outputs the
version number of the Docker CLI you are using.

Default output
The default output renders all version information divided into two
sections: the "Client" section contains information about the Docker CLI and
client components and the "Server" section contains information about the
Docker Engine and components used by the Engine, such as the "Containerd"
and "Runc" OCI Runtimes.
  The information shown may differ depending on how you installed Docker
and what components are in use. The following example shows the output
on a macOS machine running Docker Desktop:

Options:

Option	Short	Default	Description
--format	-f		Format output using a custom tem-plate: 'json': Print in JSON format 'TEMPLATE': Print output using the given Go template.

Examples:

$ docker version

```
Client: Docker Engine - Community
Version:        24.0.5
API version:    1.43
Go version:     go1.20.6
Git commit:     ced0996
Built:          Fri Jul 21 20:35:38 2023
OS/Arch:        linux/arm64
Context:        default

Server: Docker Engine - Community
Engine:
 Version:       24.0.5
 API version:   1.43 (minimum version 1.12)
 Go version:    go1.20.6
 Git commit:    a61e2b4
 Built:         Fri Jul 21 20:35:38 2023
 OS/Arch:       linux/arm64
 Experimental:  false
containerd:
 Version:       1.6.22
 GitCommit:     8165feabfdfe38c65b599c4993d227328c231fca
runc:
 Version:       1.1.8
 GitCommit:     v1.1.8-0-g82f18fe
docker-init:
 Version:       0.19.0
 GitCommit:     de40ad0
```

Format the output (--format)
The formatting option (--format) pretty-prints the output using a Go template, which allows you to customize the output format, or to obtain specific information from the output. Refer to the format command and log output page for details of the format.

Get the server version
$ docker version --format '{{.Server.Version}}'

24.0.5
Get the client API version
The following example prints the API version that is used by the client:

$ docker version --format '{{.Client.APIVersion}}'
1.43

****

docker info

Usage:
docker info [OPTIONS]

Description:
This command displays system wide information regarding the Docker installation. Information displayed includes the kernel version and number of containers and images. The number of images shown is the number of unique images. The same image tagged under different names is counted only once.

If a format is specified, the given template will be executed instead of the default format. Go's text/templateopen_in_new package describes all the details of the format.

Depending on the storage driver in use, additional information can be shown, such as pool name, data file, metadata file, data space used, total data space, metadata space used, and total metadata space.

The data file is where the images are stored and the metadata file is where the meta data regarding those images are stored. When run for the first time Docker allocates a certain amount of data space and meta data space from the space available on the volume where /var/lib/docker is mounted.

Options:

Option	Short	Default	Description
--format	-f		Format output using a custom template: 'json': Print in JSON format
			'TEMPLATE': Print output using the given Go template.

Examples:

```
Client: Docker Engine - Community
 Version:   24.0.5
 Context:   default
 Debug Mode: false
 Plugins:
  buildx: Docker Buildx (Docker Inc.)
   Version: v0.11.2
   Path:   /usr/libexec/docker/cli-plugins/docker-buildx
  compose: Docker Compose (Docker Inc.)
   Version: v2.20.2
   Path:   /usr/libexec/docker/cli-plugins/docker-compose

Server:
 Containers: 9
  Running: 1
  Paused: 0
  Stopped: 8
 Images: 5
```

```
Server Version: 24.0.5
Storage Driver: overlay2
 Backing Filesystem: extfs
 Supports d_type: true
 Using metacopy: false
 Native Overlay Diff: true
 userxattr: false
Logging Driver: json-file
Cgroup Driver: systemd
Cgroup Version: 2
Plugins:
 Volume: local
 Network: bridge host ipvlan macvlan null overlay
 Log: awslogs fluentd gcplogs gelf journald json-file local logentries splunk syslog
Swarm: inactive
Runtimes: io.containerd.runc.v2 runc
Default Runtime: runc
Init Binary: docker-init
containerd version: 8165feabfdfe38c65b599c4993d227328c231fca
runc version: v1.1.8-0-g82f18fe
init version: de40ad0
Security Options:
 seccomp
 Profile: builtin
cgroupns
Kernel Version: 6.1.21-v8+
Operating System: Debian GNU/Linux 11 (bullseye)
OSType: linux
Architecture: aarch64
CPUs: 4
Total Memory: 3.704GiB
Name: raspberrypi
ID: d5f88ac0-1495-426f-b448-a44bd20089b2
Docker Root Dir: /var/lib/docker
Debug Mode: false
 Experimental: false
 Insecure Registries:
  127.0.0.0/8
 Live Restore Enabled: false

WARNING: No memory limit support
WARNING: No swap limit support
```

****

docker cp

```
Usage:
docker cp [OPTIONS] CONTAINER:SRC_PATH DEST_PATH|-
docker cp [OPTIONS] SRC_PATH|- CONTAINER:DEST_PATH
```

Description:

The docker cp utility copies files/folders between a container and the local, or host filesystem. It copies the contents of SRC_PATH to the DEST_PATH. You can copy from the container's filesystem to the local machine or the reverse, from the local filesystem to the container. If - is specified for either the SRC_PATH or DEST_PATH, you can also stream a tar archive from STDIN or to STDOUT. The CONTAINER can be a running or stopped container. The SRC_PATH or DEST_PATH can be a file or directory.

The docker cp command assumes container paths are relative to the container's / (root) directory. This means supplying the initial forward slash is optional; The command sees compassionate_darwin:/tmp/foo/myfile.txt and compassionate_darwin:tmp/foo/myfile.txt as identical. Local machine paths can be an absolute or relative value. The command interprets a local machine's relative paths as relative to the current working directory where docker cp is run.

The cp command behaves like the Unix **cp -a** command in that directories are copied recursively with permissions preserved if possible. Ownership is set to the user and primary group at the destination. For example, files copied to a container are created with UID:GID of the root user. Files copied to the local machine are created with the UID:GID of the user which invoked the docker cp command. However, if you specify the -a option, docker cp sets the ownership to the user and primary group at the source. If you specify the -L option, docker cp follows any symbolic link in the SRC_PATH. Docker cp does not create parent directories for DEST_PATH if they do not exist.

Assuming a path separator of /, a first argument of SRC_PATH and second argument of DEST_PATH, the behavior is as follows:

SRC_PATH specifies a file
DEST_PATH does not exist
the file is saved to a file created at DEST_PATH
DEST_PATH does not exist and ends with /
Error condition: the destination directory must exist.
DEST_PATH exists and is a file
the destination is overwritten with the source file's contents
DEST_PATH exists and is a directory
the file is copied into this directory using the basename from SRC_PATH
SRC_PATH specifies a directory
DEST_PATH does not exist
DEST_PATH is created as a directory and the contents of the source directory are copied into this directory
DEST_PATH exists and is a file
Error condition: cannot copy a directory to a file
DEST_PATH exists and is a directory
SRC_PATH does not end with /. (that is: slash followed by dot)
the source directory is copied into this directory
SRC_PATH does end with /. (that is: slash followed by dot)
the content of the source directory is copied into this directory

The command requires SRC_PATH and DEST_PATH to exist according to the above rules. If SRC_PATH is local and is a symbolic link, the symbolic link, not the target, is copied by default. To copy the link target and not the link, specify the -L option.

A colon (:) is used as a delimiter between CONTAINER and its path. You can also use: when specifying paths to a SRC_PATH or DEST_PATH on a local machine, for example file:name.txt. If you use a: in a local machine path, you must be explicit with a relative or absolute path, for example:

`/path/to/file:name.txt` or `./file:name.txt`

Options:

Option	Short	Default	Description
--archive	-a	false	Archive mode (copy all uid/gid information)
--follow-link	-L	false	Always follow symbol link in SRC_PATH
--quiet	-q	false	Suppress progress output during copy. Progress output is automatically suppressed if no terminal is attached

Examples:
Copy a local file into container
```
$ docker cp ./some_file CONTAINER:/work
```

Copy files from container to local path
```
$ docker cp CONTAINER:/var/logs/ /tmp/app_logs
```

Copy a file from container to stdout. Please note cp command produces a tar stream
```
$ docker cp CONTAINER:/var/logs/app.log - | tar x -O | grep "ERROR"
```

****

3.11 Summary

In this chapter, we gave background information on OS virtualization, and some of its characteristics and examples. The two systems we used for our illustrations were LXC/LXD and Docker.

We provided a description of the LXC/LXD virtualization method and explicitly detailed LXC/LXD installation on the Raspberry Pi OS. We then illustrated LXC/LXD basic usage and gave command references for LXC/LXD. We listed LXC/LXD best practices and provided complete worked examples of advanced usage of LXC/LXD, most notably how to install a container with a ZFS backing store, how to make an LXC/LXD container "web-facing," with a public-facing IP address, and how to install a web server named Nginx in an LXD container.

We also presented container virtualization with Docker on the Raspberry Pi OS. We went through examples, primarily about how to install Nginx, a web server program, in a Docker container as a pre-built image. One of the primary examples here showed how to give an Docker Nginx container a public-facing IP address on your LAN, similar to what was done in the sections on LXC/LXD. Finally, we gave an encyclopedia-like reference to a select set of Docker commands.

Questions, Problems, and Projects

Chapter 0

0.1. Create a directory called Raspberry in your home directory. What command line did you use to do this?

0.2. Give a command line for displaying the files **lab1, lab2, lab3**, and **lab4**. Can you give two more command lines that do the same thing? What is the command line for displaying the files **lab1.c, lab2.c, lab3.c**, and **lab4.c**? (Hint: use shell metacharacters.)

0.3. Give a command line for printing all the files in your home directory that start with the string memo and end with **.ps** on a printer called **upmpr**. What command line did you use to do this?

0.4. Give the command line for nicknaming the command **who -H** as **W**. Give both Bash and C shell versions. Where would you put it if you want it to execute every time you start a new shell?

0.5. Type the command **man ls > ~/Raspberry/ls.man** on your system. This command will put the man page for the **ls** command in the **ls. man** file in your Raspberry directory (the one you created in Problem 0.1). Give the command for printing two copies of this file on a printer in your lab. What command line would you use to achieve this printing?

0.6. What is the **mesg** value set to for your environment? If it is on, how would you turn it off for your current session? How would you set it off for every login?

0.7. What does the command **lpr -Pqpr [0-9]*.jpg** do? Explain your answer.

0.8. Use the **passwd** command to change your password. If you are on a network, be aware that you might have to use the **yppasswd** command to modify your network login password. Also, make sure you abide by the rules set up by your system administrator for coming up with good passwords!

0.9. Using the correct terminology (e.g., command, option, option argument, and command argument), identify the constituent parts of the following Raspberry Pi OS single commands.

ls -la *.exe

lpr −Pwpr file27

chmod g+rwx *.*

0.10. View the man pages for each of the useful commands listed in Table 0.2. Which part of the man pages is most descriptive for you? Which of the options shown on each of the man pages is the most useful for beginners? Explain.

0.11. How many users are logged on to your system at this time? What command did you use to discover this?

0.12. Determine the name of the operating system that your computer runs. What command did you use to discover this?

0.13. Give the command line for displaying manual pages for the socket, read, and connect system calls on your system.

Advanced Questions and Problems

0.14. Following is a typical /etc/profile configuration file, this particular one is from a default installation on our Raspberry Pi system:

```
# /etc/profile: system-wide .profile file for the Bourne shell (sh(1))
# and Bourne compatible shells (bash(1), ksh(1), ash(1), ...).

if [ "$(id -u)" -eq 0 ]; then
  PATH="/usr/local/sbin:/usr/local/bin:/usr/sbin:/usr/bin:/sbin:/bin"
else
  PATH="/usr/local/sbin:/usr/local/bin:/usr/sbin:/usr/bin:/sbin:/bin:/usr/
  local/games:/usr/games"
fi
export PATH

if [ "${PS1-}" ]; then
  if [ "${BASH-}" ] && [ "$BASH" != "/bin/sh" ]; then
  # The file bash.bashrc already sets the default PS1.
  # PS1='\h:\w\$ '
    if [ -f /etc/bash.bashrc ]; then
     . /etc/bash.bashrc
    fi
  else
    if [ "$(id -u)" -eq 0 ]; then
      PS1='# '
    else
      PS1='$ '
    fi
  fi
fi
```

```
if [ -d /etc/profile.d ]; then
 for i in /etc/profile.d/*.sh; do
  if [ -r $i ]; then
   . $i
  fi
 done
 unset i
fi
```

Write an explanatory sentence in your own words describing exactly what you consider important lines in the file accomplish, including the comments (the lines that begin with the pound sign #). Examine this file on your Raspberry Pi system. How does it compare, line-for-line, with the one above? We assume here that, by default, Bash is both the interactive and login shell on your system.

0.15. What is the default umask setting in an ordinary, non-privileged account on your Raspberry Pi system, from both a login and non-login shell? Describe in your own words what the umask setting is, and how it is applied to newly created directories and files. Is the umask set in /etc/profile on your Raspberry Pi system? If not, where can the umask be set most effectively on a persistent basis, for a particular single user, both in a login and non-login shell?

0.16. Assume that all users, when they log into your Raspberry Pi system, have Bash as their default shell. What file sets the shell prompt for them on your Raspberry Pi system? Is it the file illustrated in Problem 0.14? Describe the lines in the file that actually specify the shell prompt and give a short description of the components of those lines. Experiment to find out which file accomplishes the actual shell prompt setting for ordinary users (for both interactive or login shells) and write an explicit description of what you have discovered.

Additionally, set the shell prompt for yourself in the current interactive shell, so that it contains the following:

A display of just the date/time.
A display of the date and time, hostname, and current directory.
A display where the entire prompt is in red text, along with hostname and current directory.

Then make those changes persistent for yourself in both login and interactive shells. Finally, undo the persistent changes.

As a follow-up, design your own shell prompt so that it contains the information you want in a useful display given your use case(s) and make that designed prompt persistent for yourself on your Raspberry Pi system.

0.17. Give a sequential list of the exact commands you would use to make the TC shell the default login shell for your user account on your Raspberry Pi system. Is the TC shell installed by default on your Raspberry Pi system? If not, how would you install it on a Debian-family system, such as the Raspberry Pi OS? Give the exact commands for installation of not only the TC shell, but any of the other four major Raspberry Pi OS shells available.

0.18. Execute all of the compound command examples provided at the web link https://explainshell.com/ and then use the output shown to explain all of them in your own words. Try executing the examples with meaningful arguments on your Raspberry Pi system, if possible.

Project 1

After completing Problems 0.14 through 0.16, gather your findings together in a summary report that details the default settings (within the scope of the files you have examined, and in the context of those problems) of the Bash environment on your Raspberry Pi system. For example, which actual file takes precedence by default, and what components of the Bash environment are set in that file? What are the critical default settings in the Bash environment, and what actual files on your Raspberry Pi system effect them?

Chapter 1

Nano

1.1. List ten commonly used text-editing operations you can do in Nano.

1.2. Run Nano on your Raspberry Pi system. Create and edit a block of text that you want to be the body of an email message explaining the basic capabilities of the Nano editor. This file should be at least one page (45 to 50 lines of text) long. Then save the file as nano_doc.txt. Insert the body of text you created in an email message and send it to yourself.

1.3. Log on to your Linux system and execute the Nano program on a new, blank file.

On the first line of the file, type your first and last name.

On the second line of the file, type "The Nano text editor allows

you to do simple editing on small text files efficiently" .

Use a Nano command to write the file to the default directory with the name lab51.

Print the file lab51 at your Raspberry Pi system line printer.

1.4. Do the following steps to create a file in Nano:

Step 1: At the shell prompt, type **nano** and then press **<Enter>**.

Step 2: In the text area of the Nano screen, place the cursor on the first line and type

This is text that I have entered on a line in the Nano editor.

Use the <Delete> and <arrow> keys to correct any typing errors you make.

Step 3: Press <Enter > three times.

Step 4: Type This is a line of text three lines down from the first line.

Step 5: Hold down the <Ctrl> and <O> keys at the same time (<Ctrl-O> or <^O>).

Step 6: At the prompt File Name to Write: type linespaced and then press <Enter>.

Step 7: Hold down the <Ctrl> and <X> keys at the same time

(<Ctrl-X> or <X>) to return to the shell prompt.

Step 8: At the shell prompt, type more linespaced and then press <Enter>.

1.5. Do the following steps in Nano:

Step 1: At the shell prompt, type **nano linespaced** and then press <Enter>. The linespaced file you created in Problem 1.4 appears in the Nano screen.

Step 2: Position the cursor at the beginning of the fourth line, at the character T in the word This, using the <arrow> keys on the keyboard.

Step 3: Hold down the <Ctrl> and both the <Shift> and <6> keys at the same time.

Step 4: Move the cursor with the <right arrow> key on the key-board until you have highlighted the entire fourth line, including the period. The cursor should be one character to the right of the period at the end of the line.

Step 5: Hold down the <Ctrl> and <K> keys at the same time.

This action cuts the line of text out of the current "buffer," or file that you are working on.

Step 6: Position the cursor with the <arrow> keys at the beginning of the second line of the file, directly under the line that reads **This is text that I have entered on a line in the Nano editor.**

Step 7: Hold down the <Ctrl> and <U> keys at the same time. This action pastes the former fourth line into the second line of the file.

Step 8: Use the <arrow> keys on the keyboard to position the cursor at the third line of the file.

Step 9: Hold down the <Ctrl> and <U> keys on the keyboard at the same time. This action pastes the former fourth line into the third line of the file.

Step 10: Now change the wording of lines 2 and 3 so that they read:

This is a line of text 1 line down from the first line.

This is a line of text 2 lines down from the first line.

How many lines are there in this file now, as far as Nano is concerned?

Step 11: Hold down the <Ctrl> and <O> keys at the same time.

Step 12: At the prompt File Name to Write: type linespaced2 and then press <Enter>.

Step 13: Hold down the <Ctrl> and <X> keys at the same time to return to the shell prompt.

Step 14: At the shell prompt, type more linespaced2 and then press <Enter>.

What do you see on screen? How many lines does the more command show in this file?

1.6. Complete Problem 1.5, use Nano to add two(2) more lines of text to the file named **linespaced2** below lines 2 and 3, with similar content to lines 2 and 3. Then add a line at the top of the file with your first and last name on it. Save this new file with the name linespaced3 and print it at your Linux system line printer.

1.7. What version of Nano did you use in the above work, and how did you find this out?

1.8. Use the cat command to create a short text file named **shorty** on your Raspberry Pi system, and then read that file into Nano, and add text to it. What command did you use to read the cat-created file into Nano?

1.9. Execute Nano on your Raspberry Pi system using the –m command option. What functionality did the –m option give you in Nano?

1.10. Repeat Problems 1.4, 1.5, and 1.6 by launching Nano using the -m option on the command line. When would it not be possible to use Nano with the -m option?

Vi, Vim, Gvim

1.11. Despite the availability of fancy and powerful word processors, why is text editing still important?

1.12. List ten commonly used text-editing operations.

1.13. What are the four most popular text editors available for the Raspberry Pi OS? Which one is your favorite? Why?

1.14. What is an editor buffer in Vi, Vim, and Gvim?

1.15. This problem assumes you are using the Bash shell in the Raspberry Pi OS (the default shell), and will execute the file you will create in your home directory on the system.

   a. Make sure that your search path includes the directory you are saving the following script file to, and that you have execute privileges on the file. Then, use Vi or Vim on your system and create a bash shell script file that contains the lines:

```
#!/bin/bash
echo $SHELL
cat /etc/shells
```

   Save the file as **sheller** and quit Vi. At the Bash shell prompt, type **./sheller** and then press **<Enter>**. You may have to use the **chmod** command, **chomd u+x sheller** before executing it in Bash.

   b. What appears on your screen? In particular, what shells are available?

1.16. Run Vi on your Raspberry Pi system. Create and edit a block of text that you want to be the body of an email message explaining the basic capabilities of the Vi editor. For example, part of your message might describe the difference between the Insert and Command modes. This file should be at least one page (45 to 50 lines of text) long. Then save the file as **vi_doc.txt**. Insert the body of text in an email message and send it to yourself.

1.17. Run Vi on your system and create a file of definitions in your own words, without looking at the textbook, for:

   a. full-screen display editor
   b. modeless editor
   c. file versus buffer
   d. keystroke commands
   e. substitute versus search
   f. text file versus binary file

Then refer back to the relevant sections of this chapter to check your definitions. Make any necessary corrections or additions. Re-edit the file in Vim to incorporate any corrections or additions that you made and then print out the file using the print commands available on your system.

1.18. Edit the file you created in Problem 1.17 and change the order of the text of your definitions to (d), (a), (c), and (b), using the yank, put, and D or dd commands. Print out the file using the print commands available on your Raspberry Pi system.

1.19. Execute the Vi program on a new, blank file.

On the first line of the file, type your first and last name.

On the second line of the file, type **The vi text editor has almost all the features of a word processor and tremendous flexibility in creating text files**.

Print the file to your Raspberry Pi system line printer while you are still in Vi. How do you accomplish this, in a non-GUI environment?

1.20. What Vi command allows you to move to the first line in the current buffer? What command allows you to move to the last line in the buffer?

1.21. Use the **set** command to force Vi into a 30-column by 15-line display of characters so that one screen of the display shows only 15 lines, and text is automatically wrapped onto the next line after the 30th character. How did you do this? (Hint: The **set all** command shows the current status of all Vi environment variables.)

Advanced Vi, Vim, Gvim

1.22. You changed the behavior of Vi, Vim, and Gvim by adding or modifying entries in your ~/.exrc or ~/.vimrc files, so that the changes were persistent across all sessions of the editors. You can also customize Vi, Vim, and Gvim by changing the shell environment variable named **EXINIT**. This can be achieved in the C shell by giving value(s) to the **SETENV** variable. Do the following:

a. Find the exact syntax and use of the **SETENV** command in the C shell. Then, add or modify the shell environment variable setting for the shell variable **EXINIT** so that the **showmode** user option is turned on. What is the syntax of the command you used to do this?

b. How would you test that this environment variable is actually implementing the user option change, and not what is in the ~/.exrc or ~/.vimrc files?

c. What syntax would you use for the **setenv** command to change more than one user option in the editors?

d. Are these changes in the **EXINIT** variable persistent through all Vi, Vim, and Gvim sessions? If you log out and log back into the system, does **EXINIT** still contain the changes and additions you make to it? Why, or why not?

1.23. Give the exact syntax of a Vi **substitute** command line that only replaces every instance of the discrete word **ate** on all the lines of a file, with the word **ion**, where the file has some words that end in the string **ate**.

1.24. Give the exact syntax of a Vim **substitute** command line that interactively searches and substitutes the word **cool** for the word **cold** on all the lines of a file, where there are several widely separated instances of the word **cold** in the file.

1.25. Take the following **map** command for creating a skeleton C program template and place it in your ~/.exrc file:

:map #3 <Esc>i#include <stdio.h><CR>main(argc, argv)<CR> int argc;<CR> char *argv[];<CR>{<CR>}<Esc>

where

<Esc> is used to represent the escape key, which is entered by pressing **<Ctrl>+V** followed by **<Esc>**.

<CR> is used to represent the **<Enter>** key, which is entered by pressing **<Ctrl>+V** followed by **<Enter>**.

When you enter last line mode and type **map,** and then press **<F3>**, Vim will insert the desired text into your document.

The relative number of spaces in the above **map** command definition controls the indentation of the skeleton construct.

a. Make sure that the relative indentation of the header components and other parts of the skeleton is correct.
b. Add an #include <stderr.h>, #include <stdlib.h>, and #include <string.h> as header information to the skeleton.
c. Run the **map** command in a blank Vi buffer and test it.

1.26. Run Gvim on your Raspberry Pi system. Create and edit a block of text that you want to be the body of an email message explaining the basic capabilities of the Gvim editor. For example, part of your message might describe the graphical capabilities of Gvim that make it more useful than Vim, or Vi. This file should be at least one page (45 to 50 lines of text) long. Then save the file as Gvim_doc.txt. Insert the body of text in an email message and send it to yourself.

1.27. Log on to your Raspberry Pi system and execute the Vi program on a new, blank file.

On the first line of the file, type your first and last name.

On the second line of the file, type **The vi text editor has almost all the features of a word processor and tremendous flexibility in creating text files.**

Print the file to your Raspberry Pi system line printer, from within Vi, using a single Vi command. How do you accomplish this, in a non-GUI, text-only environment?

1.28. What Vi command allows you to move to the first line in the current buffer? What command allows you to move to the last line in the buffer?

1.29. What file in your home directory allows you to customize your Vi environment variables permanently?

1.30. What do the following eight Vi commands do?

12dw, 5dd, 12o, 5O, c5b, d5,12, 12G, 5yy

1.31. While editing a file, how do you "escape" to the default Linux shell (on your Raspberry Pi systems, Bash) while in Vi, and then how do you return to the editor?

Geany

1.32. Which of the typical IDE basic features presented at the beginning of Section 1.6 are most important to you, given the programming language(s) you intend to deploy Geany with on the Raspberry Pi OS? Discuss them in detail, and how you would take advantage of an IDE instead of a text editor like Nano, or Vi/Vim.

1.33. What's the difference between a Geany document, and an ordinary code file, if any?

1.34. What are the important Geany command line options for your particular use case? See the online Geany manual at www.geany.org/manual/current/index.html for a listing of them, and what they accomplish.

1.35. What is shown in the status bar at the bottom of the Geany window, when you create a C++ program in the editor window?

1.36. How and why would you launch multiple instances of Geany, either from the command line or from the Raspberry Pi menu **Programming > Geany**?

The following five questions require that you have completed Practice Sessions 1.8 through 1.12. Note that the *default projects folder* is what Geany names the folder in /*home*/your_username/projects that are presented in the New Project window, where your_username is your login name on your Raspberry Pi system. Problems 1.37 through 1.41 provide essentially Geany project creation and cloning practice.

1.37. Take the C++ program named **count1.cpp**, created in Practice Session 1.8, and place it in a project in the *default projects folder* in your home directory. Write down the explicit steps you used to accomplish this.

1.38. Take the C++ program named **GCF4.cpp**, created in Practice Session 1.9, and place it in a project in the *default projects folder* in your home directory. Write down the explicit steps you used to accomplish this.

1.39. Take the C++ program named **third.cpp**, created in Practice Session 1.10, and place it in a project in the *default projects folder* in your home directory. Write down the explicit steps you used to accomplish this.

1.40. Take the C++ program named **third.cpp**, created in Practice Session 1.10, and place it in a project in the *default projects folder* in your home directory. Then create a clone of that project with the **cp -r** command. This new project folder, and its source project, should *not* be named **project2** or **project3**, as is seen in Practice Session 1.11, and should comprise files inside of /*home*/your_username/ projects. This is essentially the same operation that you did in Practice Session 1.11, but with a completely different source for the clone, and a different target. Write down the explicit steps you used to accomplish this.

1.41. Take the C++ programs created in Practice Session 1.12, named **input_module.cpp**, **output_module.cpp**, and **main.cpp** and place them in a new project in the *default projects folder* in your home directory. In this new project, create a new makefile that will compile these three modules into one executable image, as was done in Practice Session 1.12. Finally, run this new image from within the new project. Write down the explicit steps you used to accomplish this.

1.42. What are the characters that trigger autoindentation on the next line of code in the following languages?

C++, Python, Javascript, HTML, XML

1.43. In the program **count1.cpp** shown in Practice Session 1.8, what is the logic behind Geany's deployment of the fold regions?

1.44. What would be the advantages of opening multiple instances of Geany? Your answer should reflect what you've learned from listing the specific steps you used to most efficiently solve Problems 1.37 through 1.41.

1.45. When you only want to be running a single instance of Geany, what's the easiest and quickest way to "clear the deck" of files and projects from the last session, and start a fresh instance in the new session? This question assumes that you want to launch the fresh instance by making the Raspberry Pi menu choice **Programming > Geany**.

1.46. What is the quickest and easiest way to create a new C++ or Python program and project, after you've previously worked on different older projects and documents in Geany, and subsequently launch

Geany? Assume you have *not* taken the "clear the deck" steps from your answer to question 1.45.

1.47. Which Geany menu choice do you make in order to examine, or change, a majority of the settings that are presented in Section 1.6.4 Geany Abbreviated Reference Encyclopedia?

1.48. What does the Geany menu choice **Document > Clone** achieve, and how could it have been deployed in your answers to question 1.37 through 1.41?

1.49. Name the six component parts of the Geany window and write a short description of what each accomplishes, along with their contents.

1.50. What exact command in the Geany **Build > Set Build Commands** window executes C++ code? Give an example of that command, and its options and option arguments. Describe in your own words what the %d, %e, %f, and %f substitutions in the Command field of the Set Build Command window are, and what they accomplish.

1.51. Why would you want to use the Geany Toolbar icon **Compile**, rather than the **Build** Icon? Give examples of this for C or C++ program code.

Projects

1.
From within non-GUI, text-only Vi and Vim sessions, create a text file that you want to print at one of the available printers on your Raspberry Pi system. Then, while still in the editor, give a series of CUPS commands to manage the CUPS service, either locally or on your network, that will enable you to print the text file you created in the editor. This would involve things like starting the CUPS service if it is not running by default, checking the status of the service and attached printers with systemd commands, or changing the name of a particular attached printer, etc. What specific commands do you use to accomplish these things, in all three editors? Create a short report organizing both general and specific methodologies that someone could use to manage a CUPS service and print documents from within these editors.

2.
Repeat Project 1 using Geany.

3.
zenity is a graphical, GTK+ dialog box program that allows you to create interactive dialog boxes using Bash script files. It is installed by default on our GUI-based Debian-family Raspberry Pi OS. In this project, the zenity dialog box you will deploy will allow you to easily create new users on your Raspberry Pi system. Of course, it is assumed you have the privilege to do this account creation on your system! Use Geany to create and execute a zenity-based Bash script file, following these steps:

a. In Geany, create and save the following Bash script file, named **zen1. bash**, in your home directory:

```
#!/bin/bash
zenity --forms --title="newusers Command" --text="Add batch new
user" \
  --add-entry="Username" \
  --add-password="Password" \
  --add-entry="User Number UID" \
  --add-entry="Group Number GID" \
  --add-entry="GECOS Entry" \
  --add-entry="Default Home Directory" \
  --add-entry="Default Shell" \
>> zen_out
sed -i -e 's/\|/:/g' /home/bob/zen_out
```

b. On the command line, type **./zen1.bash**

A zenity dialog box will open on-screen. In the GUI dialog box you will create the seven fields needed to be supplied to the **newusers** command, to create new users from a "batch file" on your Raspberry Pi system. The seven inputs you supply to the dialog box will be written to a file named **zen_out**.

The seven fields, separated by the colon character (:), are:

the new user accounts name, password, UID, GID, GECOS commentary, default home directory, and default shell.

For example:

garvey:QQQ:2001:2001:CFO of Accounting:/home/garvey:/bin/bash

c. Use **zen1** to create a file of several new users you want to put on your Raspberry Pi system. Then put those users on your system!

4.

The following project can be done using this outline, which is one of several ways it can be accomplished:

a. Launch Geany on your Raspberry Pi system.

b. Create a New Project: Go to the "Project" menu and select "New."

c. Set Project Name and Location: Choose a name for your project and select the folder where you want to save your project files.

d. Add a New File: Right-click on the project in the left sidebar, select "New" and choose "Empty File." Name it with a .py extension, for example, **main.py**.

e. Write or copy and paste the Python code into the editor window.

f. Save the File: Save the Python file by pressing **<Ctrl> + <S>**.

g.   Compile or Run: You can compile and run the Python program from within Geany. Use the Geany menu **Build > Execute** to run it.

Take any of the tkinter Python script files from Section 1.6.3.3 and place it into a project in the default projects folder. Then run the program from within that project.

5.
For any two of the Practice Sessions 1.9 through 1.12, substitute the *using directive*, that allows all functions in the specified namespace to be used without their namespace prefix. For example, if in the C++ header, the following line of code is included:

using namespace std;

then lines such as

std::cout << "Enter a string: ";

in the body of the program can have the **std::** omitted before the call to function **cout**.

Once you do this substitution, rebuild and execute the selected code in those Practice Sessions.

For Practice Session 1.8's C++ program, this would yield:

```cpp
#include <iostream>
#include <string>
using namespace std ;

int main() {
    string inputString;
    char targetLetter;

    // Prompt the user for input string
    cout << "Enter a string: ";
    cin >> inputString;

    // Prompt the user for the target letter
    cout << "Enter the letter you want to count: ";
    cin >> targetLetter;

    int count = 0;

    // Loop through the characters in the input string
    for (char ch : inputString) {
        // Check if the current character matches the target letter
        if (ch == targetLetter) {
            count++;
        }
```

```
}
```

```
// Display the count
cout << "The letter '" << targetLetter << "' appears " << count << " times in the string."
<< endl;
```

```
return 0;
}
```

6.

Customize the Geany Toolbar, according to the material presented in Section 1.6.4.11, to take advantage of the additional icons available, for your own particular use case, and the language(s) you deploy Geany for.

7.

Install Visual Studio Code (VSC) on your Raspberry Pi OS, and then do a comparison of the features of Geany and VSC in terms of your use case of an IDE. The installation of VSC can easily be done from the Raspberry Pi command line as follows:

$ **sudo apt install code -y**

Once the installation is complete, to launch this IDE, from the Raspberry Pi menu, make the choice **Programming > Visual Studio Code**.

Follow this video tutorial to set up VSC, and get an overview of its basic features:

https://code.visualstudio.com/docs/introvideos/basics
VSC offers GitHub integration.

To integrate GitHub with VSC, you can use the GitHub Pull Requests and Issues extension1 of VSC. This extension allows you to share your source code and collaborate with others right within your editor. Here are the steps to get started:

1. Install Git on your machine.
2. Create a GitHub account if you don't have one already.
3. Install the GitHub Pull Requests and Issues extension for VSC.
4. Once you have installed the extension, you can authenticate with GitHub and start using some of your favorite parts of GitHub without leaving Visual Studio Code1. You can clone repositories, search for repos, and even publish repos directly from Visual Studio Code2.

For more detailed instructions on how to connect GitHub to VSC, you can refer to the official documentation provided by VSC. It provides step-by-step guidance on how to authenticate with GitHub, clone repositories, and work with source control in VSC.

8.
Deploy Geany for your use with another HLL, such as JavaScript or C, or whatever language you work with regularly. What advantage(s) does Geany confer, over and above using a text editor, for the language you choose to code in? Particularly with respect to the five key differences between text editors and IDEs that we mention at the beginning of Section 1.6. For example, would the kinds of DevOps coding projects you work on, and the teams you work with on those projects, benefit, and in what ways, from using Geany? Would integration of Geany with GitHub, or GitLab, as offered by VSC, be an advantage in the development processes your teams use? And how would this integration work? Write a short paper to explicitly answer the questions we pose in this project statement.

Chapter 2

2.1   What do you think the role of an integrator of a project would be, in terms of what a revision control system, such as git, accomplishes for a software development and maintenance program?

2.2   What do you think would be the quickest and easiest way to completely delete a local git repository on your Raspberry Pi system?

2.3   Why do you think Git would not be effective, or even work at all, in tracking content changes in C program executable image files, or in files like Word .docx files?

2.4   What git command can you use to see the abbreviated list of commits in the current branch of a repository, and their commit comments? Is this possible in GitHub, and how?

2.5   As an alternative to using git pull in Example 2.6 to obtain the source code for this book from the listed GitHub repository (https://github.com/bobk48/RaspberryPiOS), use the **git clone** command, as shown in Example 2.5, from your home directory on your Raspberry Pi system. What will be the name of the repository directory created by git on your local machine that contains the source code files?

Project 1
Create a three-branch repository of commits exactly like Project 2.1. Use any number of text files that you modify between commits on the three branches. Keep the default name for the branch master, but name the other two branches **test** and **dev**, as seen in Figure A.1

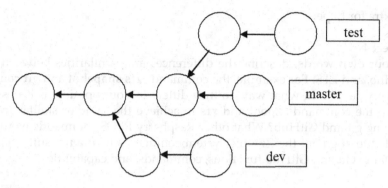

FIGURE A.1
Three-branch repository #1.

Project 2
Create a three-branch repository of commits exactly like Project 2.2. Use any number of text files that you modify between commits on the three branches. Keep the default name for the branch master, but name the other two branches test and dev, as seen in Figure A.2.

Project 3
As an alternative to using **git pull** in Example 2.6 to obtain the source code for this book from the listed GitHub repository (https://github.com/bobk48/RaspberryPiOS), fork that repository to one below your home directory on your Raspberry Pi. What will be the name of the repository directory created by git on your local machine that contains the source code files?

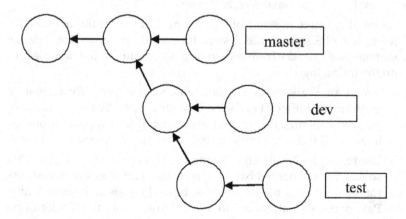

FIGURE A.2
Three-branch repository #2.

Extra for Experts

Project 4
In your own words, describe the differences and similarities between Git, GitHub, and ZFS. For example, the commands **zfs snapshot** and **git commit** are very similar. In what way do they differ? In your opinion, is it possible to use the commands **zpool** and **zfs** to achieve the same or similar results as using git and GitHub? What other Raspberry Pi OS commands would be needed to augment the ZFS file system commands to attain results that are similar to Git and GitHub functions, commands, and capabilities?

Chapter 3

LXD/LXC

3.1 Following the exact sequence of commands shown in Section 3.2.5, and the man page references given in Section 3.2.1.1, create the snapshot structure of a running LXD container of your choice. Assign a name for your choice to the snapshot and the container created. Then answer the following questions:

a. What is the IP address of one of the newly created "snapshotted" container, in relation to the container that it was created from?

b. How do the commands in this section affect the IP address of newly created containers, and why?

3.2 As an alternative method of initializing LXD, with the objective of using the ZFS storage file system for containers *on a whole external medium used as a vdev* (rather than on a file, as shown in Example 3.1), do the following:

a. Install an available and expendable second properly formatted medium, of sufficient capacity, on your Raspberry Pi system. How do you recognize this type of disk when it first appears mounted in /dev? If it doesn't mount, chances are it's unusable!

b. Use Examples 3.1 through Example 3.3 (particularly Example 3.3!), so that a zpool named lxd_pool is created on the external medium, rather than on a file on the Raspberry Pi system/boot medium. Pay particular attention to the ***Note*** in the Background material of Example 3.3. On our system, the primary objective of this problem was done with the command **zpool create lxd_pool /dev/sdb1**

3.3 You first initialize LXD as in Example 3.1, Step 5, but now you want to change some of its configuration parameters. Outline the steps you would need to take to reconfigure the LXD initial installation on your machine. Give detailed instructions for a particular configuration change, with specific command examples, that show how you would change the LXD configuration parameter.

3.4 Complete all of the steps of Examples 3.4 and Example 3.5 on your own host and LXD/LXC containers, and then use various secure methods of copying files between the host computer and the container that you enabled the sshd in. For example, use scp to copy files from host to container and vice versa. Also use the **rsync** command to copy files back and forth between host and container.

3.5 When you have completed all of the steps in Example 3.6 on your own system, modify the appropriate nginx files so that you can display a custom web page using the nginx server in the container. Consult nginx documentation to find the default location of .html files you would use for the custom web page displayed inside the Nginx LXD/LXC container.

3.6 Install Webmin in an Ubuntu LXD/LXC container, and then use the various system administration menu choice presented by Webmin to do some of the common system maintenance tasks we have shown *inside the container*. These might include creation of new users and groups, execution of operating system commands such as manipulation of systemd-controlled services, etc.

3.7 Choose an available image to install in an LXD container, such as Oracle Linux. Choose this image based upon your familiarity with that "flavor" of Linux. Then go through the steps necessary to install that system into a container. Try doing any, or all, of the LXD/LXC examples from this chapter in this image's container.

Docker

3.8 If you haven't already done so, install Docker on your Raspberry Pi system, using the instructions in Section 3.3.1. Then download an image of your choice, using the available images you see at

https://hub.docker.com/search?image_filter=official&type=image

3.9 Use the instructions in Section 3.8 to install a Docker Nginx container on your Raspberry Pi system. What IP address is assigned to your Nginx container, as shown in Section 3.8? What assigns that IP address on your LAN? Is it private, or public facing? How can you determine that?

3.10 Use the instructions in Section 3.8.1 to assign a public-facing IP address to the Nginx container you created in Problem 3.9, so that you can access an index.html file you designed yourself which is served up by Nginx to the Internet, outside your LAN. Use the instructions found in Section 3.9.2 to expose this web page on the Internet, without it being blocked by ufw on your host, or the firewall at the router or modem on your LAN.

3.11 Install a container, using the latest stable Ubuntu image available for Docker Ubuntu containers, with a ZFS backing store. How do you install ZFS on the host? Can ZFS be installed in the container as a file system used exclusively there, and not on the host? And if that's possible, are the vdevs used in the container Docker files, loop devices, or physical block devices? Explain your answers in detail. See Section 3.9.4.

Projects

Project 1

Note
This project assumes you have an account at GitHub, and can access it from the Raspberry Pi command line.
    Use the methods of this chapter, Chapter 2 on git and GitHub, and Volume 2, to do the following:

a.   Create a new LXD/LXC container on your Raspberry Pi host system that has access via ssh to and from your LAN via a public-facing IP address.

b.   In that container, create a project directory for a git repository that a user base of remote users can push to and pull from.

c.   Use the appropriate ACL commands to set the ACLs on that project directory so that local and remote users can access it and can interact with the git repository in that project directory.

d.   Design the directory structure of the repository for the intended local and remote user base.

e.   Create the git repository in the project directory according to your design.

f.   Test the git repository, both locally, and from the Internet, to confirm that local allowed users and the remote user base can work with the repository to push to and pull from it.

g.   Test that unallowed local users or LAN traffic *cannot* interact with the repository.

Project 2
On a Raspberry Pi host system, install and use ZFS as described in Example 3.1, Step 5, as the backing storage system in an Ubuntu LXD/ LXC container. Then, devise a complete strategy for backing up that container on the host. Be specific about commands and operations that you would employ to accomplish this objective, and provide, in report form, a fully developed scenario with examples. Be explicit in answering these two questions in your report:

1. In what directories are the container files, and their controlling LXD/LXC data structures and databases kept?
2. How would you use real-time "on the fly" backups to ensure that the container state is backed up?

Devise a strategy for backing up the LXD/LXC "machinery", and the Ubuntu container ZFS files, on your host system. Whether or not you have initialized and configured LXD to use a second storage medium for ZFS storage, detail the steps you would take to back up the relevant files for your container.

Project 3
Prefaced by completion of Examples 3.1 and 3.2, and following the procedures of Example 3.3, pull and run the latest available stable release of a Docker Ubuntu container, with a ZFS backing store on the host, *and* using an externally mounted USB3 medium. The container should have its own public-facing IP address. Then, use ZFS to mirror that medium onto another externally mounted usable medium of equivalent size and capacity. The result should be a mirrored media pair, with the container backed up on each.

Note
ZFS must be installed on the host system, not in the container.

Project 4
Install multiple Docker Nginx containers (at least three) on a host Raspberry Pi system, each with its own public-facing IP address. Then give each container its own index.html homepage, and use your web browser on your LAN to view these container's individual homepages.

Project 5
In your own words, describe the differences, in light of what you would use them for, between the functionality of default LXD/LXC containers and

default Docker containers. For example, which system provides a method of lighter-weight provisioning of a container? Which system provides more complete and operable default Linux operating system functioning containers? What would be the rationale for that, from the perspective of the maintainers of either system?

Index

Printed in the United States
by Baker & Taylor Publisher Services